The Business of Sports Agents

The Business of Sports Agents

Second Edition

KENNETH L. SHROPSHIRE and
TIMOTHY DAVIS

PENN

University of Pennsylvania Press

Philadelphia

Published by
University of Pennsylvania Press
Philadelphia, Pennsylvania 19104-4112

Printed in the United States of America on acid-free paper

10 9 8 7 6 5 4 3 2 1

Library of Congress Cataloging-in-Publication Data

Shropshire, Kenneth L.
   The business of sports agents / Kenneth L. Shropshire and Timothy Davis. — 2nd ed.
     p. cm.
   Includes bibliographical references and index.
   ISBN 978-0-8122-4084-9 (alk. paper)
     1. Sports agents—United States.   2. Sports—Corrupt practices—United States.
3. College sports—United States.   I. Davis, Timothy, 1954–   II. Title.

GV734.5.S58 2008
796.06' 9—dc22   2008007933

Contents

Preface to the Second Edition   vii

Introduction   1

I. Background
1. Historical and Legal Foundations   11
2. The Business   22
3. Consolidation: An Evolving Industry   37

II. Problems
4. The Basics: Competition for Clients   55
5. Unscrupulous and Criminal: The Problem Agents   72
6. Conflicts of Interest   88
7. Ethics: Attorney Versus Nonattorney Agents   97
8. Agent Wars   107
9. The Last Amateurs on Earth: Amateurism and
   Opportunity   117

III. Solutions
10. Knights of Columbus Rules? Private Sports Agent
    Regulations   131
11. The Laws   144
12. A Uniform Approach: The Uniform Athlete Agents Act   157
13. Conclusion: The Absence of a Panacea   165

Notes   173

Index   203

Acknowledgments   215

Preface to the Second Edition

The Business of Sports Agents seriously examines one of the most intriguing professions to develop as sport has become big business entertainment. The sports agent industry has been glamorized by motion picture, television, and journalistic accounts. Who would not want to be the businessperson behind the all-star athlete? This text is focused on the business and legal aspects that impact sports agents. This book is the third iteration of a work originally published by one of the current authors, Kenneth Shropshire, in 1990. In the decade and a half that has passed since the publication of that work, *Agents of Opportunity: Sports Agents and Corruption in Collegiate Sports*, much has occurred. This third work reflects that evolution.

The first three chapters of this book describe what is currently taking place in the sports agent industry. Chapters 1 and 2 examine the history of the sports agent industry, its legal foundations, and what it is that agents do. Chapter 3 considers the status of consolidation occurring among firms in the industry. Chapter 4 begins the book's examination of the problems affecting the sports agent. Focusing on client recruitment, Chapters 5 through 8 examine criminal, ethical, and agent qualification issues. There, particularly in the ethical discussion, many questions yet to be answered by the courts are raised. Chapter 9 looks at long-standing amateurism principles and how they contribute to many of the unethical activities of agents and student athletes. Chapter 10, "Knights of Columbus Rules? Private Sports Agent Regulations," sets forth agent regulations that have been put in place by private organizations such as the National Football League (NFL). Chapter 11, "The Laws," presents an overview of state laws aimed at regulating agents. This chapter also explores legal actions that may be asserted against agents without the aid of these statutes. Chapter 12 addresses the uniform law that regulates agents. The final chapter evaluates where we currently stand and where the industry is headed.

Many of the relevant statutes may be found at www.NCAA.org and elsewhere on the Internet. That site and others have the capability of regular updates that are truly valuable in this field. It should be noted that the book focuses largely, although not exclusively, on United States–based team sports. This is not intended to suggest that the athlete agent industry does not have international dimensions; it certainly does.

With the emphasis on U.S. team sports, we focus on the four major sports leagues and often list them without reference to others, including, for example, the Women's National Basketball Association (WNBA). As competition for clients in the non-major leagues increases, many of the issues impacting the major leagues will impact these emerging leagues as well.

A point of style should be noted. The legally correct name for the individual who represents the athlete is "athlete agent," not "sports agent." The individual is the agent for the athlete, not the sport. The term "sports agent," however, has developed as probably the most commonly recognized and accepted label, so the terms "athlete agent," "sports agent," and "agent" are used liberally and interchangeably throughout.

Introduction

It didn't seem so wrong. It seemed as though I worked my whole life to get where I am, and at the same time, when it was presented to me, it was like this was the time I could start to get back some of the fruits of my labor.[1]

—*Paul Palmer, former star college football running back, regarding cash payments of more than $5,000 he received from sports agent Norby Walters while a college senior*

Many variables impact the still-maturing sports agent business. This book focuses on this evolving industry, the issues affecting it, and how to improve and regulate it. In recent years the key issues and problems associated with sports agents have been visible more at the professional than collegiate level. But no matter the concerns that lie at the center of the sports agent storm, it is a business that captures the attention of many.

In the past, the dominant sports agent images were the imaginary Jerry Maguire and Arli$$. The sports agent image of the new millennium is more likely to be sports agent Drew Rosenhaus speaking on behalf of his client Terrell Owens as he sought to get a better deal for his client. The most vivid moment in that saga was a press conference with Owens in the background and Rosenhaus at the microphones responding to seemingly every query with the response "Next question?" Many observers expressed concern about the strategy the agent employed and its impact on the already tarnished image of his client. Although it generated considerable attention, the Rosenhaus microphone event should be of modest concern to those who want this business to work as it should. At the extremes, agent misconduct and malfeasance, ranging from mismanagement and misappropriation of athlete clients' assets to disparagement of other agents in order to gain a competitive advantage, fuel perceptions of an industry composed of individuals too willing to compromise ethics and competent representation for financial gain. Agent impropriety overlaps with the reality of largely newly or prospectively rich individuals not receiving the counseling they require to duplicate success on the field with success off the field.

Even with the industry focus shifting to the professional level, concerns involving the athlete representation business remain at the collegiate level as well. It is at that level where, no matter how mature we give them credit for being, young men often succumb to the sometimes corrupt actions of mature professionals. Paul Palmer's 1980s dilemma, noted in the epigraph of this chapter, remains with us in this millennium. He is not alone in having received payments that violate National Collegiate Athletic Association (NCAA) no-agent rules and now state and federal laws. Other student athletes have allegedly received inducements such as interest-free loans, automobiles, clothes, concert tickets, airline tickets, insurance policies, and dates with models.[2] In 2000, an Auburn University basketball star admitted to taking $2,500 from Nate Cebrun, a "runner" for a sports agent. The student athlete, Chris Porter, said that he used the money to pay his mother's mortgage.[3] The interaction with Porter was not Cebrun's first controversial contact with student athletes. In 1994, Cebrun, acting on behalf of certain agents, arranged a shopping spree for Florida State student athletes.[4] A recent illustration of alleged improper student athlete/agent interaction involved the benefits allegedly bestowed upon Reggie Bush during his collegiate career.

In 2006, allegations surfaced that New Orleans Saints running back and Heisman Trophy winner Reggie Bush and his family had accepted payments and benefits from marketing agents attempting to entice Bush to sign a representation agreement with them. According to media reports, Bush and his family accepted gifts, money, and other benefits totaling more than $100,000 from two marketing firms while Bush was still playing football for the University of Southern California (USC). Bush's family allegedly failed to pay rent of $54,000 during a year in which they lived in a house owned by the agent, Michael Michaels, with whom Bush did not sign a representation agreement. Bush's family allegedly agreed to repay Michaels after Bush turned professional. Media reports also alleged that Mike Ornstein, head of the agency selected by Bush to provide marketing services, provided the athlete and his family with gifts that included money for hotel expenses, airfare, and car-related expenses. If proved, the allegations could result in the NCAA sanctioning USC.[5] Amid these allegations, it was also revealed that Bush had a summer internship with Mike Ornstein's marketing firm.

The incidents involving Palmer, Cebrun, student athletes from Florida State, and Bush are points along a continuum. In 1979, after receiving $1,000 from agent Mike Trope, former University of Maryland football player Steve Atkins told *Sports Illustrated*: "I knew I did something wrong. I didn't want the NCAA to do something to Maryland, but I just needed some money to pay some bills. I didn't want to sign with him [Trope], but I just needed some money to pay some bills."[6]

An illustration from the mid-1990s involving former NFL running back Greg Hill reveals why some athletes take benefits from agents. In responding to the controversy involving agents, Hill stated: "The guys accepting pay or the guys who want to take pay, that mainly falls on you guys—the NCAA. . . . I think that's your fault because of the strict restrictions on how long guys work and how much [financial aid] guys get. Many families are too poor to give that child money. My mom couldn't give me any money. Sometimes your team has functions where you have to dress up. Some guys don't have suits. I didn't have a suit. I had to wear jeans all of the time."[7] The views expressed by Hill are not unique. From the student athlete's perspective, rules perceived as unfair and irrelevant to their life circumstances fail to deter problematic or possibly illegal involvement within the underground economy of college sport.

As reflected in Hill's comments, athletes point to what they perceive as fundamental inequities in intercollegiate athletics in explaining why collegiate athletes should be paid by the colleges and universities for which they play sports. National Basketball Association (NBA) and former Georgia Tech star Stephon Marbury told the *New York Times*, "When I signed to go to Georgia Tech, we were on ESPN twenty times, instantly. When you make the tournament they just give you money. And then they say a coach can't buy you a winter coat, even if you grew up in the hood and you don't have one."[8] Former college basketball star Eldridge Hudson summarized the attitude of at least some athletes in a *Time* magazine cover story more than two decades ago: "Once you get out on the floor, it's a job, and you expect to get paid. If a kid is busting his ass on the court, if somebody wants to buy a car, let him have it."[9] Commenting on allegations that Reggie Bush and his family accepted gifts from marketing agents, one commentator expressed similar views: "Almost all the incentives in big-time college sports point toward cheating. First, there's the perception, probably more or less accurate, that everybody else is doing it so you have to do it just to keep up. . . . Second, winning is enormously lucrative for everyone involved except the players, who happen to have the biggest influence over who wins and who loses. If you get a multimillion-dollar producer to work for you without pay, it's a fantastic deal even if you have to slip him a few thousand bucks from time to time."[10]

An affidavit submitted by NFL linebacker Johnny Rutledge focusing on payments he allegedly received during his collegiate career at the

University of Florida illustrates the improper transactions between student athletes and agents:

Beginning in 1997, my junior year, I began receiving money from Alfred Twitty, who worked for [then sports agent] Tank Black and his company PMI [Professional Marketing Incorporated] in Columbia, S.C. I initially received $200 per month, but in the summer of 1997 I asked for more. Twitty told me then that the usual amount for players like me was $600 per month. I thereafter received $600 per month through December of 1998. On occasion, I would get more than $600, like in December for Christmas and during my birthday month when I got $1,000 in cash.

Twitty began asking me about what car I wanted during my junior year, when it was possible I would consider turning pro. I decided to play my senior year instead. During my last season in 1998, Twitty again asked me what car I wanted. I eventually told him in December of 1998 that I wanted a Mercedes Benz S420.

I understood while I was receiving cash from Twitty that it was being provided by Tank Black. I met Tank Black in Tampa in the summer of 1998 at an event arranged by Twitty. Present were myself, Jevon Kearse, Fred Taylor and others from Tank's agency. At that time, Tank asked me "Is Tweet taking care of you?" I answered in the affirmative. And he told me that if I ever needed anything, I should contact Tweet.

I also talked with Tank during the balance of 1998 when he would call me by telephone and ask how I was doing. On one such call, I told him I needed money to buy furniture. Soon thereafter, Twitty came with the cash (about $700) and Reggie McGrew and I used it to purchase furniture for our apartment.

I was aware that Jevon Kearse and Reggie McGrew were also receiving monthly cash payments from Twitty. On occasion, the entire amount for all three of us would be delivered to one of us. . . .

I knew all along that it was expected by Twitty and Tank Black that I would sign with PMI when I turned pro. I informed them late in the 1998 season that I would do so. The day I signed with PMI—Jan. 4, 1999—I got the car I told Twitty that I wanted, which was a 1999 Mercedes S420 with all of the equipment I had said I wanted.[11]

Additionally, automobiles and cash payments may be supplemented by promises of the even more unsavory, such as drugs or prostitutes. Illustrative is the courtship of former University of Massachusetts basketball star Marcus Camby by agents John Lounsbury and Wesley Spears. The agents supplied Camby with prostitutes, cash payments, stereo equipment, jewelry, and rental cars in the hope that they would represent Camby once he turned pro.[12] In addition, Lounsbury and Spears, an attorney, followed another course of action often pursued by agents. They attempted to gain favor with Camby by ingratiating themselves with his family, friends, and other associates, oftentimes by providing them with gifts. Despite the agents' efforts, Camby signed with neither Lounsbury nor Spears, but with the ProServ athlete representation firm.

Criminally culpable conduct by agents also occurs. In 1987, a federal investigation of agents began after the alleged slashing and beating of an agent's associate by a rival agent. The investigation revealed that agents had threatened to "break the legs" of athletes who would not sign with them.[13] Although there is no evidence to suggest that threats and acts of violence are employed today, other criminal acts are being committed. In 2000, sophisticated stock market scams and money laundering became the crimes of the day.

Why do agents engage in illegal and unethical conduct? Why do payments by agents to athletes and other improprieties persist? Economists refer to such actions by agents as "opportunism." Oliver Williamson, in his work *Markets and Hierarchies*, defines opportunism as "self-interest seeking with guile."[14] The self-interest of sports agents is the right to receive approximately 2 to 5 percent of multimillion-dollar athlete contracts coupled with up to 30 percent of multimillion-dollar endorsement deals. As a result of this income opportunity, a wide range of techniques have been developed to secure student athletes as clients. For example, payments to athletes have become standard practice for some agents. Agent Jim Abernethy told *USA Today* back in 1987, "Everyone is being paid and signed. If anyone says otherwise, they're really stupid, blind or they're lying."[15] There is no indication that the environment has dramatically improved, as indicated by the following statement: "It is the wild, wild west out there. . . . The things agents are doing to each other, to their clients is worse than I can remember. The reason is pretty simple: there is more big money, but few hard-core punishments to serve as a deterrent to an agent who breaks the rules or breaks the law."[16] There is nothing to indicate that these payments have ceased. If anything, they are being made with a higher level of sophistication that inhibits efforts to detect the wrongdoing. The business is now much more mature, and the best understand both the hurdles they will encounter and how to circumvent them.

The absence of meaningful improvement is attributable, in part, to heightened competition for getting the rewards of representing an athlete. As will be discussed in greater detail in Chapter 3, the trend toward consolidation of sports agency firms typically affords the larger athlete representation firms advantages in securing clients. Thus, structural changes in the industry exacerbate problems derived from competition for a limited number of athletes. In the late 1980s and 1990s, industry consolidation produced deep-pocketed representation firms such as SFX, Assante, IMG, and Octagon that had the resources to spend considerable amounts to obtain and retain clients. Although certain of these firms have either lost their prominence in the agency representation business or no longer exist, consolidation persists with new players such as Creative Artists Agency (CAA) and Wasserman Media Group (WMG).

SFX Sports (SFX), a firm that at one time was one of the largest as a result of consolidation, exemplified the advantages reaped by size and resources. It reportedly advanced Peter Warrick a $500,000 line of credit on the bonus he was to receive from the Cincinnati Bengals upon signing his initial contract. The firm spent more in attempting to recapture Warrick as a client when he fired them days following the draft.[17] Competitors are not averse to turning to illegal conduct as a way of leveling what may be perceived as an un-level playing field in their efforts to sign clients. As discussed above, agents Lounsbury and Spears not only spent significant sums of money but also were willing to take risks that exposed them to criminal liability in their respective attempts to sign a representation agreement with Marcus Camby.

Changes occurring in the business of sports agency converge with the uniquely American sacred cow: collegiate amateur sports. Collegiate sport, although slowly evolving, is the last field in the world in which athletes are supposed to receive absolutely no direct monetary compensation for their athletic prowess. All the athlete may accept under NCAA rules in exchange for athletic participation is room, board, tuition, and educational fees. This concept of amateurism becomes more problematic when one understands that the Greek amateurism that many perceive American collegiate sports to be founded on may have actually allowed amateur athletes to receive compensation. Classicist David C. Young maintains that amateur athletes in ancient Greece won prizes worth as much as the value of ten years' wages.[18] If this is the case, then why is so much energy expended to ensure that collegiate athletes receive no compensation? And even if the Greeks were not compensated, why is it so important to retain this limitation today? And what of the fact that many of the athletes generating these huge collegiate athlete dollars are African Americans from lower economic backgrounds? These issues are key elements in the present agent-regulation problem.

What is being done to stop undesirable agent activities? First, state and federal prosecutors are taking action. For example, beginning in 1999, the agent most aggressively pursued by state and federal forces was William "Tank" Black.[19] His premier client was NBA star Vince Carter. Carter fired Black as the details of the evidence alleged against Black unfolded.[20] High-profile prosecutorial action goes back as far as 1989 when sports agents Norby Walters and Lloyd Bloom were convicted and sentenced for racketeering, conspiracy, mail fraud, wire fraud, and extortion after a trial that showcased sports and entertainment figures such as then University of Michigan head football coach Bo Schembechler and singer Dionne Warwick. That conviction, ironically, was ultimately overturned. In addition to prosecutorial action, colleges and universities are taking direct action against agents. In 1999, the University of Southern California sued Robert Caron, attorney and unregistered agent, alleging that he improperly induced certain of its student athletes to violate NCAA rules.[21]

Second, twenty-nine states, prior to 2001, had passed or were contemplating some sort of legislation to regulate athlete agents. As addressed in Chapter 11, these laws focus on regulating illegal activities of agents. Unfortunately, legislation that has been either enacted or proposed has done little to ensure agent competency. In fact, except for the higher price tag, registering to be a sports agent is often as simple as obtaining a license to fish: complete a form, pay a fee, and you're a "licensed" sports agent. It is the exception for states to require applicants to pass a competency exam. The number of states that have enacted athlete agent legislation has increased with the promulgation of the Uniform Athlete Agents Act (UAAA) in August 2000. As of February 27, 2007, the UAAA had been adopted in thirty-five states, the District of Columbia, and the U.S. Virgin Islands. During 2007, the UAAA was introduced in three additional states.[22] A principal goal of this act, which was prepared by the National Conference of Commissioners on Uniform State Laws, is to create uniform standards for regulating athlete agents. Proponents of the act hope that uniform standards will curtail the noncompliance with existing state legislation.

Third, the NCAA is is now clearly conscious of some of its more antiquated concepts of amateurism and has made a number of revisions to its rules in recent years.[23] In addition, the sports agent question is an important element in the NCAA's ongoing regulatory review process. For example, the NCAA continues to be focused on steps to address the increasing influence and threat of corruption posed by "street agents,"[24] individuals who serve as the intermediaries between sports agents and athletes before and after they enter college. Beyond that there is also a movement afoot to develop basketball academies for stellar high school basketball players, an anticipated impact of which is a reduction in the power and influence of street agents and Amateur Athletic Union (AAU) coaches. Interestingly, individuals as juxtaposed as NBA Commissioner David Stern and former athletic shoe executive Sonny Vaccaro support the idea, whereas superagent Arn Tellem of WMG opposes it.[25]

What can be done to stop the corruption associated with sports agents? Improprieties occur because the opportunity exists to make money. The solution, in the broadest terms, is simple: remove the opportunity to prosper by "cheating." As the following discussion reveals, layers of regulatory mechanisms will help to stymie the improprieties that are so prevalent in the sports agent industry. At the collegiate level, these mechanisms can be combined with efforts aimed at eliminating the opportunity for agents to benefit from improper conduct by implementing reforms that recognize the economic, social, and structural realities of college sports. Once the focus goes beyond college sports, the reform emphasis must be on agent competency and honesty. As you will read, this is much more simply said than done. The reality is that the system may always have major flaws.

Part I
Background

Chapter 1

Historical and Legal Foundations

A Brief History of the Business

The sports agent profession is not a new one. What is relatively new are the high finances and intense competition that pervade the profession. Most attribute the genesis of the athlete agent industry to theatrical promoter, impresario, and showman Charles C. "Cash and Carry" Pyle. Pyle, the agent for many athletes in the early part of this century, most notably the legendary football star Harold "Red" Grange,[1] the "Galloping Ghost," was a charter member of the NFL Hall of Fame. It was Pyle who negotiated a $3,000-per-game contract for Grange to play professional football with the Chicago Bears in 1925. In addition, he negotiated for Grange to receive more than $300,000 in movie rights and endorsements including a Red Grange doll, a candy bar, and a cap.[2] Other Pyle sports clients included tennis stars Mary K. Brown and Suzanne Lenglen.[3] Lenglen was the Wimbledon singles champion from 1919 to 1923. She signed with Pyle in 1926 for $50,000 to become the first professional tennis player.[4] Another example of an early sports agent was cartoonist Christy Walsh. Walsh, according to *Sports Illustrated,* advised baseball Hall of Famer Babe Ruth to invest in annuities prior to the stock market crash of 1929.[5]

During the 1960s, the number of sports agents increased, and individuals from diverse backgrounds and professions entered the industry. For example, considerable press coverage was given to Hollywood movie producer J. William Hayes, the agent for actor Vince Edwards (who portrayed television doctor Ben Casey), when Hayes orchestrated a $1 million holdout by Los Angeles Dodgers' pitching superstars Sandy Koufax and Don Drysdale.[6] In a holdout, a technique used to gain leverage in negotiations with a team, the athlete is, in effect, "held out" from playing with a team until the parties negotiate an agreement on the terms of the player's contract. The Koufax-Drysdale holdout was precipitated by a demand for a salary of $167,000 per year for each player for three years. This figure represented an amount that was $42,000 more than the salary earned by the highest-paid player of the day, Hall of Famer Willie Mays. As part of their negotiating strategy, Koufax and Drysdale signed with Paramount Pictures to act in a movie if their contract demands were not met.

Yet even in the mid-1960s, the use of an agent by an athlete was a conspicuous enough event to receive coverage in *Time*.[7] Before settling the Dodgers' contract dispute with Koufax and Drysdale, Dodgers' president Walter O'Malley told *Sports Illustrated*, "We can't give in to them. There are too many agents hanging around Hollywood looking for clients."[8] O'Malley's prognostication regarding the future was prescient.

The development of the sports agent as a recognized professional has by no means been smooth. A standard anecdote in the industry, disputed by some, is told about the legendary coach of the Green Bay Packers, Vince Lombardi. It was time to negotiate center Jim Ringo's contract for the coming year. The player came into the office with a gentleman wearing a suit. When Lombardi asked the player to identify the gentleman, Ringo responded that he had come to help in the contract negotiation. The story has it that Lombardi excused himself, stepped into the next room, and made a phone call. When he returned he informed Ringo that he was negotiating with the wrong team because he had just been traded to Philadelphia.

Lombardi was not alone in his view of agents. Another team executive, Don Klosterman, of what was then the NFL's Houston Oilers, told *Time*, "We spend $200,000 a year in evaluating talents and some uninformed agent is going to tell *us* what a player's worth? They're just parasites, in it for a fast buck."[9] Many believe that Klosterman's blunt and early view was fairly accurate.

Obviously, acceptance of the sports agent by management has come a long way since the days of O'Malley, Lombardi, and Klosterman. It is now more common than not for a player to be represented by an agent. Professors Schubert, Smith, and Trentadue, in their book *Sports Law*, concluded that the evolution of the sports agent profession is not accidental, but simply a natural response to dramatic developments witnessed in the professional sports arena during the twentieth century.[10] The authors cited several events that have transpired to account for agents' prominent position in the sports industry.

First was the demise of the extensive use of reserve and option clauses in standard player contracts through the early 1970s. These clauses bound athletes to teams in perpetuity without an opportunity to have their contracts affected by open-market bidding. Beginning in the mid-1970s, however, courts and arbitrators began to invalidate the perpetual nature of these clauses. In the 1970s, athletes in the major team sports—professional football,[11] basketball,[12] and hockey[13]—successfully asserted that mechanisms such as draft and reserve clauses constituted improper restraints of trade in that they limited players' ability to market their services freely. *Mackey v. National Football League* is illustrative of the judicial response to such legal challenges.[14] In *Mackey*, the player compensation rule known as the "Rozelle Rule" provided that "when a player's contractual obligation to a team expire[d] and he signe[d] with a different club, the signing club [had to] provide compensation to the player's former team."[15] The *Mackey* court held that the rule constituted an unreasonable restraint of trade in violation of Section 1 of the Sherman Act. In reaching this conclusion, the court stated: "[The Rozelle Rule] operates as a perpetual restriction on a player's ability to sell his services in an open market throughout his career."[16] With the opening provided by favorable court decisions, athletes obtained increased bargaining power.

Second, competition from newly created leagues in football, hockey, and basketball presented athletes with an appealing alternative to participation in the established leagues. Athletes were able to tell owners that they would command fair-market compensation or they would take their services to the rival leagues. This demand led to higher salaries, which were simultaneously enlarged by the voracious appetite of the newly formed leagues to sign players of some fame. Examples include the signing of then collegiate all-American Joe Namath by the upstart American Football League and the later signings of NFL veterans Paul Warfield, Larry Csonka, and Jim Kiick by the rival World Football League for relatively astronomical salaries. Economist Roger Noll of Stanford University wrote in 1988 that interleague competition was an important cause of increases in player salaries. During the National Basketball Association–American Basketball Association wars from 1967 to 1972, the average professional basketball player salary increased from $20,000 to $90,000.[17] During the United States Football League (USFL) and NFL war between 1982 and 1985, the average salary for players rose from $90,000 to $190,000.[18]

The surge in salaries over the last twenty years has only fueled the recent competition by agents for clients. Although the most significant sums of money are paid to upper-echelon athletes, as a result of television contracts, merchandising, and favorable minimum salaries negotiated into collective bargaining agreements, salaries have increased significantly over the past twenty years for both upper-echelon and non-star athletes. For example, in 1983, the NFL's number-one draft pick, John Elway, received a $1-million signing bonus. The number-one NFL pick in 2004, Carson Palmer, received a signing bonus of $10 million. The number-one NFL draft pick in 2005, Alex Smith, signed a six-year deal for $49.5 million, of which $24 million was guaranteed money (which includes bonus income). In 1983, football players considered $300,000 big money. The average salary for all NFL players in 2005 was

$1,400,000. The average salary in 2005 for quarterbacks, running backs, and offensive tackles exceeded $3 million.[19] In Major League Baseball the average player salary was $2,699,292 in 2006. The minimum salary for the 2006 season was $380,000.[20] "Players in the four major team sports, the NFL, [MLB, NHL, and NBA] were paid a total of $7.685 billion in 2005. This represents an increase of 125% over the $3.412 billion paid to players in these sports in 1995–96."[21] Of course such a substantial increase in player salaries has a direct relationship to the fees generated by agents. Athletes paid an estimated $385 million in fees to agents for their services in 2005.[22]

Third, the strength of the unions went from informal to the powerful position most hold today. Although the major sports unions have varying degrees of strength, they have all had an impact on increasing player salaries, particularly median salaries. The unions have also been responsible for solidifying the role of agents by leaving the role of salary negotiator to the agents and not retaining it for themselves, as unions traditionally do.

Fourth, higher salaries made it necessary for athletes to obtain professional guidance in a range of financial matters. Just as with any other highly compensated individual, it is generally wise for the professional athlete to obtain competent tax and other financial advice. The financial advice that the athlete requires is complicated by the fact that a playing career in most sports averages less than five years. With this in mind, the planner may have to take extra precautions to protect the athlete's earnings.

Fifth, additional sources of revenue began to emerge both for the leagues and for individual players. Media interest in including sports as part of regular television programming expanded very rapidly, pouring enormous amounts of revenue into the leagues. Using the muscle of their bargaining units—players' associations—athletes benefited handsomely from this revenue bonanza. Furthermore, the increase in the degree of media exposure afforded athletes contributed to increasing their popularity, which resulted in a booming commercial endorsement business for players. Today this exposure includes the personal websites of athletes and other online opportunities. "In 2005, the top seventy-five athletes, coaches, and sports personaliites earned fees totalling $598 million from endorsements. During the week leading up to the 2006 Super Bowl, 167 NFL players and draft prospects earned fees totaling $2.3 million for 360 appearances."[23] In 2006, Nike's financial commitment to endorsement obligations internationally was reported at $1.9 billion. Reebok reportedly spent $490 million on endorsements.[24] These five elements and the increasing complexity of the clauses required to protect athletes in player contracts caused the demand for agents to increase.

Two agents who might be appropriately referred to as the "modern fathers" of the sports agent industry for team sports were Boston-based agent Bob Woolf and New York–based agent Martin Blackman. The late Bob Woolf's beginnings in the business are chronicled in his 1976 book *Behind Closed Doors*.[25] A former criminal lawyer and college basketball player, Woolf entered the sports agent business in 1964. He maintained that he was the first attorney to specialize in the area and that as of 1976 he had negotiated more than 2,000 contracts. Woolf entered the field by serendipity when professional baseball player Earl Wilson came to his office for standard legal advice following an automobile accident. According to Woolf, "When we talked we discovered we had a lot of attitudes in common. One day we found ourselves discussing methods by which an athlete could defer income and that, I guess, is where the whole thing began."[26] Some of Woolf's most famous clients included Carl Yastrzemski, Jim Plunkett, Julius Erving, and Derek Sanderson.

Wheras Woolf is noted as a pioneer in the representation of athletes in contract negotiations, Martin Blackman is best known for his pioneering negotiation of endorsement deals for athletes. His most famous connection of athletes with products is the series of Miller Lite television commercials featuring retired professional athletes of the "tastes great, less filling" genre. Many point to the early deals put together by Blackman as the foundation for the growth in endorsement contracts today.

Probably the most successful agent of the 1970s was Mike Trope. Trope writes about the successes and tribulations of his career in his autobiographical *Necessary Roughness*, published in 1987.[27] Trope entered the business in 1973 at the age of twenty while still a student at the University of Southern California. Not only did he enter the business at an unusually young age for any profession, but he did so with an unusually prominent client: Johnny Rodgers, the 1972 Heisman Trophy winner. This began an amazing string of signings by Trope of six Heisman Trophy winners and other first-round draft picks in the sport of football. Trope negotiated a $1.6 million contract plus a Rolls Royce for Rodgers from the Canadian Football League's Montreal Alouettes. His other clients included running backs Ricky Bell, Tony Dorsett, and Earl Campbell.[28]

Perhaps it was Trope's success, other agents' jealousy, or simply the truth that accounted for what may have been the first widely circulated stories regarding improprieties by agents in obtaining clients. When anyone young in any business is successful, it is natural to ask how it was done. And whenever there is a young "whiz kid" in any industry, he or she probably will be subject to intense scrutiny. Perhaps this explains why Trope was alleged, among other things, to have made payments to athletes to induce them to sign with him.

In his book, Trope readily admitted that "some things" occurred. He also made it clear that he did not consider the rules of the NCAA to be the law of the land, and so he had not, in his mind, done anything illegal. Unfortunately, he was only the first of a long line of agents to make this flawed argument. Trope alleged that his competitors started the stories about his improper activities and maintained that he was not alone in being involved in activities that violated NCAA regulations.

One successful competitor, and one who remained in the business even after Trope retired, is agent Leigh Steinberg. Like Trope, he started out at a relatively young age. While a law student at the University of California at Berkeley, he developed a relationship with an undergraduate student and star athlete, quarterback Steve Bartkowski. He was an adviser in Bartkowski's dormitory. Bartkowski became Steinberg's first major client, and at the age of twenty-five, Steinberg negotiated a then-record $650,000 per year contract with the Atlanta Falcons of the NFL.

Steinberg continued to have great success and was noted not only for negotiating what were considered outstanding contracts for his clients but also for being a master of public relations. His unique contracts often required that athletes donate a portion of their professional contract earnings to their colleges or high schools. It was not simply the terms of these contracts that brought Steinberg public notoriety but also the numerous positive quotes in the press and appearances on television shows such as *Lifestyles of the Rich and Famous*. One of the hottest tickets at the NFL's Super Bowl was a ticket to the annual party hosted by Steinberg. Through such self-promotion, Steinberg manufactured an early reputation as one of the few "honest" agents. He's been able to do this despite negative public relations revelations in trials and drunk-driving arrests.[29]

While Steinberg and Trope became successful as individual agents, two other sports agents developed firms that became sports marketing powers: Mark McCormack's International Management Group (IMG) in Cleveland and Donald Dell's Washington, DC–based ProServ.[30] IMG got its start representing athletes in professional golf. McCormack's first client, in the early 1960s, was Arnold Palmer. Because of the firm's marketing and management successes with Palmer, other golfers soon followed, including Jack Nicklaus and Gary Player. The firm eventually branched out into other sports and other areas of representation. IMG has represented clients as diverse as the Wimbledon Tennis Championships and the Vatican.

Donald Dell is an attorney and former captain of the U.S. Davis Cup tennis team. It is understandable, then, that ProServ got its start in tennis. Dell's first client was Arthur Ashe. Building on his success with Ashe, Dell began to represent other tennis players and, like IMG, eventually began to branch out into other team and individual sports. IMG remains a solo player after undergoing an ownership change following the death of McCormack, while ProServ has been acquired, divided, and portions acquired again.

By 1980, other agents had become prominent. Some of them specialized in specific sports, whereas others represented athletes in several sports. The agent ranks continued to swell, with even boxing promoter Don King becoming certified as an agent by the National Basketball Players Association (NBPA).[31] Beginning in the 1980s, agents began to have their names closely associated with the athletes they represented. If one attends a sports agents' conference or an event where there are potential professional athletes, one can walk away with a wide array of business cards with firm names such as Sports Plus, The Sports Management Group, Superstars, Inc., and Sportstars. The owners of most of these types of firms are part-time agents and full-time stockbrokers, attorneys, accountants, insurance agents, dentists, or members of virtually any other profession. As we have seen, with the increase in the number of individuals in the industry, the hostility between agents has also increased. Some agents jokingly refer to their ongoing battles as "agent wars."

Another event has begun to impact the industry as well: the growth of women's professional sports. For example, agents were quite valuable during the existence of the WNBA's rival, the American Basketball League. They remain so in sorting through offers for their clients to play in Europe, Asia, and South America. Curiously absent from these ranks are significant numbers of female sports agents.

The new millennium brought about a series of mega-mergers of superstar successful agents. At one time we even saw David Falk and Arn Tellem joining forces with publicly traded entertainment enterprises such as, in their case, SFX. The phenomenon repeated itself again in 2007 with superagents Tom Condon, Jim Steiner, Ben Dogra, and Casey Close all ending up at CAA.[32] These mergers only highlighted the dominant role that the concept of sports as entertainment has come to play.

Fact has blended with fiction to discredit the business with anecdotes, but not until the 1989 trial of agents Norby Walters and Lloyd Bloom were many of the anecdotal stories confirmed to the public at large. Only agents and athlete clients fully realize how intense the competition has become or what types of recruiting tactics continue today. Many agents who have unsuccessfully tried to recruit clients without making payments or taking other steps in violation of NCAA rules and state laws cannot imagine someone legitimately making a living as a sports agent. Is this the reality or only sour grapes? The chapters that follow explore conduct spurred by competition that led to the convictions of agents Walters and Bloom and, more recently, of "street agent" Myron Piggie

TABLE 1
NUMBER OF AGENTS AND PLAYERS, JANUARY 2006

	Registered Agents	Players on Total Roster
NBA	350 (fewer than 100 are estimated to have a client)	400
NHL	150	700
NFL	800–1,000 (50 percent have clients in league)	1,900
MLB	300	1,200 on 40-man rosters

Source: Timothy Davis, *Regulating the Athlete-Agent Industry: Intended and Unintended Consequences*, 42 Williamette L Rev 781, 793–94 (2006) (the article includes citations to specific sources of the information).

and agent Tank Black. Also examined in greater detail is the consolidation ebb and flow among sports agencies. We also look at the call for state regulation of agents. Before these matters are addressed, we take a brief look at the principles that provide the legal basis for the athlete/agent relationship. First, however, we need to have an idea of the number of agents and athletes involved in the major professional sports (see Table 1).

The Legal Basis of the Relationship

A great deal of criticism was directed toward Leland Hardy, the agent who negotiated the contract between then–top draft pick NFL running back Ricky Williams and the New Orleans Saints. Critics assailed the length and the incentive-laden nature of the contract that resulted in Williams making a base salary far less than a player of his caliber could demand. In defending Hardy against criticism that questioned the agent's competence and negotiation skills, Williams stated as follows:

> I'm first and last when it comes to my decisions. . . . I don't work for my agent. My agent works for me. This was my decision and my decision alone. . . . When I got drafted, I told Leland I was going to get the deal done in the next two weeks. So we waited a little while longer . . . and after the course of negotiations [with Saints salary cap expert Terry O'Neil], Leland called and said, "I'm going to give you some options on contracts to look at," and when I told him what kind of a deal I wanted, he told me I shouldn't do it.[33]

Williams reportedly told Hardy to reject a deal that would have paid him a guaranteed salary of $25.6 million over seven years. Instead, Williams signed a contract that paid him an up-front signing bonus of

$8.8 million and required him to meet certain performance objectives in order to earn more than the yearly base salaries.[34] As it turned out, Williams did not have the Hall of Fame career that would have been required to receive the maximum payouts under the incentive-laden deal. (The terms of Williams's deal are discussed in detail in Chapter 2.)

Williams's statement is instructive for two reasons. First, Williams demonstrates an appreciation of the most fundamental principle of the agent's relationship with his principal: ultimate decision-making authority rests with the principal. In addition, Williams's statement illustrates that the relationship between sports agents and the athletes whom they represent is governed by the same core concepts that govern other principal/agent relationships. Thus a personnel officer who, acting as an agent, hires an employee for a corporation, and a building leasing manager who, acting as an agent, rents residential or commercial buildings for its owner are bound by the same legal principles relevant to the sports agent's relationship with his or her client.[35]

The agency relationship is defined as "the fiduciary relationship which results from the manifestation of consent by one person to another that the other shall act in his behalf and subject to his contract, and consent by the other so to act."[36] The Restatement (Second) of the Law of Agency also provides definitions of agent and principal. The principal is "the one for whom action is to be taken."[37] In the sports context, the athlete is the principal. The agent is "the one who is to act" for the principal.[38] "The essential nature and character of the agency relationship is that the principal authorizes his agent to contract on his behalf with one or more third parties."[39]

These definitions tell us that the agency relationship is consensual— typically expressed in a contract. This is certainly the case in the sports context in which the major sports leagues have developed model contracts for the agent/principal relationship. For example, the National Football League Players Association (NFLPA) has developed a "Standard Representation Agreement" for mandatory use by agents and their football player clients. In addition to provisions governing the fees to which an agent is entitled, the NFLPA agreement sets forth general principles including the concept that the "Contract Advisor" acts "in a fiduciary capacity." The Uniform Athlete Agents Act provides the following definition: "'Agency contract' means an agreement in which a student-athlete authorizes a person to negotiate or solicit on behalf of the student-athlete a professional-sports-services contract or an endorsement contract."[40]

The above definitions relating to agency also inform us that the most basic obligations that agents owe to their principals are defined not only by the contract but also by the fiduciary characteristics of the relationship.

A fiduciary is defined as "one who acts primarily for the benefit of another."[41] Consequently, the essence of the principal/agent relationship spawns a fundamental obligation that the "agent owes his principal the fiduciary duty of undivided loyalty and the duty to act in good faith at all times. This fiduciary relationship is imposed by law upon the agent because the very nature of the agency relationship involves the principal entrusting his fortune, reputation, and legal rights and responsibilities to his agent whose actions, for better or worse, vitally affect the economic well-being and reputation of the principal."[42]

As alluded to above, Ricky Williams's statement also reflects the basic notion that it is an agent's duty to carry out the desires of its principal.[43] This certainly makes sense, as the agent acts not to carry on its own business affairs but those of the principal.[44] Thus it is the agent's duty to act in accordance with his or her principal's instructions even if the agent believes they are unwise. As stated by two commentators, "An agent has the duty to obey all of his principal's lawful instructions no matter how arbitrary or capricious any of those instructions seem to the agent or anyone else. . . . By contrast, if the principal's instructions are illegal, immoral, unethical, or opposed to public policy, as where the principal instructs his agent to bribe another to obtain business for his principal, the agent has no duty to obey."[45] Moreover, by acting on its principal's behalf, the agent assumes a duty that it "possesses a degree of skill commensurate with the job to be done and that he will use such skill with diligence."[46] In exercising this duty of reasonable care and skill, it is important to emphasize that the agent does not guarantee or ensure that he or she will achieve the result desired by the client unless the agent has expressly agreed to do so.[47] Rather the agent has fulfilled his or her duty by acting with the care and skill employed by a reasonable person under the same circumstances.[48]

Agent Michael B. Siegel notes the tension created by this agency norm. "I can't play for him [the athlete] and he can't negotiate for me. But I think it's important that a guy [athlete] be in a position so that he can determine whether he wants to go left or right."[49] Siegel knowingly concludes, "if they say they want to go left and I disagree, I will give them every reason why they should go right. If after I lay it out for them and we discuss it and they still want to go left, then it's fine because they have made an educated decision."[50]

Another basic duty of the agent to the principal seems particularly relevant in the sports context. The agent must account to its principal for all of the principal's funds that come into the agent's possession as a part of the agency relationship.[51] Other basic duties that the agent owes to the principal include the duty to comply with the law, the duty to notify the principal of all matters that may affect the principal's interests, and the duty not to delegate the performance to another without the consent of the principal.[52]

Finally, the agent owes a duty of loyalty and good faith to its principal. This duty precludes an agent from acting on behalf of parties adverse to his or her principal.[53] Courts have attempted to incorporate these core concepts into rulings addressing matters ranging from agent malpractice to conflict of interest. Further, as discussed in Chapters 11 and 12, some state legislatures, as well as the recently promulgated Uniform Athlete Agents Act, attempt to explicitly spell out these obligations.

Chapter 2

The Business

"That's what agents are for."

—*Latrell Sprewell, then of the New York Knicks, explaining why he failed to inform his team and teammates about missing a week of practice prior to the 1999–2000 NBA season*

For many people, the life of a sports agent conjures up visions of a Hollywood lifestyle complete with fast cars, fancy clothes, and beautiful women. The motion picture *Jerry Maguire* and the television series *Arli$$* did much to further glamorize the profession. SportsCenter snippets of agents in action, such as Drew Rosenhaus, have enhanced this even further. Some sports agents refer to their profession as "the business," in much the way natives of New York or San Francisco refer to their towns as "the city." Longtime successful agent Leigh Steinberg once described the stereotypical agent as "short and slick, he wears a gold chain around his neck and a diamond ring on his pinky finger; he's armed with a stream of fast talk and a package of promises to fatten his wallet at the expense of the athlete."[1] Statements made in a more recent interview suggest that Steinberg continues to view agents with something that falls short of admiration. "One of the major problems of contemporary agentry is the lack of collegiality. . . . With most agents, they seem to be psychologically incapable of finding the good or acknowledging the strengths of their competitors, and it's really sad. I didn't want my wife to marry me because I convinced her [that] all other men were [jerks]."[2] But this is a stereotype. Successful agents Ben Dogra and Eugene Parker, for example, are known for being low profile. Arn Tellem, like former NFL head coach Bill Walsh, is known for being cerebral. In terms of personalities, the industry is not short on diversity.

It is the flashy and competitive lifestyle that many agents point to as a prime reason for their success in obtaining athlete clients. These images, as will be discussed, have also been largely responsible for the negative perceptions of sports agents.

Who Needs an Agent?

Although sports agents often exude the heady glamour of life in the fast lane, in reality agents attract clients primarily by performing valuable services for athletes who are enmeshed in increasingly complex business activities off the field. Agents provide a level of parity in negotiations between athletes and clubs or other entities for whom athletes have contracted to perform. Club management representatives have had years to become expert negotiators, sometimes negotiating dozens of contracts per year. The athlete may have only one opportunity to negotiate a contract in an entire professional career. A sports agent, however, may have negotiated many sports contracts and is often a match for the negotiating experience of the management representative. Even an agent who has not negotiated dozens of contracts in sports may have experience negotiating contracts in other business settings. Rarely does a student athlete possess similar talents.

Reginald Wilkes, now a prominent financial adviser to professional athletes and others, was a premedical student at Georgia Tech University. When he graduated from college, he had no idea that he would be drafted and subsequently named the NFL's rookie of the year. Even with his serious academic background, Wilkes recalls, "I don't think I was mentally prepared to choose an agent or negotiate a contract." He adds that it would be difficult for any student fresh out of college to attempt to negotiate a contract without an agent.[3]

A different perspective, however, was offered by then veteran NFL wide receiver Carl Pickens, who defied conventional wisdom by negotiating a contract without any direct form of representation. Following a release from his acrimonious relationship with the Cincinnati Bengals, Pickens signed a five-year deal worth $20 million with the Tennessee Titans. During the negotiation process, Pickens fired his second agent and may have received advice from a third, the agent who then represented Tennessee Titans' head coach, Jeff Fisher.[4] In commenting on whether he had anyone review the contract, Pickens stated that he knew what to look for after eight years in the league. "This is my third time going through this situation. . . . I'm the one that has to deal with the deal at the end of the day, so I kind of know what I want. I can come down here and sell myself. I don't need an agent to tell me yea or nay over a contract I can read and understand."[5]

Scholars indicate that the athlete salary negotiation is the classic scenario in which the use of an agent is appropriate. In their article "When Should We Use Agents? Direct vs. Representative Negotiation," Jeffrey Rubin and Frank Sander conclude that it is most appropriate to use an agent "when special expertise is required, when tactical flexibility is deemed important and—most importantly—when direct contact is likely to produce confrontation rather than collaboration."[6]

This is not to say that the use of an agent is mandatory. Until the agent became an accepted part of sports, athletes often negotiated their own contracts with management. They might or might not have had the documentation reviewed by an attorney or other knowledgeable third party. Notable recent "self-negotiators" have included Ray Allen of the Milwaukee Bucks; the previously noted Carl Pickens of the Cincinnati Bengals; and Tedy Bruschi, who negotiated a two-year, $3.4-million contract to play for the New England Patriots and who at times consulted with an attorney.[7] Self-negotiators in earlier times were Danny Ainge of the Boston Celtics, Alan Trammel of the Detroit Tigers, and Mike Singletary of the Chicago Bears.[8] In 2003 two baseball free agents, pitcher Curt Schilling and slugger Gary Sheffield, both negotiated their own free-agent deals.[9]

Another illustration involves Matt Morris, who pitched for Major League Baseball's (MLB) St. Louis Cardinals and joined the San Francisco Giants in 2006. Morris reportedly dismissed his agent due to uncertainty as to where the "agent's company was going" and handled negotiations himself.[10] Morris reportedly said that Cardinals' general manager Walt Jocketty "sent me a proposal I thought was fair. They've always treated me well, even with my injuries and everything."[11] Morris recognized that he may have left money on the table by not using an agent, but he remained satisfied with the deal he struck. "I'm sure if I had an agent, he'd be scratching at the door trying to get as much as he could but that's not the person I am and that's not the relationship I want with the club, either."[12] At the time, Morris signed a contract that guaranteed him $27 million over a four-year period.

Nevertheless, there are reasons why self-negotiation may not be a good idea. In addition to the need for "expertise" and "tactical flexibility," the avoidance of confrontation is particularly applicable in the sports setting. The athlete must play for the team once the negotiations are complete. It is often necessary in these negotiations for the athlete's representative to sing the praises of the athlete. To counter this, in the paradigm of bargaining, the management representative must discuss the skills the player lacks, whether factual or not. When the goal is to make the athlete a member of the team, both literally and ideologically, it is easier for both parties to negotiate when the player does not actually have to brag or invite management's criticism.

An intermediate measure between self-representation and employing an agent is to use a family member or close friend for contract negotiation. Former MLB player George Brett is one of the more prominent athletes who took this route.[13] Similarly, hockey's Eric Lindros has been represented by his father. NBA great Dominique Wilkins had various contracts negotiated by his mother. Mike Conley, Sr., announced his entry into the business in 2007 representing both his son, Mike Conley, Jr., and Greg Oden in the NBA draft.[14]

Others urge athletes to avoid agents and have their contracts negotiated or reviewed by lawyers. Edward Garvey, the former executive director of the NFLPA, was one of the most vocal critics of the use of people who call themselves agents. His harshest criticism of agents homed in on the large fees that they charge. Garvey recommended that athletes use attorneys who will charge a standard hourly rate for negotiation services.

Pitcher Brad Radke used an attorney to negotiate his contract with the Minnesota Twins.[15] Former University of Maryland basketball star Steve Francis hired Washington attorney Jeff Fried to provide a range of services.[16] The NBA's Ray Allen received considerable notoriety in 1999 for employing a lawyer to review a contract that he had negotiated with the Milwaukee Bucks basketball franchise. Allen's use of a team of attorneys, whom he reportedly paid up to $500 per hour to review his contract, and his retention of a business manager and accountant, provoked varying reactions.[17] Some heralded Allen's conduct as the beginning of a trend that would contribute to diminishing the power and influence of agents. Others, perhaps unable to be so prescient, nevertheless viewed Allen's decision as a wise business move that allowed him to take control of his affairs, a view shared by Allen: "It was merely a good business decision. . . . I don't need an agent. I know how much money I'm going to make. If you're smart, and know what you're doing, you can negotiate what you're worth."[18] Others, however, were quick to caution that Allen's decision was prudent only because of the convergence of a unique set of circumstances—the NBA hard salary cap and Ray Allen's intelligence, business acumen, and strong family structure.[19] Allen admitted that his decision might not be appropriate for other athletes and in particular in sports other than basketball. For example, an NBA player who would not be awarded the maximum amount permissible under the collective bargaining agreement might be better suited to use an agent who can negotiate and act as a buffer when the player and team disagree on a player's worth.

NBA player Grant Hill is represented by attorney Lon Babby, who has carved out a niche in representing professional athletes in contract negotiations at the litigation-oriented Washington, DC, firm of Williams & Connolly.[20]As of early 2007, Babby's other athlete clients include the NBA's Tim Duncan, Shane Battier, Tony Battie, Malik Rose, Josh Childress, Pat Garrity, Luke Ridnour, and Andre Miller; MLB's Melvin Mora, Chris Nelson, Chris Ray, Rickie Weeks, and Chris Young; and several

WNBA stars including Chamique Holdsclaw, Tamika Catchings, and Nikki McCray.[21] Although Babby charges $400 or more per hour for his legal services, he asserts that the total cost is considerably less than the standard 2 to 4 percent agent fee typical in the NBA.[22] Babby charged Hill a reported $100,000 to negotiate his first contract, a six-year, $45-million deal with the Detroit Pistons. The standard 4 percent would have cost Hill $1.8 million.

Nevertheless, according to some agents, charging an hourly fee has disadvantages including hampering the development of both a business and a personal relationship between attorney and client. This view is held by former attorney agent Leonard Armato, who once represented Shaquille O'Neal of the NBA. "Some clients prefer to have the knowledge that there's a fixed cost and not worry whether conversations, communications or meetings are work and are billable or were social and not billable. . . . An hourly fee is much easier when a client puts a contract on your desk and says, 'here, negotiate this deal.' But when you provide a range of services, the relationship between the agent and athlete often runs a range beginning in business and ending in friendship."[23]

Lon Babby believes that another advantage of athlete representation by an attorney is that an attorney attempts to avoid appearing as the "bigger-than-life agent who calls the shots for his clients. 'The player is the brand name that should be known, not the agent's.'"[24]

A related issue involves the advantages that may accrue to an athlete who hires an attorney, whether the attorney acts merely as an agent or in a dual capacity as an attorney and agent. A former professional basketball player is reported to have expressed the following view regarding lawyers who represent athletes: "Lawyers do the same things agents do: they lie, connive, cheat, and hurt athlete clients."[25] Despite the cynicism expressed in this statement, scholars have identified several advantages that can result from an attorney who represents athletes. From the perspective of competence, the education and training necessary to become an attorney arguably prepares lawyers to substantively understand increasingly complicated collective bargaining agreements used by professional sports leagues.[26] Moreover, unlike nonlawyer agents, attorneys representing athletes possess the duty to know the law or consult with others who know the law regarding a broad range of potentially relevant matters that traverse collective bargaining agreements, such as the Americans with Disabilities Act and workers' compensation.[27]

Other potential advantages to attorney representation include:

1. Attorneys, in contrast to agents, are held to standards, such as the American Bar Association's Model Rules of Professional Conduct, which arguably make them more accountable to their clients.

Consequently, athletes who feel their interests have not been adequately protected by an attorney have greater avenues of recourse available, such as registering complaints with bar associations, in addition to filing malpractice claims;

2. Information such as formal evaluations may be available to assist an athlete in researching the competence and ethics of an attorney; and,

3. In contrast to nonlawyers, lawyers are better equipped to avoid conflicts of interest and will be held to higher standards of accountability to avoid conflicts of interest. In instances in which an attorney represents more than one athlete client, "[i]f a conflict of interest is present, a lawyer-representative must fully disclose the conflict to the athletes and obtain an acknowledgment of the conflict and an express waiver of the conflict of interest from each athlete."[28]

Notwithstanding the perceived benefits of the alternatives to representation by an agent—no representation, familial representation, and attorney representation—they remain the exception. The most common practice is for the athlete to be represented by an agent. One of the conclusions of a 1977 congressional inquiry into professional sports was that "player agents are now generally accepted as permanent, highly visible, and at times positively beneficial element[s] in the sports labor relations process."[29] Former Senator John Culver stated in another setting, "when performed properly it's about as honorable a thing as you can do so these kids [student athletes] are not exploited."[30]

In the aftermath of Ray Allen's use of an attorney, newspaper headlines asked whether agents are an endangered species. In a commentary, attorney, former basketball star, and former agent Len Elmore opined that various factors may converge to radically reduce the prominence and significance of agents.

To bring down the pro sports agent house of cards, players need only to sincerely question "what are we getting for the percentage of gross compensation that we pay to our agents?" In an environment where they must constantly restate their value proposition, a majority of agents are going to be hard-pressed to prove fairly and comparatively how they enhance a player's bottom line or his overall career.

Certainly instances exist where some players feel that a few agents in fact enhance careers, but the grumblings are growing louder than the praise. . . .

The day has come when superstars can meet face-to-face with an activist owner and without an agent reach the basics of an agreement. In the NBA world of "max-out" players, a ceiling is placed on what a free agent can earn. Even in the "never-never" ("as in never leave money on the table") land of Major League Baseball the same remains true. With professional help from a lawyer, accountant or even an economist, a superstar might agree with an owner to only 80 to

90 percent of what an agent could have gotten him, and wind up in no worse position than if an agent did the deal. . . .

Thanks to their collective-bargaining agreement and the millions of marketing dollars it receives pursuant to it, the National Basketball Players Association is in a financial position to hire a law firm or two to negotiate individual contracts for far less than the aggregate dollars spent by players for their individual agents. Players could use the savings to contract for all the services agents now propose to provide such as public relations, endorsement opportunities and financial advice. The NCAA and its member institutions would beam with glee because this development would all but erase the headaches caused by agent involvement with high school players and college players with eligibility remaining.[31]

Others involved in the industry share the views expressed by Elmore. In commenting on whether rookies need agents, agent Keith Kreiter stated, "Every contract is just a form agreement. My plummer [sic] could negotiate a first-round pick's contract as good as the best negotiator in the county can."[32] Notes another agent, "It used to be that it came down to good negotiation on the part of the agent, . . . but now (with the rookie scale) those skills have been taken away, so that puts the average agent on par with the David Falks and Arn Tellems of the basketball world."[33]

Elmore's comments could represent the future of the industry. However, for now it appears that agents will continue to play a prominent role in representing professional athletes. The phrase "value added" is often employed to explain the enduring prominence of agents who stress that "he or she offers management services as well [as negotiation services], everything from finding a hotel room for a player's mother for when she flew into town to shopping an athlete when trade time looms."[34] Notes another agent, "contract negotiation becomes secondary in a changing sports world accentuated by the merging of sports and entertainment, and by new technologies that create expanding opportunities to exploit the athlete's image for financial gain in contexts extending beyond the sport in which he or she plays." Moreover, agents remain important because of the influence they yield.[35]

Agent Bill Strickland comments on the broad scope of an agent's activities: "I have in my career done everything including physically moving a client, that is driving a moving truck and loading and unloading the furniture onto and off of the truck, which was a rare case. . . . [I have handled] prenuptial agreements and rape cases, sued [an athlete's] family members, attended funerals, simply shown support for an athlete, sat with mothers, parents and significant others who may not understand the process going on with a player. I've done a little bit of everything."[36]

Interesting questions regarding the duties of agents have been raised in recent years. As addressed in Chapter 1, some of these questions came up in the context of the representation of Heisman Trophy winner Ricky Williams by agent Leland Hardy.[37] Williams was the fifth player selected in the 1999 NFL draft. More importantly, however, he was the lone draft pick of the New Orleans Saints. The team traded away all other picks as they coveted Williams, and this was the only way the team could be assured of selecting him. Most viewed this as an opportunity for Williams, through his agent, to exert tremendous leverage. Not only did the Saints' action show how much they wanted Williams, but the team obtained an additional benefit. Rather than having to negotiate contracts with and pay up to eight new players, it only had to negotiate with and pay one player, Williams.

From a negotiation perspective, the contract to be negotiated had a substantial upside for Williams. But instead of securing a contract with substantial amounts of guaranteed monies, Williams's contract was incentive laden. In essence, Williams, beyond a sizable signing bonus, would have to earn every dollar above the minimum base salary. First, the contract was of a seven-year duration with a club option for an eighth year. It included no escape or out clauses favoring Williams.[38] The contract included base salaries ranging from the NFL minimums of $175,000 to $400,000. If the Saints had exercised their exclusive option for the eighth season, Williams would have received $3.5 million in 2006. The rest of the contract consisted primarily of incentive clauses that would have been triggered if Williams had achieved extraordinary results. For example, the contract provided that Williams would have earned $1 million if he had rushed for 1,600 yards, $1.5 million for 1,800 yards, $2 million for 2,000 yards, $2.5 million for 2,100 yards, and a maximum of $3 million if he had achieved the single-season rushing record, which at the time of the contract was 2,105 yards.[39] Another clause involved Williams matching or surpassing three of four production levels achieved by then Denver Broncos star running back Terrell Davis during Davis's first four seasons: 6,413 yards rushing, 7,594 yards rushing and receiving, a 4.8-yard rushing average, and scoring 366 points.[40] If he had reached these goals, Williams's salaries during his fifth, sixth, and seventh seasons would have equaled or surpassed the earnings of Davis, who had signed a nine-year $51.6-million contract in 1998.[41] Williams was unable to stay healthy and failed to achieve the incredible statistics required to trigger the incentives.[42] For example, Williams failed to even remotely approach the numbers of Terrell Davis. In contrast to Davis, Williams rushed for 3,129 yards and had total yards gained of 4,221 entering his fourth season.[43] Williams also forfeited $100,000 in 2001 for failing to comply with a provision requiring him to maintain a designated weight of 240 pounds. After Williams was traded to the Miami Dolphins, his contract was reworked by Leigh

Steinberg to make the incentives more achievable and the penalties less harsh.

Most faulted agent Leland Hardy for this deal, which at least one commentator characterized as widely considered one of the worst negotiated for a top draft pick.[44] As discussed in Chapter 1, Williams indicated in an interview in the *SportsBusiness Journal* that Hardy had simply structured the deal according to his instructions: "This was my decision and my decision alone."[45] This being the case, Hardy was acting in the role as the agent is traditionally defined.

Williams's view of Hardy later changed. In the year 2000, Williams reportedly filed a countersuit against Leland Hardy and Percy Miller (aka Master P) alleging incompetence in Hardy's negotiation of Williams's initial contract with the New Orleans Saints.[46] Williams's countersuit was purportedly in response to a suit in which Hardy and Miller asserted that the player failed to pay a $75,000 installment toward the commission arising out of his signing bonus.

Two weeks after Williams's contract was signed, Hardy failed an open-book take-home test given to agents on the NFL's collective bargaining agreement and substance abuse policy, and the NFLPA's agent regulations.[47] Hardy was suspended for thirty days from representing NFL players and was required by the NFLPA to retake and pass the exam.[48] Miller closed No Limit Sports a few years after his clientele fled the agency in the wake of the Williams's contract negotiation.[49]

The agent concept in sports is similar to that which has long existed in the motion picture, theatrical, television, and music sectors of the entertainment industry, as exemplified by the influential William Morris Agency. The duties that agents undertake in the entertainment industry, however, are often more specific than those of the agent in sports. In the entertainment industry, traditionally it is common for a performer to employ a group of advisers, including an agent, a personal manager, a business manager, and an attorney, in contrast to the athlete who may employ *an* agent.[50] The combined fees for the entertainer's group of advisers have been estimated to equal 30 to 40 percent of the entertainer's gross income.[51] The "agent" in the entertainment industry is loosely defined as the person who finds employment for the entertainer.

Another distinguishing characteristic relates to the nature of regulation. The agent in entertainment has been regulated by state laws for some time. Because of the nature of the entertainment industry, an agent can be regulated by the laws of only New York and California, the states in which the entertainment industry is centered. This situation contrasts with that of the sports industry, in which an agent may need to conduct business (for example, contract negotiation) in many states. As discussed further in Chapters 5, 11, and 12, this aspect of the sports agent industry has resulted in regulatory problems and influenced the promulgation of the Uniform Athlete Agents Act (UAAA) in 2000 and the Sports Agent Responsibility and Trust Act (SPARTA) in 2004. This is certainly not to say that all is perfect in the entertainment industry relative to the sports industry. The personal manager in entertainment wears many of the same hats as the sports agent. According to the entertainer Kashif, personal managers often enter the business like sports agents, with no experience at all. Kashif quipped that it would not surprise him to hear a personal manager say, "Yesterday I was a garbage man, today I'm a manager." Fortunately, it is a generally recognized practice in the entertainment industry for the personal manager to hire professionals to handle the tasks of the combined team.[52]

Increasingly, sports agents provide services beyond the negotiation of the professional contract.[53] These additional services may include the following: providing advice regarding financial matters such as tax, investment, insurance, and money management; obtaining and negotiating endorsement contracts; medical and physical health and training consultations; legal (including criminal) consultation; post-playing career counseling; counseling players regarding their particular sport; counseling players regarding their media image; and counseling players on matters pertaining to everyday life.[54] All of these services and more are certainly required, in varying degrees, by today's professional athletes.[55] Once the player signs a contract, the agent may continue to have ongoing obligations, depending on the nature of the specific athlete/agent agreement. Some agents are finished with their duties once the player contract is negotiated and simply receive their fee. Others maintain an ongoing relationship, providing certain of the laundry list of functions described above, particularly financial, endorsement, and counseling services.

A negative aspect of the business is what some agents refer to as "babysitting," such as taking the 1:00 A.M. telephone call about the bad game the player had that night. Sports agent and attorney David Ware expands on the related statements of Bill Strickland: "The good agents have to accept that as a part of the business. If you don't like being in the personal service business, it's [being a sports agent] not the business for you. You may not think the 1:00 A.M. phone call from a player is important, but obviously he does."[56] The burdensome nature of this role was expressed by another agent as follows: "An athlete calls you at 12:30 in the morning and says, 'I've got this girl in my hotel room and now my wife's here. What do I do?' Or, 'I've got my shoes in Detroit and I'm in Orlando. What do I do?' It's a full-time service position. Being called an 'agent' is misleading. It's a combination. You're agent, manager, social worker, family counselor, psychologist. All under one hat."[57]

On the other hand, not all agents view this role from a negative perspective. As noted in Chapter 1, some sports agents use their babysitter function as a tool for recruiting players. In this regard, it becomes a part of the value added that an agent can offer in contrast to a player representative such as an attorney, who only negotiates a contract for a player. Thus, they accept the fluid role of agents. Notes one agent, agents have evolved into "'full-service providers,' handling their clients' finances, endorsement and marketing opportunities, and even personal affairs. . . . An agent is wearing many different hats. Contract negotiation is one of the minor roles that an agent performs."[58]

Some athletes do not need such services and consequently do not want to pay for them. NBA player Pat Garrity, in commenting on why he selected attorney Lon Babby to represent him rather than an agent, remarked, "I didn't want someone always checking up on me. . . . I'm a mature person and can take care of a lot of things myself."[59] Others welcome having an agent available to help deal with everyday matters from paying monthly bills to assisting in the purchase of a home.

Not all sports agents can provide all the services an athlete may require. That too causes some confusion in the business. Most people today accept that professionals such as doctors or lawyers specialize in particular areas. You may go to a general practitioner who will refer you to a surgeon to take care of the actual problem you are enduring. Likewise, your tax attorney may refer you to a trial lawyer. There are agents, however, who will attempt to provide services they are not qualified to perform for fear that they will lose their athlete clients by referring them to an expert. This is especially true when the expert is (or is secretly anxious to become) a rival agent.

Full-Service Firms

Some agents maintain that athletes not only want their contract negotiated but also want to have the agent manage their income as well. Obviously, this is appropriate when the agent is qualified. In other cases, however, the agent may not provide adequate service in this capacity. In fact, the agent may be violating state or federal laws or relevant codes of ethics if not properly licensed to perform this duty. To remedy this and similar problems, agents have recognized that special steps must be taken if they want to provide more than contract negotiation services. One solution is the full-service sports management firm, the largest and most prominent being Cleveland-based IMG. There are others as well, including Octagon, WMG, and CAA. These full-service firms provide, under one roof, individuals who negotiate contracts and deal with financial issues, endorsements, and whatever else athletes might encounter during and even after their careers. In addition, these firms possess the resources that allowed IMG to plow millions of dollars into the development of a controversial 190-acre sports academy. The facility gives it a competitive advantage not only against smaller agencies but also against larger rivals Octagon, WMG, and CAA, which send their clients to independent training sites with which they have forged relationships.[60] The newer firms also promise entrée to the entertainment industry. Many of the most successfully marketed athletes, such as football's Peyton Manning and golf's Arnold Palmer and Tiger Woods, are clients of these firms.

The key benefits of a full-service agency are twofold. First, the athlete is presumably able to receive the best service possible without having to shop around for various specialists. Second, the agent does not lose any part of the client's business. In fact, the athlete often pays an additional fee for any services beyond the initial contract negotiation. Where the cost of a contract negotiation may range anywhere from a low of 2 percent to a typical high of 5 percent of the total value of a contract (depending on maximum limits imposed by player associations in certain team sports), often an endorsement will cost the athlete as much as 30 percent of the value of the contract negotiated.

The marketing services sports agents provide are not just a matter of pairing an athlete with some product that will pay the price. Although no special license is required to be involved in product endorsements, an athlete can be harmed by an inexperienced representative. David Falk, founder of SFX Sports, once observed that "sports marketing is a very specialized business. There is a very broad range of opportunities."[61] Falk noted that product choice is important and that the agent must be careful in determining "what kind of an athlete is appropriate to be utilized for a particular [product] campaign."

Not only is the product choice important, but so is the type of relationship the athlete has with the product. The athlete/product relationship may range from a one-day appearance at a local automobile dealership to what Falk calls the "autograph relationship" with a product. The autograph relationship is one in which a product is named for a particular athlete, such as the Air Jordan athletic shoe manufactured by Nike and named after NBA star Michael Jordan, a long-time Falk client

The agent must be particularly conscious of client overexposure. There is a view in the sports and entertainment industry that a client who is overexposed, or who appears in the public eye too frequently, will not be able to demand high endorsement dollars. The full-service sports marketing firms pay particular attention to this issue.

By way of example, Octagon used the in-house resources available to its clients in devising a comprehensive marketing plan for the NFL's top pick in 2001, Michael Vick. Octagon's director of media and business development created pre- and post-draft strategies for shaping and marketing Vick's image. These strategies included creating a series of comedic commercials that revolved around Vick and the Heisman Trophy, developing a plan to broaden the scope and extent of public service announcements that Vick would make, controlling media access to Vick, and working with the Atlanta Falcons (the team with which Vick signed) to develop and implement marketing plans for Vick.[62]

Praise for full-service firms is not universal. In fact, it is not difficult to interpret the practice of providing all services under one roof as a classic case of conflict of interest. Reginald Wilkes, the former NFL star, makes the analogy of a union that hires a money-management firm to run a pension fund. It is unlikely that the union would want the same firm also to evaluate the fund's performance, establish investment guidelines, and evaluate those guidelines as well. As Wilkes points out, such a setup "invariably breeds an air of conflict of interest. The full-service agent firms are the exact same thing as far as I'm concerned."[63]

Edward V. King, Jr., a San Francisco–based attorney who has successfully sued several agents for athletes, agrees with this as well. "It's like having all the foxes in the hen house. What you lose with a full service firm is a proper check-and-balance system."[64] Despite this warning, however, even King maintains that often the full-service firm is the best place for the athlete to go.

Another alternative available to the athlete who wants agent services that go beyond contract negotiations is to pull together his or her own team of professionals. If the athlete is able to retain the appropriate mix of professionals, a natural check-and-balance system is established. Each professional necessarily has some overlap with the others as well as the opportunity to review portions of one another's work in an unbiased manner. The athlete in this situation may, for example, hire an attorney to negotiate the player contract, an accountant to handle finances, an investment firm to handle investments, and one of the sports marketing firms to handle endorsements.

But the current allure of these mega-firms cannot be overrated. First, the difficulty in competing with these firms is being acknowledged by the large number of smaller, boutique firms merging with them. Second, in many instances this is what the athletes want. An example in 2000 was Vince Carter. Long-time journeyman agent Merle Scott was able to "close the deal" with Carter when Scott announced that he was becoming an employee of IMG. Scott as the solo agent could not match the marketing resources of the worldwide enterprise.[65]

The size and financial resources of larger firms afford them a very distinct competitive advantage: they routinely forgo charging the commission that they can collect from recent draft picks in the NBA. These firms are willing to take the risk that they will collect more three to four years later when rookie players sign more lucrative contracts. Whether this situation will occur is dependent, of course, on whether the athlete maintains his relationship with the agent firm. The following comments regarding the 2001 NBA draft illustrate how agents hope for larger returns in the near future.

> Since almost every first-round pick receives a salary that is 20 percent more than the scale each year, the No. 1 pick in this year's draft likely will make $11.92 million over three seasons. The agent's share would be $158,990, or $52,996 per year. Meanwhile, an agent that negotiated a $11.92 million for a veteran would make some $476,971 on a 4 percent commission from the deal. Therefore, profiting is dependent upon an agent retaining the player until he becomes a free agent. "It's my understanding that most agents don't charge for rookie contracts," said agent Lon Babby . . . . "[B]ut in return, there is some kind of moral imperative that the player will be around for his free agent contract," Babby said in the ESPN.com report, "and that the agent will be appropriately paid for that."[66]

In the NBA, turnover has been relatively low. In other words, athletes tend to maintain their relationships with the agents who initially represented them. Forgoing the fee is a luxury that agents operating independently or in small firms may find difficult to afford.

The willingness of larger sports agencies to forgo rookie fees also supports the idea that for many firms the commission is of secondary importance. "The real action, the chance to earn double-digit commissions, is in moving an athlete into promotional opportunities elsewhere—sneaker and movie deals."[67]

A recruitment tool employed by major firms that has been subjected to intense scrutiny is the marketing guarantee described as follows:

> The use of marketing guarantees, "cash advances that agents give players for future income when they sign," have been characterized as out of control and an improper inducement by many opposed to the practice. Opponents to the use of marketing guarantees argue that agents offer them to prospective clients, such as those expected to be selected in the second and third rounds fo the NFL football draft, with doubtful abilties to earn endorsements in the six figures. Although some independent agents are believed to use marketing guarantees as a means of breaking into the business and securing their first client, they are often viewed as a mechanism that favors larger firms. As explained by one independent agent "[m]arketing guarantees are a problem for any independent agent, many of the agents out there that are having to compete with the large firms are pointing directly to marketing guarantees as reasons they are not getting recruits."[68]

One other impact these mega-mergers are having is a negative one on the number of agents, particularly African Americans and females, who are able to enter or continue successfully in the agent business. As one former African American agent said in returning to the full-time practice of law in 2001, "It was difficult enough battling one on one with agents, particularly the white ones who might play the race card, but how can my two man operation possibly compete against Fortune 500 companies?"

Conclusion

With these historical and business foundations established, the next chapter focuses on the consolidation that has dominated the industry over the last several years. The initial flurry of mergers and acquisitions subsided. It has been followed by a period of downsizing and dismantling of firms such as SFX Sports and Assante as well as by a second wave of mergers and acquisitions. These developments will also have a lasting impact on the business.

the future given the convergence of factors (for example, increased competition, players' association regulations, and collective bargaining agreements), David Falk said, "I do think there will be a consolidation in the business. I do think that one of the things that's going to differenti-ate agents is their ability to do things other than negotiate contracts, whether it's financial services, marketing, public relations, or entertain-ment."[6] Falk's view proved to be prescient.

ProServ Inc. and IMG were the pioneers of the full-service sports agency firm, which makes available, under one roof, all the services players are likely to desire. Visits to the websites of corporations that have established divisions that provide athlete representation and re-lated services are instructive with respect to the comprehensiveness of the services that such firms are capable of offering and the advantages afforded thereby over many of their smaller competitors. Although it no longer represents players in the major team sports, IMG's website fo-cuses on the benefits that come from being represented by a company with diverse and far-reaching resources. "Using imagination, creativity and energy, IMG's mission is to leverage the unparalleled power of our worldwide resources, capabilities and assets to benefit our clients, cus-tomers and partners in the areas of sports, entertainment and media. Our diversified global company employs over 2,500 talented people in 30 countries, operating in two major business segments, Sports & Enter-tainment and Media."[7]

In 2007, Octagon's website touted its history in the industry, its re-sources, and the comprehensive nature of its athlete representation services.

Octagon's philosophy is deeply rooted in the principal [*sic*] that the client comes first. The agency's long-standing stature in the industry, its global expertise and influence and its professional competencies have kept Octagon at the **fore-front of the representation business for four decades.** As trusted advisors, Octagon builds a **strategic plan** to manage the overall careers of our athletes and personali-ties during their active tenure and beyond, by providing unparallel client-tailored services including: Contract negotiations; Marketing initiatives and endorsement programs; Public relations and charity involvement; Financial planning, wealth ad-visory and asset management; Television opportunities; Content creation; Prop-erty development; Event management; [and] Speaking engagements.
Octagon owns and manages more events around the world than any other agency. This enables us to develop powerful, integrated marketing packages for our clients. In addition, Octagon's Athletes & Personalities division also pro-vides corporate business development solutions and athlete and entertainment talent procurement programs.[8]

Factors other than the need to increase potential revenues from client representation have influenced the perceived need for consolidation.

As the Internet, cable, and satellite technology increase the amount of media, products, and services available to people around the world, opportunities for athletes have grown considerably. Having the potential to offer athletes high-level service and to position athletes for numerous endorsement opportunities, large companies without much prior experience in the sports agent industry have made major inroads into the sector and captured considerable market share.

To establish their presence as credible service providers in the athlete management industry, these large corporations needed to accumulate a well-known client list quickly. In the sports agent industry, firms receive new clients in large part based on their existing client list. Without any athlete clients to speak of, the principal, and perhaps only, way for these firms to quickly attain an all-star client list was to purchase the top sports agent firms.

The enticements offered to induce existing sports agent firms to merge with or to become divisions within larger corporations include significant amounts of cash. Leigh Steinberg is reported to have sold his business in 1999 to Assante Corporation in a $120-million deal.[9] Other inducements included equity in the purchasing company and incentives. An example of these types of inducements was Assante's purchase of Dan Fegan's basketball practice. In exchange for all of the assets of Fegan's practice, Assante was to pay "an undisclosed amount of cash and issue 171,200 Subordinate Voting Shares in Assante." As it was further described at the time, "[t]he purchase agreement also provides an earn-out. The considerable earn-out will be earned to the extent that Fegan & Associates Inc. attains certain financial targets over the five years following closing. The earn-out will be paid in a combination of an undisclosed amount of cash and up to 1,428,835 Subordinate Voting Shares."[10]

This structure was typical of the deals in the market for companies being acquired during the 1990s' wave of consolidations. The initial down payment to the acquired company was made with cash, the acquiring company's stock, or some combination of the two. Subsequent payments to the acquired company were to be paid out at future dates, and the amount earned was determined by a formula pegged against the acquired company's future performance. These "earn-outs" generally paid the acquired company some amount (again, in cash, stock, or some combination of the two) based on whether target revenue figures were met.

More importantly, consolidation offered existing sports agencies enhanced opportunity for longevity. Consolidation within a larger corporate structure allows the sports management division the chance to offer its athlete clients numerous new services, as well as the resources to invest in capital-intensive programs such as web applications, the production of their own sports events, and athlete training facilities.

Frank Craighill realized that his company's historical 20 percent growth would not be sustainable without capital due to the increasingly complex logistics of the athlete agent industry.[11] Consequently he sold Virginia-based Advantage International to Octagon for $30 million. Other well-known sports agencies at the time, such as Steinberg, Moorad & Dunn, Tellem & Associates, and Falk Associates Management Enterprises (FAME), also elected to be bought by large conglomerates to remain competitive.

The Marquee Group began this trend of consolidation in the mid-1990s with its purchases of Washington, DC–based ProServ and Connecticut-based Sports Marketing and Television International.[12] After Marquee's purchase, larger conglomerates with one piece of the puzzle realized the enormous potential of the sports agent industry. SFX Entertainment, an events promoter, Assante Corporation, a money-management firm, and Octagon, a piece of the Interpublic Group's global marketing web, each made considerable investments during the 1990s to establish their presence as full-service athlete representation firms.

Along with purchasing sports agent firms, the conglomerates added marketing agencies and other businesses to the mix. Including athlete and marketing agencies within their corporate structures gave these firms the ability to sell entire packages to their large corporate customers. According to Ray Clark, whose Dallas-based sports services firm was purchased in 1999 for $12 million by New York–based Omnicom Group Inc., "Consolidation is running rampant because corporate clients want it. They don't want 15 sports marketing agencies. They want one that can solve all their needs."[13]

Besides their corporate clients, these conglomerates were also able to offer special events and exhibitions to the public. SFX sold sports fantasies on the Internet through its website, eSuperstars.com. There, sports fans could bid on events such as the opportunity to play golf with their favorite PGA player or take batting practice with their hometown MLB team.[14]

It would be a bad investment for the purchasing company if it were unable to receive value from the synergy suggested by the difference in acquired price and market value. Although it seems that some conglomerates may have overspent to receive a well-known client list, the greatest value the conglomerates received in some instances came from the gravitas gained by adding high-profile agents to their management rosters. For example, the reputations of agents such as Steinberg and Falk were attached to the companies that acquired them.

As long as their reputations are positive, that is positive for the acquiring company.

A few methods aim at keeping high-profile agents with the company. In the sports agent industry, key personnel are required to sign non-compete agreements, restricting their ability to work in the industry or take clients with them for a negotiated period of time after leaving the firm. Such a strategy might be effective in the short term, but defections have occurred. Probably the most publicized defection was agent David Dunn's departure from Assante with dozens of clients. Perhaps the most promising method for retaining agents is to give them an equity stake in the company with promises of future equity through stock and stock options. Generally, this is the logic behind the earn-outs discussed earlier. It works most effectively at publicly traded companies such as Interpublic Group, but might not be as valuable to owners of firms purchased by private companies, including IMG. Holding equity in a public company, these executives need to worry about stock price changes and how possible skirmishes might affect the outsider's view of the company.

The Key Players

Consolidation of the sports agency business in the 1990s involved the merger of a number of smaller firms into four companies: SFX, Assante, IMG, and Octagon. These companies molded their sports groups to compete in the revamped industry by combining sports agents firms, sports marketing firms, and sports branding firms. Although each found its way into the industry through different outlets, sports agent pioneers were at the forefront. In the second round of consolidations the lead players did not have long histories in sports. One, CAA, was entrenched in the entertainment industry whereas another, WMG, had its grounding in a sports niche, action sports. The third, Blue Equity, seemed to view its agency acquisitions as just business expansion. There are certainly others who emerged and disappeared from the scene. Below we describe the key players in the first round of consolidation and then the most powerful newcomers.

THE INITIAL ROUND OF CONSOLIDATIONS

SFX

SFX was one of the early aggressive players in this space. But as will be noted, its role in the sports agent business turned out to be fleeting. What became SFX Sports began as the result of the acquisition of regional musical venues around the United States.[15] Within a short time span, the company became the leading concert promoter in the U.S. market, owning 120 venues globally, including 16 amphitheaters in the top 10 U.S. markets, as well as owning or operating venues in 31 of the top 50 domestic markets.[16] Analysts expected SFX's revenues to increase by 9 percent in 1999, resulting in a lower net loss of $39.2 million.[17] In addition to concert promoting, SFX sold Broadway subscription series and individual productions in 55 markets.[18] SFX also owned production rights to Broadway shows such as *Ragtime* and *Phantom of the Opera.*

SFX entered the sports agent business in May 1998, purchasing FAME for a reported $82.9 million in cash and one million shares of stock, worth $38.75 million at the time, and $15 million over five years if FAME's cash flow hit certain earn-out levels.[19] In the deal, SFX received one of the most coveted sports agents, David Falk, and his most prominent client, Michael Jordan.

In July, shortly after the acquisition of FAME, SFX announced it would purchase the Marquee Group for approximately $100 million in stock.[20] The Marquee Group specialized in managing sports events, representing athletes and broadcasters, and producing television programs.[21] Originally a marketing company, the Marquee Group used $62 million it had raised in two public offerings to begin a consolidation boom by acquiring ProServ and Athletes & Artists, a firm that represented hockey players and sports broadcasters, including Al Michaels and Chris Berman.[22] Prior to the merger, the Marquee Group also spent £5 million in an effort to become global by buying the two companies of English football's best-known agents, Jon Holmes and Tony Stephens.[23]

SFX's purchases in 1998 received attention from investors, competitors, and the United States government. Leigh Steinberg told a reporter in May 1998, "[SFX's acquisition of FAME] highlights the synergy between Big Entertainment and Big Sports, to the extent that sports have become content and programming in a much larger world."[24] On September 22, 1998, shares of SFX dropped 13 percent as the company's plans to consolidate the sports agent industry seemed to be in peril. At one point, SFX even received a notice of a preliminary inquiry from the Department of Justice's antitrust division into its proposed purchase of the Marquee Group.[25]

Even under the watchful eye of the government, SFX continued its buying spree of sports agencies when it purchased Randy and Alan Hendricks's agent firm, Hendricks Management Company, in June 1999 for $15.7 million, plus $5 million in deferred payments with the chance to earn additional bonuses. This deal was followed by the purchase of Tellem & Associates in October for an undisclosed sum.[26] By buying these firms, SFX added even more all-star talent to its long client list. Tellem's roster of clients consisted of thirty-five basketball players and twenty baseball players, which included clients such as Albert Belle, Kobe Bryant, and Nomar Garciaparra. The success of the combined efforts of Falk and Tellem was exemplified during the 2001 NBA draft. SFX represented the overall number-one draft pick, Kwame Brown, and five other lottery picks, which constituted 46 percent of the NBA draft lottery. In addition, SFX represented ten of the twenty-eight players—36 percent—taken in the first round of the NBA draft.[27] In commenting on SFX's "smashing success," Falk remarked that the "acquisition of Arn [Tellem's] agency has significantly strengthened our presence in professional basketball."[28] Tellem's remarks focused on the marketing clout of SFX as a reason for its success in the NBA draft: "We were about to make deals, especially in the card area, that were unprecedented in the history of sports."[29]

At the same time, SFX also increased its marketing capabilities by acquiring the marketing firm Integrated Sports International (ISI) of New Jersey in the middle of 1999 and later Sean Michael Edwards Design, Inc. (SME). SME focused on sports-related brand-identity building. Its list of clients in 1999 included the four major sports leagues, World Championship Wrestling, PGA Tour of America, and several top university programs.[30] In 2001, SFX purchased Signature Sports Group, which managed thirty professional golfers and golf events. This purchase followed SFX's acquisition in 2000 and 2001, respectively, of Greg Norman Production Company and Tony Rosenberg Promotions.[31]

As a result of its various acquisitions and other efforts, by mid-2001, SFX possessed an impressive client list. Its athlete clients included Michael Jordan, Dikembe Mutombo, Alonzo Mourning, Eddie Griffin, Eddy Curry, Kwame Brown, Roger Clemens, John Rocker, Kobe Bryant, Jason Giambi, Nomar Garciaparra, and Larry Walker. At one point SFX represented one-sixth of the players in both the NBA and the MLB (approximately 15 percent of the players in each league).[32]

With its knowledge of the entertainment industry and well-known list of agents and clients, SFX made a number of strategic moves. The company dubbed this compilation of companies SFX Sports and appointed David Falk as its CEO. The upshot of the loss of individual corporate identity was "branding."

As alluded to earlier and as discussed in Chapter 6 in greater detail, consolidation has not been without its problems. The August 2000 acquisition of SFX by the conglomerate Clear Channel Communications eventually led to a restructuring of SFX Sports and David Falk's taking on the title of "Founder" in the restructured company.[33]

That was not the conclusion of the story for SFX. At the end of 2005 Clear Channel spun off its entertainment division (including the SFX Sports division) into a separate, stand-alone company called Live

Nation.[34] All of the company's high aspirations came to a halt as the leading agents that had been acquired began to depart for other opportunites. The most severe loss was Arn Tellem. His agreement allowed him to buy his practice back, which he did in 2005. Amid much speculation, he then sold his practice to the Wasserman Media Group. That departure alone may have been enough for SFX to rethink all, but also departing were the hockey practice of Jay Grossman in 2002 and the Hendrickses in 2003. The final key pieces departed in 2006 with football agents Ben Dogra and Jim Steiner buying back their practices and selling them to CAA.[35]

Assante Corporation

Of the major players in the agent business, Assante, along with SFX, was arguably the firm that made the most dramatic and significant transition over the last several years. The firm went from a big presence, with high-profile acquisitions of the firms led by Leigh Steinberg, Dan Fegan, and Eugene Parker, to a complete departure from the sports representation business.

Without any connection to the entertainment industry, Assante surprised the sports world with its $120-million purchase of Steinberg, Moorad & Dunn in October 1999.[36] Assante, a publicly traded company located in Winnipeg, Manitoba, at that time managed more than $3.4 billion and had $22.9 billion under administration with its 2,500 employees operating in more than 150 offices in North America.[37] Unlike the other acquisitions, insiders believed Assante's purchase of Steinberg's group was not solely a strategic move into the potentially high-profit sports agent industry. Some thought the firm's motives were to increase the amount of assets it managed and to attract high net-worth individuals using the high-profile image of the athletes.[38] Assante supposedly contemplated being able to profit by signing athletes to contracts and from the investments their clients made with the company, while receiving free advertising.

Assante realized few reputable large sports agent firms remained in the industry, and if it wanted to try its strategy, it needed to move quickly. Steinberg, whose client list at the time consisted of 150 active and retired athletes (primarily NFL talent), managed players such as Troy Aikman, Drew Bledsoe, and Jake Plummer.

As he observed his independent competitors being acquired by large companies, Steinberg realized that to remain competitive he needed a large amount of cash, an amount available only in a conglomerate. Steinberg told reporters that the merger would help his twenty-four-year-old firm expand as advertising, television, and other media deals had become more important than the contracts he negotiated with the players' teams.[39] To take advantage of the new wave of endorsement opportunities available at Assante, Steinberg planned to involve his players in anything sports related, including TV sports quiz shows, TV biography shows, and even putting the diaries of his players on the Internet.[40]

As for the development of Assante's sports group, Steinberg stated in an interview that he would oversee expansion into television and Internet sports-related programming, the acquisition of ten or twelve more firms, and Assante's involvement in the management and marketing of athletes in all lines of professional sports.[41] In line with its promise, Assante purchased Maximum Sports Management, a sports agent firm based in Fort Wayne, Indiana, and owned by African American Eugene Parker. Then the third-largest athlete representation firm in the NFL, Maximum managed 60 players in football and basketball, including stars such as Deion Sanders and Emmitt Smith. Assante strengthened its position in the representation of NBA players with the purchase of Dan Fegan's firm at the end of 2000 for an estimated $10 million.[42] NBA athletes under contract with Fegan in 2000 included Kenyon Martin, Austin Croshere, Dale Davis, Chris Dudley, Howard Eisley, Jerome Kersey, Joe Smith, and Shawn Marion.[43] Earlier in 2000, Assante purchased M. D. Gillis & Associates of Kingston, Ontario, a company that at the time represented 35 NHL players.[44] Assante also purchased NKS Management, Inc. and Philpott, Bills & Stoll, two Los Angeles–based companies that specialized in managing the business affairs of entertainers. In 2000, Assante moved to enhance its financial services capabilities with the purchase of Klarberg, Raiola and Associates, a New York City financial planning firm that served mostly athletes and entertainers.[45] Assante entered into a joint venture with Omnicom's The Marketing Arm. The purpose of the newly formed Assante Marketing Solutions was to match Assante Sports and Entertainment Group's athletes and properties with endorsement marketing, and sponsorship opportunities.[46]

After much fanfare with its entry into the business, the parent company hired Dr. Harvey Schiller, whose primary task was to unwind the existing agreements and pull Assante out of the representation business. In 2003, Leigh Steinberg repurchased his practice for a reported $4.077 million. In 2005, Eugene Parker and Roosevelt Barnes bought their firm, Maximum Sports Management, from Loring Ward (formerly Assante Corporation). In 2005, Greg Genske, Scott Parker, Brian Peters, and Sandy Climan assumed control of most of what remained of Assante's sports representation business when they bought Legacy Sports, formerly Steinberg & Moorad.[47] In August 2006, Loring Ward divested itself of what remained of its former Assante Sports Group when Barry Klarberg bought his financial services business for $5.5 million.[48]

IMG

IMG, based in Cleveland, Ohio, is the largest agency in the world with 2,600 employees working in over 30 countries. Accounting for over $1 billion in revenue, IMG boasts a prestigious list of sports clients, including Tiger Woods, as well as corporate clients, including US West, Texaco, and Nokia.[49]

Already an established full-service firm, IMG mildly participated in the consolidation boom, acquiring an Atlanta-based Olympic consulting firm and a California TV production outfit that specialized in sports in early 1998.[50] Subsequently, IMG purchased Charlotte, North Carolina–based Muhleman Marketing Inc., known for marketing NASCAR racing and helping teams with licensing arrangements.[51] With a well-known reputation and a good sense of understanding the trends in the industry, IMG maintained a client list of over 1,000 athletes.[52]

IMG began to change dramatically following the death of founder Mark McCormack and the subsequent acquisition of the firm by Ted Fortsmann via Fortsmann Little. The transaction, annnounced September 30, 2004, had Fortsmann acquiring the company "from Trusts established by McCormack, and from the family of Arthur J. LaFave, IMG's Vice Chairman."[53] The latter reported the sale price was $750 million.[54] After being acquired, the company underwent management changes and reached a crossroads when the longtime head of the team sports division, Peter Johnson, departed. This occurred in January 2006 shortly after Fortsmann brought in George Pyne, formerly chief operating officer (COO) of NASCAR, with almost exactly the same title Johnson held.[55] The departure of Johnson triggered clauses in the contracts of other prominent IMG agents, allowing them to leave. This included football agent Tom Condon, one of the most powerful agents in the sport, followed by Casey Close, the head of IMG's baseball practice. Both ultimately sold their businesses to CAA.[56] When IMG's hockey practice departed, Pyne announced, "it is fair to say it is unlikely and not in our current strategic plans to focus on any of the team sports athlete representation businesses in the U.S."[57] At the heart of this decision was not so much the departure of the clients, but the small margins that any business is capable of earning through contract negotiation in the regulated team sports area. IMG is an existing business with options, and that is apparently what it is pursueing.

Octagon

A subsidiary of the New York–based Interpublic Group, Octagon is composed of several sports-related companies purchased by Interpublic over the last few years. Interpublic, the parent of three of the world's largest ad agency giants—McCann-Erickson World Group, Ammirati Puris Lintas, and the Lowe Group—covers almost every aspect of brand marketing, including promotional marketing, direct response, media buying, public relations, and sports marketing.[58] In 1998, as sports acquisitions were getting underway, the company tallied $10 billion in billings from its 2,500 employees working in 75 offices located in 35 countries.[59] Major customers have included General Motors Corporation, Coca-Cola, Burger King, and Mercedes-Benz.[60]

One of the first companies to acquire sports agent firms, Interpublic Group realized the trend in advertising and moved quickly to stay ahead. Interpublic purchased its first sports agent firm, Advantage International, in 1997. Advantage, which represented the core of Octagon, managed clients in several sports, including tennis stars Anna Kournikova and Michael Chang and NBA all-star David Robinson.

Adding to its portfolio, Octagon initially purchased the following companies: CSI, a London company with ninety employees in five cities worldwide that specializes in selling and distribution and sports TV rights, in February 1998;[61] API Group in London, a sports marketing firm, on May 21, 1998; APA, a sports management group founded by former Olympic sprinter Alan Pascoe, in 1998; Pros Inc., an agency representing golf stars such as Tom Kite, Justin Leonard, and Davis Love III, in March 1999; and Brands Hatch Leisure PLC, recognized at the time as the largest single organizer and promoter of motor sport events in the United Kingdom in December 1999.[62] Octagon also entered into partnerships with Koch Tavares, a leading sports marketing agency in Brazil, in early 1999 and with the Italian-based Flammini Group, an agency specializing in motor sports. It also acquired the exclusive TV rights for home matches of English football clubs in the Union of European Football Association's UEFA Cup in September 1999.

In the midst of its buying spree, Octagon publicly released its new organizational strategy in September 1999. Octagon announced it was going to rebrand its sports marketing and entertainment groups into Octagon Marketing, Octagon Athlete Representation, Octagon CSI, and Octagon Motorsports. The Octagon name was also added to each of the subsidiary's 34 sports firms, which at the time accounted for 800 employees and $700 million in estimated annual billings.[63] In this restructuring, Advantage became Octagon Athlete Management. Frank Lowe, CEO of Interpublic's Lowe Group, remained CEO of Octagon.

These moves positioned Octagon as one of the top sports agencies and marketing firms worldwide. Lowe felt that his decision to brand the name of the company was a logical step. "Having spent the last two years building a group whose focus is on providing a marketing-led approach to sport, we all felt that the time is now right to launch what is essentially a new brand of sports marketing."[64] Along with sports marketing, Octagon offers a high level of service in athlete representation, consultancy, event management, property representation, TV rights, sales and distribution, TV production and archive, rights ownership, and licensing and merchandising.[65] Octagon represents more than 250 athletes, including those previously mentioned along with star athlete Sergei Fedorov.[66] Among its 100 blue-chip multinational clients, Octagon represents IBM, Guinness, and MasterCard.[67]

In 2000, Octagon made aggressive moves to establish its presence in the major American team sports. During 2000, it purchased Sullivan & Sperbeck to increase its representation of NFL players, and the baseball division of Bob Woolf Associates and baseball agent Gregg Clifton's business to increase its representation of MLB players.[68] These purchases added ninety players to Octagon's client roster—twenty-five NFL players, forty hockey players, and twenty-five MLB players. These acquisitions also added to Octagon's roster of high-profile athletes including baseball players Tom Glavine, David Wells, Benito Santiago, B. J. Surhoff, and Turk Wendell.[69]

In late 2001, Octagon demonstrated its willingness to expand beyond traditional areas of athlete representation when it purchased Carlisle Sports Management, one of two major independent companies that represent athletes who compete in extreme sports.[70] This acquisition represents Octagon's effort to establish a foothold in the potentially lucrative extreme sports marketplace.

Of all of the firms aggressively involved in the early consolidation phase, Octagon may be the company that has most adhered to the model that led it to acquire firms in the first place.

The New Consolidation Players

Creative Artists Agency (CAA)

Creative Artists Agency flirted with entry into the sports agent business for a while. Its stellar entertainment client list has included Nicolas Cage, George Clooney, and Jennifer Aniston. The synergy of its dominant business, representation of entertainers, was always relatively clear. CAA began to move forward aggressively with this concept by acquiring the practices of football agents Tom Condon from IMG and Jim Steiner and Ben Dogra from SFX.[71] The appeal to athlete clients is the access that the longtime entertainment agency has had to those opportunities. The management team for this side of CAA's business includes longtime Fox Sports executive David Rone, Howard Nuchow of Mandalay Sports Entertainment, and Michael Levine of Van Wagner Sports Group.

Wasserman Media Group (WMG)

On its website, WMG describes itself as "a leading sports management company, representing the most talented athletes across baseball, BMX, motorcross, skateboarding, soccer and surfing."[72] It initially seemed that action sports would be the focus of WMG, but with the dynamics of the marketplace, other opportunities developed. WMG's key acquisition in the team sports area occurred in early 2006 with its purchase of Arn Tellem's practice.[73] Following that transaction, WMG acquired other major firms including the soccer practice of Richard Motzkin, Sportsnet, as well as the baseball practice of Tom Reich and Adam Katz, Reich & Katz.[74]

Blue Equity

On its website Blue Equity describes itself as "a private equity firm committed to actively investing both growth capital and business expertise in enterprises with solid development potential. We form strategic partnerships with existing management teams, leveraging our expertise and relationships in order to stabilize, strengthen and grow lasting value."[75] That is the apparent spirit under which the firm has moved to acquire companies focusing on a variety of sports over the past several months. Its most significant acquisitions include Joel Segal's Wordwide Football, Bill Strickland's football and basketball practice, and Donald Dell's tennis practice, formerly SFX Tennis.[76] In just a matter of months, Blue Equity went from a business with no athlete clients to one of the top firms with a diversified client list.

Synergy

The emergence of CAA in the agency business is probably the fullest manifestation of the synergy that many in this business have been referring to for years. For example, Wilhelmina Artist Management, a modeling agency, raised eyebrows when it signed NBA star Stephon Marbury.[77] At the peak of his career, NFL running back Eddie George signed with Wilhelmina. While sports agents Lamont Smith and Peter Schaffer continued to represent George in contract work, Wilhelmina provided exclusive representation with respect to endorsements.[78] Wilhelmina's signing of top amateur golfer Matt Kuchar to an exclusive marketing contract was seen as a significant move by the company into the sports business. This move by Wilhemina also suggested, however, that notwithstanding the comprehensive nature of the "one-stop" service offered by firms, a market may exist for athletes interested in having multiple representatives. A representative for Wilhemina remarked that "We are not wanting to be in the sports agent business, but we would love to work with sports agents to help them on the marketing and endorsement side of their talent."[79]

Other companies better known for business relationships in more traditional segments of the entertainment industry have flirted with the business. Unlike Wilhelmina, which stated that it had no interest in attempting to get athletes into television and movies,[80] other companies, such as CAA, have made just such a pitch and are attempting to secure clients. Well-established talent agencies such as Michael Ovitz's Artists Management Group (which added a sports management division), International Creative Management (ICM), and William Morris Agency sought to exploit connections in the television and movie industry to convince clients that these firms are better qualified to pursue their interests in these areas than are traditional agencies.[81] Despite some problems, such as cultural differences between the sports and entertainment worlds, some predicted increased representation by talent agencies of athletes. At the beginning of this millennium, an ICM executive noted, "I think as the entertainment business and sports business come closer and closer together, through ownership, through fan support, through marketing, there will be more and more desire for athletes to be part of the world of entertainment. . . . In five years, we're going to have a lot more athletes coming to us as they learn what we're up to. And we're going to be a lot more selective in who we take on."[82]

Conclusion

Some companies, such as the athletic apparel giant Nike, entered the fray briefly but are no longer involved in the athlete representation side of the sports business. Others will clearly come and go as well. An example of the type of problems, many unanticipated, that might arise from the consolidation of the industry was brought to the forefront with complaints from at least two players' associations regarding potential conflicts of interest. Unions representing NFL and NHL players complained about such conflicts that arose as a result of SFX's representation of "players as well as owners of NHL venues."[83] At least in part as a result of such complaints, SFX reorganized. Consolidation—such as the purchase by CAA of multiple football practices—is likely to renew concerns that such an agency will yield so much leverage in negotiations that it "could dictate the market."[84]

A future issue of concern is the anticompetitive impact on any market that once had many players and is reduced to a few. The potential antitrust issues, however, are not ripe in this arena. There are still many smaller players successfully battling for clients against the acquiring giants. As competition stiffens and smaller firms become unable to compete, antitrust actions could begin to be filed.

No matter how the structure of the industry evolves, the basic manner of doing business—one key point person recruiting a single athlete—does not appear to be evolving. The truth be told, recruitment of the athlete still occurs the old-fashioned way: person-to-person, one-on-one recruitment of clients. The complexities and problems associated with recruitment and representation are our next topics of discussion.

Part II
Problems

Chapter 4
The Basics
Competition for Clients

> *It's a huge problem. . . . We have a contract with players, and there's got to be some honor among thieves. But there is not. And I think that that goes on daily.*[1]
> —*Agent David Falk responding to a question regarding attempts by agents to steal other agents' clients*

The nature of "the business" continues to evolve, and a major influence on its evolution is the competition for clients. As the above quotation suggests, competition among agents is fierce and can lead to unethical behavior. In 2005, Major League Baseball Players Association (MLBPA) Executive Director Don Fehr commented that the number of complaints concerning improper agent conduct, including "stealing clients, telling lies about other agents and giving players improper inducements," is a significant and growing problem.[2] In fact, because of the competition, many individuals with outstanding business or academic records are not able to sign a student athlete as a client. Johnny Rutledge's affidavit that appears in the Introduction reveals unsavory recruiting steps that some agents employ.

As any athlete will attest, a prospective agent is not a difficult person to find. According to a former NFL defensive back, the athlete representation industry is "the perfect arena for a con man."[3] Consequently, the athlete's threshold question to the agent is often "Who else do you represent?" This valid inquiry is sometimes the greatest barrier to entry for the prospective agent. One prospective agent described breaking into the business as being like the schoolyard basketball game "ice." In that game you are not allowed to begin to tally the baskets you score against your opponent until after you sink the first one. Sports agents face a similar dilemma: until you negotiate a contract for your first client you are frozen out while others with clients continue to score.

Dr. Michael Jackson, a professor and the director of the sport and recreation administration program at Temple University, has advised Temple students and others in the agent selection process. He once described the difficulties prospective agents encounter: "Surgeons have cadavers to experiment on. Our players are not cadavers. The agents have to have experience."[4] Agent Bucky Woy wrote about the importance of that first client in his book *Sign 'Em Up Bucky: The Adventures of a Sports Agent*: "As far as Consulting Services' [Woy's firm] success in the sports agenting field is concerned, I owe everything to Mr. Easy [professional golfing great Julius Boros]. When he agreed to let me represent him in many business dealings, people took a new look at Bucky Woy and this Consulting Services outfit he was pushing. . . . He opened all the doors for me with the players who had been viewing me with suspicion during my first year in business."[5] It is not surprising that Woy's entire book is dedicated to Boros. Similarly, sports agent attorney Bob Woolf closed his autobiographical work *Behind Closed Doors* by thanking his first client, baseball player Earl Wilson.[6]

Agents entering the industry today tend not to have the benefit of a mentor who not only provides professional guidance but also assists them in securing their first client. In fact, new entrants often find it difficult to hold on to the clients they are fortunate enough to sign. New agents' frequent lament is the loss of clients to agents willing to use improper means to induce athletes to sign with them. One agent described the cruel realities of the industry as follows: "Some agents need that first client so badly they will waive their 3 percent commission. They will steal clients outright and dispense . . . 'trinkets,' such as arranging lines of credit and the purchase of expensive cars. Even the big boys do this."[7] What is particularly frustrating is the loss of clients not because of a lack of competence but because athletes want "cars and an apartment to live and they want money."[8]

In addition to having to contend with the unsavory conduct of their competitors, new agents must also deal with the credibility and track record of established agents. Some agents, most notably Leigh Steinberg, boast that they do not solicit clients. These agents insist that athletes come to them because of their reputations. Baseball Hall of Famer Frank Robinson learned about his agent Ed Keating while appearing on the old television game show *Sports Challenge*. Edward King once said that "typically, an athlete chooses Agent A over Agent B because Agent A has done more favors for the athlete or his family or has been friendlier."[9]

Because of the lucrative fees many agents receive,[10] the level of competition among sports agents to provide services and to obtain that first client has become extraordinary. As with any industry, as the field of competitors for a limited number of clients has increased, so have the cutthroat methods of competition.

Payments to Athletes

Letters do not work, agents say, because student athletes "don't write back and they receive dozens of pieces of mail." Even an eye-catching brochure featuring models, yachts, and sunny beaches in Miami, including an invitation to the athlete to come visit, does not always attract the student athlete's attention. Mike Rozier, a winner of the Heisman Trophy, estimated that he received 1,200 letters while at the University of Nebraska, "most of which came from people I had never heard of, and who did not even know me, or want to know me. All they wanted was to line their pockets with the money that I soon would earn in professional football."[11]

Agents maintain it is the face-to-face meetings that are most successful. Norby Walters's vivid description of what many agree occurs in face-to-face meetings between a prospective agent and student athlete remains revealing: "The kid knows everybody's breaking all the rules so he's primed and ready for a businessman to come along. He's talking turkey as soon as you sit down. 'How much for my family? How much for me? How much interest? Do I have to pay it back?'"[12] A similar view was expressed by another agent. "There is a player today who was taken in the seventh round . . . who I'm sure spent $80,000 on a car and has a line of credit of $50,000 and whose signing bonus will proably be $25,000, before taxes. He gave a wish list to somebody, and they said, 'Fine.' Now there's trouble brewing. . . . He is what we call classically in debt."[13] In his autobiography, Hall of Fame NFL linebacker Lawrence Taylor described the nature of the interaction between an agent and a prospective client. His first encounter with his soon-to-be agent Ivery Black came between Taylor's junior and senior years in college. Taylor explained that Black made it clear that the rules of the NCAA do not allow the giving of money, so his policy was to *lend* athletes money until they were drafted, after which they would repay the loan. This is a standard explanation of what appears to be a common practice.[14]

It is this type of transaction, and variations of it, that many see as the prime barrier to entry into the field by ethical professionals. One former agent maintains, "The mentality on the part of the athlete is for 'right here and right now.' What can you do for me now?" He sees one of the agent's greatest contributions to the client is providing a perspective beyond the here and now. Any payment in the manner described would result in violations of the UAAA, SPARTA, and other state agent statutes.

The stories of what agents provide to athletes for their signing range from anecdote to fact. A 1999 feature story in the *Wall Street Journal* highlighted allegations of a new client recruitment method, promises of "romantic liaisons" with supermodels from New York's Wilhelmina Models Inc. modeling agency.[15] Agent Eric Fleisher made these allegations claiming that he was the victim of unfair competition. *Sports Illustrated* reported that Norby Walters and Lloyd Bloom paid more than $800,000 in varying sums to approximately fifty athletes, five of whom were first-round picks in the 1987 NFL draft.[16] Similarly, agent Jim Abernethy claims that he spent more than $500,000 over a one-year period in recruiting clients.[17] Other specific overzealous recruiting techniques reportedly include the following: the offer of one-third of an agent's management corporation to George Rogers;[18] a series of incidents involving Florida State football players that culminated in one agent taking several players on a $6,000 shopping spree at Foot Locker in 1994;[19] agent Robert Caron's alleged cash payments totaling $3,900 to University of Southern California football player Shawn Walters;[20] the payment of a $2,500 promissory note to University of Alabama basketball star Derrick McKey;[21] Auburn basketball player Chris Porter's acceptance of $2,500 from an agent;[22] agent Jeffrey Nalley's purchase of $1,000 worth of clothing for Penn State star Curtis Enis;[23] the offer of $65,000 to former Louisiana State linebacker Michael Brooks;[24] allegations that one Florida player received wheel rims valued at $1,500 and another received weekly payments totaling up to $500 per month from an agent;[25] the promise to Wayne Waddy, a running back at Texas Christian University, of $75 for each touchdown he scored;[26] the promise to a Memphis State University basketball player of $500 per month with a $200 Thanksgiving bonus and a $1,000 Christmas bonus;[27] the alleged payment of $54,000 to University of Iowa running back Ron Harmon, his girlfriend, and family members;[28] and an additional $1,500 paid to Harmon for revealing a teammate's phone number to an agent.[29] Harmon was also reportedly offered $2,000 to aid the agent in recruiting linebacker Larry Station.[30] And now we have the allegations associated with the recruitment of Reggie Bush (see discussion in Chapter 1).

In his autobiography *The Boz*, former NFL and college star Brian Bosworth explains that other athletes are sometimes involved in the student athlete recruiting process: "You get hit on constantly by agents in college, or by friends of agents. Even pro players call and try to sign you with their guy. Howie Long [then] of the Raiders called me to see if I wanted to hook up with his guy. I didn't even *know* Howie Long, much less his guy."[31]

Another client recruitment technique is the payment of a fee to the student athlete's coach or some other person with influence over the athlete. In 1988, *Newsday* exposed payments made by agent Lance Jay Luchnick to coaches. *Newsday*'s investigation revealed that Luchnick agreed to pay one coach, Ron Davis, a percentage of basketball player Cliff Livingston's contract if he could deliver him as a client. Livingston was "eager to help his old coach," and when he learned of this deal, he signed with Luchnick.[32] Davis reportedly received more than $14,000 for his role in bringing the two together.[33] Similar accusations were initially raised in 1998 against once prominent South Carolina–based agent Tank Black.[34] Deals of this nature factored into the NFLPA's promulgation of rules requiring agents to disclose their runners (see discussion in Chapter 10).

A recruitment technique employed with increasing frequency is agents' use of street agents to help them to secure clients. NCAA rules do not prohibit an agent from having contact with an athlete. However, the UAAA, SPARTA and many pre-UAAA state athlete agent regulations require agents wishing to have contact with a student athlete, whose collegiate athletic eligibility has not expired, to register, pay a fee, and notify administrators at the student athlete's college. In order to circumvent such rules, or merely as a means of establishing a relationship with athletes, agents will use a street agent or "runner." The role of the runner often is to funnel money and gifts from an agent to an athlete as a means of establishing an indirect relationship between the athlete and the agent, thereby placing the agent in a more advantageous position than his competitors. Runners can be high school coaches, summer league coaches, friends, roommates, family members, girlfriends, or anyone who can "win over players with flattery, cash and other gifts."[35] Notes Washington, DC–based agent Bill Strickland, the improper use of runners places agents who do not use runners at a disadvantage.[36] A college sports official adds, "Sometimes the player is unaware of the source. . . . The benefit to the agent . . . would be at a later time, when he would make it clear to the player that he or she should show gratitude, or there could even be threats."[37]

Runners who provide favors to student athletes, who have not exhausted their collegiate eligibility, can lead to dire consequences for athletes' schools. In 2003, the NCAA Committee on Infractions sanctioned Fresno State University. In imposing sanctions, the committee relied, in part, on evidence that a runner had made cash payments to student athletes enrolled at the university and to an athlete's grandparents. The committee also heard evidence that an agent paid $1,500 to an academic adviser to perform work for two Fresno State student athletes.[38] NFLPA regulations now make agents liable for the actions of their runners.[39]

The case of Myron Piggie is revealing in this regard. The name Myron Piggie is synonymous with some of the worst incidents that can occur in

the athlete representation world, particularly when it comes to intermediaries that funnel star athletes. Piggie was a coach of a youth basketball
team in Kansas City, but he also had a criminal record that caught up
with him. Piggie was also the classic street agent who possessed enough
control over young future collegiate stars and professionals that he
could play a major role in influencing which schools they ultimately attended and which agents they signed with for professional representation. The crimes to which he pled guilty and that caught the attention of
basketball fans were defrauding the NCAA and four universities because
he compromised the status of amateurs by providing them with cash
and other gifts.

Piggie had been hired by a wealthy philanthropist, Tom Grant, to coach
a youth basketball team. Piggie had no experience, but he did have a
criminal record. Following his team's success, Nike signed Piggie to a five-
year, $425,000 consulting agreement. Piggie was close to the talent that
Nike wanted to have wear its products and to serve as endorsers if they
reached superstar status. Ultimately Piggie was removed from the fray as
he was incarcerated based on his fraudulent activities. In 2001, Piggie was
sentenced to thirty-seven months on a single count of conspiracy to commit mail and wire fraud and one year for failure to file income tax returns. The terms were served concurrently without the possibility of
parole. He was also required to pay restitution in the amount of $320,000
to four universities, a prep school, and the IRS. The U.S. Attorney who
went after Piggie stated, "We look at someone like Myron Piggie as a pimp
and the players as prostitutes."[40]

It is important to note here that many AAU programs are run by honorable, well-intentioned people. Sonny Vaccaro, who has worked with
major shoe companies supporting these programs, has seen both sides.
Vaccaro urges us not to lose sight of the success that many have had in
helping kids progress through life with the support of these programs.[41]

For younger players, financial inducements such as cash and shoes
are often enough. When they are not, these forms of payment sometimes have been accompanied by threats. Chicago Bears free safety Maurice Douglas testified at the Walters-Bloom trial that Lloyd Bloom told
him, "if I didn't return the money and the cars, he'd have somebody
break my legs."[42] The reference to money and cars related to a $2,500
initial payment and other periodic payments made by Walters and
Bloom; the pair also leased a car for him.[43] The *Chicago Tribune* reports
that Walters and Bloom made "veiled references to their friends [in Las
Vegas] as well."[44]

Of course, not all agent/player relationships are the product of improper inducements. Many athletes and their parents evaluate the capabilities of potential agents as one would in the hiring of any professional.

They sometimes use extensive, formalized interview programs to select their agents.[45] Nevertheless, these interview techniques appear to be the exception.

We close this section with an account that provides a textbook example of the tangled web created when agents employ improper techniques to secure clients and when athletes succumb to the temptations that accompany such techniques. Indeed the affairs surrounding the relationships between Marcus Camby and agents John Lounsbury and Wesley Spears (neither of whom was apparently aware of the other's efforts to sign Camby) epitomize the solicitation techniques described above, including agent gifts and payments to an athlete, the drawing in of an athlete's family and friends, the use of threats to secure representation, and alleged athlete complicity.

In a *Sports Illustrated* article,[46] Lounsbury and Spears characterized Marcus Camby as the "ultimate greedy athlete, constantly with his hand out." In describing his interaction with Camby, Lounsbury is quoted as saying, "Marcus was very good. . . . I would call him all the time, and he'd have a few sentences, a little time. But when he wanted money, he increased the amount of time he gave me. He knew how to play me. He'd ride around in my car, tell me what I wanted to hear, then take the money. 'I'm struggling, man.' Those were Marcus's famous words. That's what he said anytime he called and needed something. 'I'm struggling, man.'"[47]

In the same magazine account, Camby admitted to having received favors from Lounsbury, including a stereo system, cash payments of between $300 and $500, and meeting a woman procured by Spears for sex at Spears's home. Camby denied, however, that Lounsbury gave only when requested to do so by Camby. Said Camby, "I didn't have to ask for anything. I had so many people offering me things without asking. I got offers from big-time agents, names you would recognize. I got offered cars, houses for my mother, college tuition for my sisters. When you're getting all those offers, why would you need to ask for anything."[48] Camby also denied that he received $40,000 in cash and gifts that the agents asserted they spent on him.

Camby's relatives and friends also became entangled in the web. Camby's mother, Janice Camby, reported that Lounsbury, despite her protests, insisted she take money from him. Lounsbury admitted to purchasing gifts for and giving $1,500 in cash to Janice Camby.[49] Lounsbury allegedly offered money to one of Camby's childhood friends. Spears engaged in similar efforts to win favor with Camby's other friends. One of Camby's associates indicated that the athlete never intended to sign with Spears. He described the nature of the interactions with Spears as a "two-bit shakedown" of the agent.[50] Camby admitted to the essence of this characterization: "I wasn't asking for nothing. . . . He would give it. It was basically my friends who were milking him. . . . They have been my boys since I was growing up. It was an opportunity to do things for them. Taking the cash, cars, and jewelry . . . , 'was all part of the hustle' fun by Wray and Murray [Camby's friends]. Things just got out of control. So far out of control. No one knew it would twist this way."[51]

Finally, Camby's entanglement with Spears also involved allegations of extortion. Spears is reported to have exploded and made threats against Camby when he discovered that the athlete would not sign with him. According to one news account, Spears threatened Camby, saying

> he had $75,000 invested in Camby and his friends, and Camby promised him face to face he would sign with him. . . . He also . . . [said] he had Camby on video taking money from him and witnesses from clothing stores. . . . Spears insisted that refusing to select him as Camby's agent will result in a lawsuit "that will tarnish Camby's image . . . and UMass will get in trouble."
> Spears [told] Camby, "You told me you are going to sign with me, and you are going to sign with me. . . ."
> "UMass would go down and you wouldn't be the number-one pick and no endorsements. The thing that bothers me most is that you lied to me."[52]

As is often the case, however, the techniques used to solicit an athlete and to win favor with his associates were to no avail. Despite favors and threats, rather than securing Camby as a client Spears was charged with extortion and promoting prostitution. As a result of a plea bargain, charges were dropped against Spears on the condition that he complete two years of probation and one hundred hours of community service.[53] Lounsbury did not fare much better. He was forced into bankruptcy, a consequence, he says, of giving gifts to Camby.[54] After Camby signed with ProServ, he gave $28,500 to Lounsbury, reportedly so that the agent could avoid being killed by loan sharks.[55] Lounsbury surrendered his certification as an NBA agent. A separate unrelated incident, in which he was charged with providing airline tickets to two University of Connecticut basketball players, also resulted in Lounsbury settling charges filed by the Connecticut Department of Consumer Protection.[56]

The Racial Undertone

There is an omnipresent racial edge to this business that should be noted. Readers must remain aware of the White agent/Black athlete dichotomy even when it is not highlighted. One-time agent Norby Walters fit the stereotype. Walters signed an astounding number of first-round draft picks as clients during his first year in the business. Through his firm, General Talent International, Walters represented such Black stars as Janet Jackson, Patti LaBelle, and Ben Vereen. Many pointed to the middle-aged Walters's success with African American entertainment acts as a "magnet" for young African American athletes, who reasoned, "if he can do it for them, he can put me in a Rolls Royce too." Walters entered into a partnership with Lloyd Bloom, a former Studio 54 discotheque bouncer. In a 1989 article, the *New York Times* stated, "the plan seemed so simple. Mr. Walters, a prominent music booking agent, would join forces with Mr. Bloom, an enthusiastic, young former football player. Together the two men, both white, would woo black college athletes with the promise that they could do for the athletes what the booking agent had done for such black entertainers as Luther Vandross and Kool and the Gang."[57]

Robert Ruxin, in his book *An Athlete's Guide to Agents*, tells the story of an agent who attempted to make student athletes believe he was Black. According to two student athletes who encountered the agent, "I thought he was black, having spoken to him on the phone. . . . His actions were black. . . . Like, he walked with a slight limp. You know, how a lot of blacks walk, kind of cool. A strut."[58] This is the omnipresent undercurrent in the business: White agents and African American clients. A key feature of this undercurrent is the relatively low percentage of African American athletes who patronize African American sports agents. The question that reverberates was prominently stated in the subtitle of a *Howard Law Journal* article, "A Search into Why Black Athletes Do Not Hire Black Agents."[59] At the heart of this question is a belief that there would be a natural affinity between this world of Black athletes who numerically predominate certain sports (for example, basketball and football) and well-qualified Black agents. The fostering of these relationships, however, has been impeded by stereotypes and the long-time dominance of White agents over Black agents.

In *In Black and White: Race and Sports in America*, the stereotype issue is explained as "the white man's ice is colder." Specifically,

A classic story, most often credited to Malcolm X, provides an insight into the black community's perception of the competence of our own professionals. The story has it that in a small southern town on some hot summer day, people stood in a long line wrapped around a corner to purchase ice. On the other side of town a black ice vendor sat with plenty of ice, doing very little business. When a black patron in the long line was asked why he would stand in the long line rather than purchase the ice in his own neighborhood, he responded, "Well everybody knows the white man's ice is colder."[60]

At the heart of the stereotypical belief that it is more advantageous for athletes to secure White representation is what some Black agents allege is being said by some White agents. According to African American athlete agent Fred Slaughter: "[White agents] just tell the kid, 'Only a white man can make that deal for you.' They have actually said that. And some kids, kids who are sitting in a well-furnished office with computers clicking and listening to a guy with gold teeth say that, they'll think, 'Wait a minute: if he's saying that, he must be right.' There are a lot of problems. It's been rough."[61]

Alleged statements that a Black agent's race would impede his ability to represent clients effectively lie at the heart of a lawsuit filed by Black agent C. Lamont Smith against a White agent. Smith's lawsuit alleges that former IMG agent Tom Condon, in an effort to dissuade a prospective professional NFL player from "hiring plaintiff, stated in his presence that plaintiff alienated the general managers of NFL clubs by 'playing the race card' during contract negotiations. Smith alleged that Condon made similar comments in the presence of other potential clients."[62] Condon denied the allegations.

A federal district court dismissed two of Smith's claims because they were not filed in a timely fashion and thus were barred by the applicable statute of limitations. With respect to the surviving claim, the court rejected the defendant's argument that Smith failed to make a prima facie case of defamation. Applying Pennsylvania law, the court stated that a statement is defamatory if there is a tendency of it to harm the reputation of another or to dissuade third parties from dealing with that person.[63] The court concluded that Condon's alleged statements "would cause others to question [Smith's] integrity in his business dealings with NFL clubs and would deter prospective professional football players from associating with plaintiff."[64] The court also found that the alleged statements would constitute slander per se because "they would adversely affect [Smith's] fitness to conduct properly his duties as an agent."[65]

Although the number of successful African American agents may have increased in recent years, racial tensions persist in the sports agent business. Like other sectors of society, any examination that does not consider these racial issues is necessarily incomplete. This is particularly true when it comes to the business of sports. The reality is that it remains exceptional for African American athlete agents to represent top draft picks in the major sports.

In an interview conducted in early 2000, Eugene Parker stated, "there were few if any black agents at the highest level, so the challenge has been twofold: first, to convince team officials of his competence, and second, to convince players of the same thing."[66] Black agent Roosevelt Barnes added, "you have to let [team management] know from the beginning that you know what you're doing. Once they understand that, they deal with you above board."[67] Barnes further said that "convincing players and their parents of his abilities has been more difficult."[68]

Other agents have remarked that the articulated reasons for why high-profile athletes do not select Black agents have shifted over time. Agent Bill Strickland offered the following analysis: "The argument used to be that there was an absence of competent black agents. . . . I don't think that's the case any longer. But now you see players saying 'There are no black owners, so white guys can deal with other white guys better.' "[69] David Ware added the following commentary: "While there has been some progress, the progess is glacier-like. . . . For every one that we get, there are 150 that not only do we not get, but we don't get to talk to."[70]

The ever present racial undercurrent surfaced in the case of Carl and Kevin Poston, African Americans who attracted considerable attention due to what some perceived as an overly aggressive negotiating style in their representation of several high-profile African American athletes. The Postons were criticized for running an agency that, at its height, had a roster of more than forty players, none of whom were White. The Postons' response to such criticism was "we'd love to represent [White stars] Peyton Manning and Zach Thomas. We don't get the time of day from white players and their families."[71]

A report in the *SportsBusiness Journal* is revealing. In its 2006 "By the Numbers" sports industry analysis, only one African American agent was listed among the top ten agents in the NBA, the NFL, Major League Baseball, and the NHL based on salary of players represented.[72] Bill Duffy was the sole African American identified on these lists; Duffy ranked number ten on the list of NBA sports agents. None of these lists included an individual with a Spanish surname.

Sports agent Bill Strickland sees it cutting both ways: "we still have black athletes who don't feel that black professionals can do the job. Some guys think the white man's ice is colder, when ice is ice. Some agents who are incompetent say let's get down because we are both black."[73] NFL player Ray Crockett reported that Kirk Wright, a hedge fund manager, played the race card in persuading Black athletes to invest with Wright's company International Management Associates (IMA). The $15 million that Crockett and two other athletes invested was part of an estimated $115 million to $185 million managed by Wright that went missing. According to Crockett, "Race was a big part of IMA's image. Kirk would say his company had to be above board because as a successful black company, people were watching them."[74] The impact of Wright's alleged improprieties and those of stockbroker Calvin Darden, who misappropriated $300,000 of Latrell Sprewell's money, extends beyond the individual athletes who suffer financial losses. Unfortunately, improper conduct by Black agents or financial advisers makes it more difficult for all Blacks in the industry because it may foster racial stereotypes that linger within the industry. The title of the *Sports Illustrated* article chronicling the Kirk Wright incident, "Brother Beware," is indicative of the overly broad indictment that is sometimes imposed on all Blacks in this profession because of the negative actions of one.

The Gender Barrier

The gender of an agent plays a role in competition as well. Although female agents are beginning to emerge in the athlete representation industry, men continue to dominate. An October 1998 *SportsBusiness Journal* article reported that although women represent a few players, they lag far behind in representing players in the major moneymaking leagues, the NBA, the NFL, MLB, and the NHL. At the time of that article, only one of the 225 agents registered with the NHL Players' Association (NHLPA) was a woman. The statistics were similar for the other major sports. In 1998, women represented only 2 percent of the agents registered with the NFLPA. Only five women represented players on forty-man rosters in MLB.[75] It is the case on some occasions that the female representative is the wife, mother, or sister of the player. There does not appear to have been much change since 1998. In 2007, the percentage of certified female representatives in the NFL was at 3 percent, with only a total of two women having active clients.[76]

Explanations vary for what amounts to a "glass ceiling when it comes to [women] representing male athletes" in the major sports.[77] In the 1998 article, one female agent, Leslie Giordano, who at the time had negotiated contracts for eight NFL players over a four-year span, attributes the paucity to the fact that "no one has encouraged them [women] to do it." Rather than gender discrimination, Giordano noted the difficulty for anyone, male or female, to break into the business. "No one has said to my face that [discrimination] may be a factor why I haven't signed a particular player. . . . I feel like I'm just now starting to do something. It takes a while."[78]

Wendi Huntley, who represents a number of players in the WNBA, expressed a similar concern regarding the inequitable treatment of women in the competition for male "big league" clients. She noted that as she was attempting to recruit an NFL draft pick, the athlete told her that a competing agent had said, "You don't want to be represented by a girl, do you?" According to Huntley, "an assault based on the number of NFL players I represent would have been one thing but on this basis . . . that's comedy."[79]

Huntley also reflected on a key issue that many female agents must deal with: making sure the athlete understands that the relationship is to be all business. "I don't want any clients talking about, 'hey, baby.' Let's be clear, I am their agent, not their baby."[80]

The *SportsBusiness Journal* article indicated that another explanation offered by male and female agents for the lack of female agents is the greater comfort level male players have with men. "A player-agent relationship is an intensely personal one, and individual players unlike major corporations and organizations, are not under any public pressure to hire women."[81] Others reject comfort level as a legitimate basis for a male not to hire a woman agent. "For years people said they were uncomfortable with and didn't want to work with people of other races or women, and that's not good enough. . . . It will take strong women with a lot of determination to break through the barrier."[82]

Huntley perceives a "sisterhood" among WNBA players and female agents. "But time will tell. The women are not making enough money for the big-time male agents to really come in and compete. In the WNBA it is estimated that half of the players in the draft were not represented by agents and those who were had agents primarily in order to explore international leagues beyond the WNBA. Since the demise of the rival American Basketball League (ABL) there is no leverage necessitating WNBA management to negotiate in the manner the industry is accustomed to on the men's side."[83]

As with race, a degree of bias toward women remains in society. Like other sectors of society, however, as women become more successful and experienced in this field, their presence should increase. Unfortunately, bias is a difficult barrier to overcome.

Agents' View of Their Business

One of the ironies of the sports agent business is that not only do outsiders look down on it but so do many agents, if not always seriously, often sarcastically. Agent Andy Miller, whose clients include or have included NBA players such as Kevin Garnett, Sebastian Telfair, Brendan Haywood, Al Harrington, and Chauncey Billups, is reported as having said that 90 percent of agents are "scum of the earth."[84] Veteran agent Joe Linta stated in a 1998 interview that "I am very afraid of what the business has become. . . . It has gotten out of hand—the amounts of money involved, how crazy agents are."[85] One of the most successful agents, Leigh Steinberg, once expressed a similar view when he called the sports agent business "the ultimate sleazoid profession."[86]

Agent Scott Boras has come to epitomize what some consider the worst and others consider the best attributes of agents. Boras represented Alex Rodriguez in negotiations that led to the then record-setting ten-year, $252-million contract for the shortstop to play for the Texas

Rangers. The agent's fee reportedly came to $12.6 million for his work on that single transaction.[87] Boras's negotiations on behalf of other players have led to some of the other biggest contracts in professional baseball. For example, he negotiated the first $100-million deal in baseball on behalf of Dodgers' pitcher Kevin Brown in 1998. Boras also negotiated a $119-million, seven-year deal for Carlos Beltran with the Mets. In 2006, Boras was ranked as the number-one agent representing MLB players based on player salaries. His sixty-four players on active MLB rosters at the beginning of the 2006 baseball season had annual salaries totaling approximately $246 million.[88]

Boras's successful negotiations on behalf of his clients have resulted in him being disliked by many and described as a "man who doesn't have a soul . . . so he sells his clients."[89] On the other hand, others recognize that he zealously represents his clients through his hard work, brilliant negotiation strategies, knowledge of the business of baseball, and preparation.[90]

As was mentioned in the Introduction, for many, within and outside of the industry, Drew Rosenhaus has come to represent the modern image of the sports agent. This perception was amplified for many when, in November 2005, Rosenhaus attempted, during a televised press conference, to defend his client NFL player Terrell Owens after the athlete had been dismissed from playing for the Philadelphia Eagles for conduct detrimental to the team. Some argued that Rosenhaus's behavior in representing Owens tarnished the image of both athletes and agents. "It takes agents like Rosenhaus to give athletes a bad name, making them look like all they care about is money and self-promotion."[91] As for the image of agents, some argue Rosenhaus has "become the poster boy for a brand of agents best embodied by Bob Sugar, the scruple-lacking, camera-loving slime ball portrayed by Jay Mohr in the movie, 'Jerry Maguire.'"[92] It should be noted that notwithstanding the negative image many have painted of Drew Rosenhaus, he continues to be a highly effective and successful agent. In 2006, he was identified as one of the twenty most influential sports agents as evidenced by his roster of about eighty NFL players, including many high-profile players.[93] Many praise his ability to zealously represent his clients and negotiate quality deals for them.

Some agents have decided to opt out of the industry due to the harsh realities that now define it. In commenting on his decision to discontinue player representation, former basketball player and agent Len Elmore stated, "In all candor what chased me from the industry was the shrinking revenue caused by wage scaling and my unwillingness to pay a young kid to become my client. I simply did not desire, nor could I afford, to 'stoop to conquer.' Betrayal by client family members and significant others who, in my opinion, sought to control the wealth and attendant power amassed by 'their boy' also had negative impact. Thus, I was left with a harsh business reality. It was time to fold them and move on."[94]

David Ware told a group of agents at an NFLPA meeting that he resented accusations that agents are a "little higher than snakes and a little lower than scorpions." Ware continued, "If you don't like the business, you should get out." In noting how much he enjoyed what he did, Ware argued that the agent has an "obligation to be a zealous advocate of his client."[95]

Ware's statements came in response to the constant grumbling of many agents regarding the difficulty in signing clients "honestly," that is, without making payments that violate state agent regulations and cause athletes to violate NCAA regulations. In any case, Ware had success in recruiting clients. His representation of 1988 Heisman Trophy winner Barry Sanders in his negotiations with the NFL's Detroit Lions was just one of his achievements. Ware and agent C. Lamont Smith were the first African Americans to represent a Heisman Trophy winner. In 1999, Ware also took over the representation of some clients who had been represented by Tank Black.

In reality, however, many people calling themselves agents are not successful, and they have not found the business to be financially rewarding.[96] The position of sports agents entering the business illustrates why there is not a lot of success. Numbers are a key factor. There are, at varying times, more agents than there are athletes in a given league; thus competition for clients is intense.[97] Moreover, even if an agent does sign a client, there is no guarantee that the agent will make any money. If the athlete does not make the team after a contract has been negotiated, neither the athlete nor the agent gets paid absent an initial signing bonus; because the agent is generally paid a percentage of the athlete's earnings, the agent earns nothing if the athlete earns nothing. As was noted, in exceptional circumstances the agent may be paid on an hourly basis like most attorneys or accountants, and in such cases the agent may be compensated for the time expended. However, such arrangements are rare.

Ironically, it is possible for an agent to exert the most effort for the athlete that is going to bring the lowest fee—the rookie free agent who is *not* drafted out of college. Often such a rookie will enlist a sports agent to help find a team that is interested in giving the athlete a tryout. The agent must then contact more than two dozen teams in the appropriate leagues to try to find one or more that will give the player a tryout. If, after the tryout, the player does impress the team, then the agent can negotiate a contract for the player. But even then there is still the chance that the athlete will not make the team's final cut and the agent will not earn a fee for his or her efforts. Compare the work and the risk involved here to an early round draft pick where there is no shopping for a team or a tryout, and the agent's responsibility is to negotiate a contract in the athlete's best interest. Although the contract negotiation itself may be difficult and time consuming, the compensation to the sports agent will inevitably be higher than in the rookie free-agent situation.

In the sport of baseball, some agents exhibit the patience of Job while their clients serve time in the minor leagues, often for years. During this time, the agent takes little or no fee while waiting for the call from the major league team to come. During this waiting period, the agent is probably—in addition to providing the player with gloves, bats, and other equipment—providing financial support. Most agents accept this toil with rookie free agents and minor leaguers as part of the price an agent must pay to become a success in the business. Among themselves, however, some complain about what a "pain" their athlete clients are. Ware notes that he for one "resent[s] guys who talk about the business and still take a fee for it."[98] Baseball agent Stanley O. King views the investment in his baseball clients as an "annuity," except, he notes, "the baseball type doesn't always pay off."[99]

Those individuals engaged in athlete representation take differing routes in pursuing the business, and they also possess mixed feelings about their profession. Many attorneys who enter the athlete representation profession will begin their careers at a traditional law firm that has carved out a niche for sports representation or one that will allow an individual attorney to pursue athlete representation while also working on the firm's other business matters. Often these attorneys will either leave to open up their own firm or become associated with a company that has more of a focus on athlete representation.

The above description tracks the experiences of Kevin Robinson who became what he characterized as a "sports attorney" in 1999. He began his representation of athletes at a law firm in Denver. After he secured his first athlete client, the firm decided to terminate the sports representation aspect of its business. The firm's managers decided it was not worth the expense and time to continue in the business. Thereafter, Robinson began to pursue sports representation with A. J. Mills, Jr., P.C. of Boulder, Colorado.

Robinson considers himself fortunate to have become associated with a sports management firm because it allowed him a better opportunity to secure clients. This association helped him to overcome a significant obstacle to breaking into the business: the reluctance of experienced agents to bring on board and mentor aspiring agents for fear that the latter will "sign clients and then leave the firm."[100] Robinson sees this reluctance to mentor as a manifestation of the competitive nature of an industry that he describes as "hostile." He also recognizes that competition by agents for clients and the desires of athlete clients (many of whom based their representation decisions on information they obtain from agents) cause many agents to provide improper inducements as a means of signing clients. "There are a lot of agencies and firms that have their grips on players, [by offering improper inducements], by the time they are sophomores in college."[101] Consequently, "it becomes difficult for other agents to compete."

Although aware of the unflattering realities of the athlete representation business, Robinson has not become jaded. He remains optimistic regarding the profession because of the positive role he believes he can play in the lives of his clients. "Our goal is that these young men become responsible, productive business men . . . and productive members of society."[102] Robinson also believes that some clients possess views that align with these goals: "You have . . . a set of athletes . . . who have an advisor and [look] at appropriate things like experience, what types of contracts [the adviser has] negotiated in the past . . . [and the adviser's] competency."[103] Robinson's perservance paid off. Subsequent to the publication of the first edition of this book, Robinson became a partner in Ascent Sports Management, which was founded by Jack Mills.[104] Even some experienced agents retain a more positive view of the profession. Notes one, "[many] of the agents in the business are good guys who take good care of their clients."[105]

Conclusion

This chapter set forth the basics of the competition among agents in the business. Although the financial upside can be huge, only a few sports agents reap truly large financial rewards. The next chapter discusses the legal mechanisms employed to sanction agents.

Chapter 5

Unscrupulous and Criminal
The Problem Agents

Problems associated with unethical agents have clearly seeped into the public consciousness. Newspapers and television news programs, both sports and nonsports oriented, report with regularity on problems that ultimately stem from agents' intense competition for clients. Widely reported incidents include the criminal case of agent Tank Black, athlete agents who mismanage and misappropriate client funds, agent conflicts of interest, and agents who bestow cash and gifts upon student athletes and thereby precipitate the NCAA's imposition of sanctions against the colleges for which these athletes play. These incidents have alerted the public and those intimately involved in the sports industry to the ethical and credibility challenges that confront the athlete agent industry.

As discussed in detail in Chapters 11 and 12, certain of these incidents led to a rush to stop sports agent problems by regulating the industry. By the end of the 1980s, more than a dozen states had enacted statutes that attempted to regulate the activities of sports agents.[1] Entering the new millennium, this number more than doubled.[2] Conspicuously absent from this flurry of legislative activity—focused on protecting the interest of academic institutions—are efforts to engage in a far-reaching reassessment of the multiple dimensions of the ethics and competency issues that confront the athlete agent industry. The narrow focus of legislative efforts is exemplified in the state of Florida's initial agent legislation: "The Legislature finds that dishonest or unscrupulous practices by agents who solicit representation of student athletes can cause significant harm to student athletes and the academic institutions for which they play. It is the intent of the Legislature to protect the interests of student athletes and academic institutions by regulating the activities of athlete agents that involve student athletes at colleges or universities in the state."[3] Even though Florida adopted the Uniform Athlete Agents Act in 2002, as elaborated upon in Chapter 12, the underlying purposes of the UAAA mirror those articulated in Florida's original agent legislation.

Despite the benefits to be derived from state-promulgated agent legislation, it often ignores other improprieties spawned by agents who are unscrupulous, unethical, unqualified, criminal, or some combination of the four. The payment of monies to student athletes by sports agents is the most publicized impropriety committed by sports agents. As alluded to above, however, additional wrongs occur frequently. Historically, these improprieties have included the mismanagement of athletes' income and excessive agent fees.

Income Mismanagement

The stories associated with the mismanagement of athletes' income are no more disturbing than stories linked with the mismanagement of the assets of other high-income individuals such as physicians, lawyers, and other businesspersons. Incidents of income mismanagement in sports, however, receive much more publicity because of the notoriety of the parties involved. In 2005, Calvin Darden pled guilty to grand larceny and scheming to defraud. Darden stole more than $7 million from his employers and investors. Darden emphasized his ability to obtain business from high-profile clients such as Shaquille O'Neal and actor Samuel L. Jackson as a means of obtaining loans from his employers. The promised high-profile client list never materialized. The case received more attention than it otherwise would have because of Darden's alleged connections with athletes and actors, and because he victimized then New York Knicks player Latrell Sprewell in the amount of $300,000. Darden was sentenced to four to twelve years in prison, ordered to repay $6 million to his victims, and barred from future work in the securities field.[4]

A well-publicized case of financial mismanagement occurred in the 1980s involving Technical Equities Corporation, a growth-oriented holding company run by sports agent Harry Stern,[5] which declared bankruptcy in 1986. Technical Equities allowed individuals to invest in high-tech, manufacturing, and real estate deals. Many of the firm's athlete clients invested their life savings in the company. The firm's financial collapse involved not only seventy sports figures but also nearly seven hundred others, including doctors and lawyers.[6] Mr. Stern agreed to plead guilty to criminal fraud charges and was sentenced to a five-year prison term.[7]

Calvin Darden's and Harry Stern's misconduct and the alleged misconduct of Kirk Wright, who reportedly defrauded about five hundred investors, including seven NFL players, of $115 million to $185 million, illustrate that not only athletes are victimized. Yet the widely reported instances of agents and financial advisers mismanaging athletes' finances inevitably raise the question of whether athletes are more susceptible to such misdeeds. In answering this question, it is important to avoid casting athletes who become victims of poor financial advice or fraud as dumb jocks. Lack of experience is more of a factor than lack of intelligence. Athletes' lack of experience becomes particularly troublesome when combined with the increasingly complex financial world into which many young athletes are cast when they become professionals. It is a world that very few are prepared to navigate effectively because they tend to focus on preparing for success on the playing field rather than managing financial matters. One financial adviser to athletes suggests that in addition to lack of experience in evaluating businesses and investments, athletes' willingness to seek risky investments makes them an attractive target of unscrupulous financial advisers. "Athletes hold risky jobs and that lifestyle can promote picking risky investments. . . . You are talking about men who are in a high-risk business. When you have that competitive edge, you want to roll the dice a bit more."[8]

Also at the heart of many athletes' financial headaches is the fact that agents are subject to few educational or professional requirements, must adhere to vague ethical standards, and are subject to minimum regulation. A Beverly Hills entertainment attorney who also served as a sports agent commented, "I don't like to be lumped and called a sports agent. I was the Rams' general counsel for eight years. What I saw coming through the door representing the player was an embarrassment."[9] One attorney who represents athletes in agent abuse cases also criticizes deficiencies in the ranks of players' representatives: "'There's no scientific study of the percentage of players that have been abused somehow in their investment, but it's in the high 90s,' he asserts. 'Virtually all of them are abused. The question is to what degree.'"[10]

The nebulous "financial advisers," according to agent Mark Bartlestein, prey on people "who are very inexperienced and very vulnerable. They get in there and recruit players harder than anyone."[11] The following account given by NFL player Antoine Winfield describes a tactic allegedly used by financial advisers and agents to secure athletes as clients. "Winfield says [Dunyasha] Yetts gave him money by losing on purpose in card games. 'In college, we were broke, there's no money,' he explains, 'and if someone comes around and throws money in your face, you are going to take it.' Winfield says he and Yetts went on trips to Las Vegas and the Bahamas, courtesy of Yetts. 'He was giving me suits' valued at $1,500 and free Ohio State football tickets that, Winfield says, he sold. 'He was giving cash,' Winfield went on. 'If we needed the money, he would pay the rent.' Winfield says he realized his acceptance of the gifts violated NCAA rules. 'We knew it was illegal,' he says, adding: 'If you got caught, you would be in trouble.'"[12]

The problems associated with financial advisers raise particular cause for concern because they may fall through the regulatory cracks. These advisers often are not agents and therefore are not subject to player association certification or state regulatory requirements. The law does not position unions to play the same regulatory role with financial advisers as it does with agents. Notes Charles Banks, a traditional financial planner, "It's the new bad fad. As the fees on the agent side come down and salaries go up, everyone is getting in on the financial side and no one is really looking out for the player who doesn't understand the difference between a stockbroker, an investment manager and a life insurance salesman."[13]

As will be discussed in Chapter 10, the NFLPA in 2001 undertook a major new initiative aimed at addressing problems associated with financial advisers. As discussed below, complaints filed by the Securities and Exchange Commission (SEC) also suggest that the activities of financial advisers may be more thoroughly scrutinized in the future.

A February 2002 issue of *U.S. News and World Report* contained an investigative report concerning NFL players victimized or allegedly victimized by financial managers.[14] The report revealed that cases involving acknowledged and alleged mismanagement of players' investments follow similar patterns. The alleged surefire deal fails; investment funds are used to cover personal expenditures, which allows financial advisers to maintain a certain (often lavish) standard of living; and investment funds are used to cover other failed transactions.

One of the more notorious cases of alleged irregularities identified in the *U.S. News* article that seems to fit this pattern involved financial adviser Donald Lukens. An SEC complaint filed against Lukens alleged that athletes were among the individuals whom he "duped" into making high-risk investments.[15] The complaint specifically claimed that Lukens "violated federal securities laws by systematically defrauding at least 100 (and perhaps more than 200) clients and brokerage customers collectively of tens of millions of dollars in a series of investment schemes during at least the mid-to-late 1990s."[16] According to the SEC complaint, "in soliciting these funds, Lukens routinely and falsely described the investments as 'safe' and 'secure,' promising high returns, provided baseless personal guarantees, made other materially false or misleading statements, and failed to disclose material information, including significant risks."[17] Lukens allegedly misappropriated or diverted for personal and business use the money given to him for investment purposes. In his answer to the SEC complaint, Lukens denied having engaged in any wrongdoing.

Lukens was also alleged to have formed Global Sports & Entertainment, a financial and investment advisory firm, in the mid-1990s. Global is thought to have represented at least forty professional athletes at various times. Global's athlete clients reportedly included the NBA's Kurt

Thomas and Byron Russell.[18] Lukens was accused of having defrauded NFL player Simeon Rice of $2.4 million.[19] Additionally, Lukens, who filed for bankruptcy, listed among his creditors the following former or current professional athletes: Eric Dickerson ($1.835 million), NFL player Sean Gilbert ($350,000), NFL player Steve Atwater ($1.2 million), and NFL tight end Shannon Sharpe ($300,000).[20] Lukens eventually settled the case filed by the SEC by agreeing to pay $4.75 million.[21]

The SEC also sued agent John W. Gillette, Jr., alleging, among other things, that he "made materially false and misleading statements and converted clients' funds to his own use."[22] After pleading guilty to thirty-eight counts of grand theft and forgery, Gillette, who was charged with having duped more than $11 million from his clients ($5.6 million of this amount was invested by NFL players), was sentenced to ten years in prison in 1998. He was paroled in 2001.[23]

Lukens and Gillette shared something other than being sued by the SEC—they used a similar tactic to make an inroad with clients. They resorted to religion. They expressed a belief in Christian values as a means of obtaining the trust and business of professional athletes. In the mid-1980s, a newspaper reporter gave the following account of an agent whose solicitation tactics included a religious appeal:

Dallas agent Joe Courrege won the trust of several [Dallas] Cowboy players through his devout Christianity. Courrege played religious tapes in his car while driving players around and arranged to have one of them, safety Bill Bates, appear as a guest on TV evangelist Pat Robertson's 700 Club. Last year Bates and three other players filed suit against Courrege for allegedly defrauding them of $200,000 through the use of fictitious names and bogus corporations in 14 real estate investments; Bates reached an out-of-court settlement with Courrege, but the suits of his three other former clients are pending. "What I found out is that he beats you over the head with his Bible and has his hands in your pocket at the same time," Dallas linebacker Jeff Rohrer, a plaintiff in one of those suits, told the Fort Worth Star-Telegram. Courrege has denied wrongdoing in all the cases.[24]

Football player D'Marco Farr described his initial interaction with Donald Lukens as follows: "He came off as a God-fearing man. He liked to quote Bible Scriptures and whatnot. That really spoke to me."[25] Some are uncomfortable with the use of sprituality as a recruiting mechanism. "The mere fact that someone aligns themselves with God or the Bible doesn't necessarily mean they conduct good business practices."[26] For some, Gillette represents the paradigmatic case of the agent whose espoused spirituality was incongruent with his business ethics. On the other hand, some agents and financial advisers who freely express their spirituality are sincere and provide competent service to their clients.

Another illustration of the aggressive posture taken by the SEC involved Dunyasha Yetts (discussed previously), who allegedly "violated the federal securities laws by operating [as] an unregistered broker-dealer in Dublin, Ohio, and defrauding at least 14 customers of approximately $1.8 million in an investment scheme that continued from 1998 through to early 2001."[27] Yetts allegedly formed and operated Worldwide Financial Group and World Wide Sports Group.[28] The SEC claimed that Yetts fraudulently induced customers to invest with him and Worldwide Financial.[29] The complaint further asserted, "Yetts did not invest those funds for his customers' accounts. Instead, Yetts misappropriated or diverted their funds for personal and business expenses."[30] NFL player Antoine Winfield, who was identified as Worldwide Financial's largest client, was allegedly defrauded of $1.35 million.[31] Yetts denied that he defrauded Winfield.[32]

On May 20, 2003, a federal court judge entered a final judgment against Yetts and the two entities he operated. They were ordered to pay $2,980,627. Yetts was also assessed a civil penalty of $110,000. Yetts consented to judgment without admitting to or denying the SEC's allegations.[33] The NFLPA decertified Yetts. Conduct on which the NFLPA focused in revoking his certification reportedly included Yetts's mismanagement of Winfield's funds and money given to Winfield to induce him to sign a representation agreement with Yetts.[34]

In August 2001 former NFL running back Terry Orr was sentenced to fourteen months in a federal prison after pleading guilty to one count of wire fraud. He was also ordered to attempt to make restitution to three of his former teammates on the Washington Redskins and to another investor. Three former football players—Raleigh McKenzie, Art Monk, and Brian Mitchell—each had invested $50,000 in a deal involving a shoe company. Their investments were lost when the shoe company failed. In addition, Orr used some of the money invested by the former players and another investor for personal expenditures and to satisfy debts arising from another failed investment. For example, Orr used $22,000 of the $50,000 obtained from Monk to make mortgage payments; $15,000 was used as a down payment on a Suburban SUV.[35]

A *U.S. News and World Report* article identified the following as instances of alleged or proven improprieties by financial advisers:

- An SEC investigation regarding whether Von Cummings mishandled $1 million of former NFL running back Robert Smith.[36]
- The case of Linda Frykholm, who defrauded several investors, including Brian Simmons of the Cincinnati Bengals, of a total of $15 million that was used "to finance a lavish lifestyle"[37]
- The SEC arbitration in which Sean Jones, a financial adviser and former NFL player, was ordered to pay $550,000 to former NFL

cornerback Cris Dishman, who alleged that Jones failed to disclose the high level of risk associated with certain investments[38]
- Money lost by NFL players who entered into investment deals with Luigi DiFonzo, who committed suicide in August 2000[39]

Often issues of competence and ethics merge to create disastrous results for athlete clients. One of the most notorious mismanagement stories involved then South Carolina–based agent William "Tank" Black.[40] Like Norby Walters and Lloyd Bloom, Black began to have success at a rapid rate. The principal business entity through which Black operated was Professional Management, Inc. (PMI). Like many other firms that depend on one, if any, marquee client for most of the firm's existence, initially Sterling Sharpe was PMI's lone recognizable client. Yet prior to his downfall, Black's firm was on track to represent an unprecedented five NFL first-round draft picks. Black had also acquired first-rate clients that included the NBA's Vince Carter and NFL stars Fred Taylor, Duce Staley, Ike Hilliard, and Terry Allen.

The unraveling of Tank Black's emergence as a superagent began simply enough when NFLPA lawyer Richard Berthelsen stated at a meeting of football agents that he could not take action against agents who made under-the-table payments because the agents present at the meeting never named names. At that point Ray Anderson, then of AR Sports in Atlanta, stood up and said, "I'll give you a name, Tank Black."

Anderson's statement led to an NFLPA investigation of Black and PMI. Thereafter, investigations were launched by the Securities Exchange Commission (SEC), the Internal Revenue Service (IRS), the Federal Bureau of Investigation (FBI), the United States Attorney's Office, and authorities in the states of Florida and Louisiana. The allegations asserted against Black went beyond claims of under-the-table payments. Black was accused of fraudulently leading clients to believe they were investing in a publicly traded security, leading clients into a pyramid scheme, and, perhaps most damaging from a prosecutorial standpoint, laundering drug monies.

Michael Fuchs, an SEC lawyer involved in the Black case, told *Sports Illustrated*, "Professional athletes are prime candidates for financial fraud. Many are unsophisticated in financial matters and suddenly find themselves with a six- or seven-figure salary. They're young, they're trusting, and they've been taken care of most of their lives."[41] Cumulatively, Black's clients allegedly lost millions of dollars as a result of having placed the ultimate degree of trust in a single individual who seized the opportunity to take advantage of their trust in an extraordinarily grievous manner.

The various investigations of Black prompted Reverend Jesse Jackson, the Florida branch of the NAACP, and others to raise the question of racial motivation. Some felt that the investigation of Black constituted another illustration of the "system" trying to pull down an African American who was achieving unprecedented levels of success. One of Black's attorneys succinctly expressed this view: "Tank is setting records and beating these white [agents] at their own game."[42] In fact, it appears highly unlikely that race played any role in the initial attention directed toward Black. Ray Anderson, an African American, was motivated by a desire to protect his own business interests when he reported a competitor he believed was involved in wrongdoing. This is not to say that race is not a factor in the athlete agent business. Race impacts many aspects of the industry including access to opportunities for agents of color, whom agents pursue as clients, and whom clients select as agents. Yet allegations of racism based on the vigorousness of the prosecution of Black appeared unfounded. As Berthelsen told *Sports Illustrated*, "this case with one individual has more violations of our regulations than all of our previous cases combined."[43]

Black and James Franklin, general counsel of Black's PMI, pled guilty and admitted that they assisted convicted drug traffickers and others in moving cash from drug proceeds.[44] Black admitted to playing a part in laundering more than $1 million. In June 2001, Black received a six-year, ten-month sentence after he pled guilty to money laundering charges asserted in the case before U.S. Federal District Chief Judge Lawrence Zatkoff.[45] He was also fined $15,000. In January 2002, a Florida jury convicted Black of "conspiring to commit mail and wire fraud and of conspiring to defraud the U.S. and obstruct a Securities and Exchange Commission investigation."[46] A federal judge sentenced Black to five years in prison, which the former agent would begin to serve after his completion of the earlier six-year, ten-month sentence. The latter conviction grew out of allegations that Black stole upward of $13.5 million from football players, including Ike Hilliard, Fred Taylor, and Robert Brooks, whom he represented as a financial adviser.[47] James Franklin was sentenced to thirty-two months in prison, two years of post-prison probation, and a fine of $10,000. In a separate Florida action, a federal judge sentenced Alfred "Tweet" Twitty, Black's assistant, to six months of house arrest for helping pay former University of Florida football players while they were still students and for defrauding NFL players of millions of dollars.

Other matters have raised competency and ethics issues. Githaiga Ramsey was charged by the California State Bar with eighteen counts relating to his allegedly having bilked more than $2.2 million out of former NBA player Jason Caffey. According to Caffey, Ramsey misappropriated, for the agent's personal and business expenses, money from a joint account they had established. Ramsey resigned, without admitting fault, from his law practice in order to avoid disbarment and to bring the state bar proceedings to an end.[48] A civil suit filed by Caffey against Ramsey was settled.[49]

In the Walters-Bloom trial, Joel Levy, an accountant for both Lloyd Bloom and his client, then Kansas City Chiefs running back Paul Palmer, testified about the misuse of client funds. Levy maintained that Palmer gave Bloom $125,000 to start a credit restoration business. With these funds, Bloom allegedly made a $82,242 down payment on the lease of a $160,000 1987 Rolls Royce Corniche, commonly referred to then as the most expensive vehicle in the world. He also used the funds to pay other personal expenses, including "credit-card debts, clothing and karate lessons."[50] Levy testified further that Bloom "had a sickness with money and trouble handling his own money."[51]

LEGAL MECHANISMS

Criminal Prosecution

As illustrated by the Tank Black case, in several alleged cases of financial mismanagement, the legal system has been deployed as a means of holding agents and financial managers accountable for their misconduct. Sometimes the legal process is invoked in the form of criminal prosecution. In this regard, the federal indictments issued against South Carolina–based Summit Management Group and its principals are illustrative. In a fifty-six-count indictment, federal prosecutors alleged that several high-profile athletes, including baseball player Mookie Wilson and football players Charles Woodson and Stephen Davis, were collectively defrauded of $3 million to $5 million by the management firm.[52] Federal prosecutors alleged that "as a part of a scheme and artifice to defraud and obtain money from professional athletes," Marion D. Jones and James E. Brown fraudulently represented that Summit "had assembled a highly qualified team of trained professionals, including certified public accountants, attorneys, investment portfolio managers, pension fund experts, asset managers and consultants for real estate investments, tax and estate planners, insurance managers and career counselors, to insure the financial growth and success of its clients."[53] More specifically, the indictment charged that Summit committed mail fraud, wire fraud, bank fraud, and money laundering.[54]

Prosecutors apparently began the investigation in 1999 following Stephen Davis's complaint that Summit had misappropriated his money. According to the indictment, certain athletes granted powers of attorney to Summit. For example, Corey Jenkins, a first-round draft pick of the Boston Red Sox, allegedly handed over for Summit's management the

$575,000 signing bonus he received from the club. The indictment alleged that Summit failed to use portions of the money to pay the athlete's bills, including house and car payments, as it had agreed.[55] The indictment also charged Marion Jones and James Brown of Summit with violating fiduciary duties owed to their clients. Other athletes allegedly victimized and their claimed losses included Reggie Taylor ($283,772), Jamie Watson ($736,485), Corey Jenkins ($130,000), and Stephen Davis ($107,719).[56]

Conviction of the charges asserted against the Summit Management defendants carried the potential of imprisonment and fines. For example, the federal indictment identified the maximum penalty for each count of mail fraud as imprisonment for five years and a fine of $250,000. In addition, prosecutors sought forfeiture of a minimum of $445,947.27 from Marion Jones and James Brown, which represented proceeds traceable to their alleged money-laundering offenses. A minimum of approximately $1.2 million was sought in forfeiture from Jones, Brown, and another defendant, Andre Lewis.[57] This amount allegedly represented "proceeds the Defendants obtained, 'directly or indirectly, as a result of [bank fraud offenses].'"[58] In January 2001, the defendants named in the indictment pled not guilty to the federal charges.[59] Brown, the former vice president of Summit, later pled guilty to one count of mail fraud in exchange for his testifying against the other defendants and agreeing to pay restitution to the athletes.[60] Thereafter, Lewis, a former banker, was convicted on eight counts, sentenced to six and a half years in prison, and required to pay restitution of about $460,000.[61] Finally, Jones, Summit's former president, pled guilty to one count of bank fraud and was ordered to pay restitution in exchange for offering testimony against another defendant. Jones did not admit guilt and insisted the athletes had squandered their money.[62]

Another criminal prosecution ended in the conviction of Atlanta-based agent Fairron Newton. A federal grand jury issued an indictment charging Newton with fraud, tax fraud, money laundering, and filing false tax returns. Newton arranged for the salaries of NFL football players (including Charlie Garner, Tim Bowens, Fred Baxter, and Shaun King) to be paid directly to his company, Options Plus Financial Services. Newton promised to pay the players' bills, debts, and expenses. In 1995, without the knowledge of the players (who were in no way involved in criminal misconduct), Newton began filing fraudulent tax returns in order to generate tax refunds that were received by Options Plus.[63] In June 2001, Newton was sentenced to serve two years in prison, ordered to pay restitution of more than $240,000, and ordered to serve two hundred hours of community service.[64]

Criminal prosecution against Howard J. Golub, who at one time served as a financial manager for approximately seventy athletes, resulted in his being sentenced in January 1989 to ten to twelve years in prison and ordered to pay restitution in the amount of $163,600 to clients following a guilty plea.[65] Golub had been indicted by a grand jury on five counts of fraud and nineteen counts of theft. His clients included baseball players George Foster and Lance Parrish, basketball players Louis Orr and Cedric Maxwell, and football player Rich Karlis.[66]

One of the earliest agent-related criminal prosecutions took place against agent Richard Sorkin.[67] While acting as a sports agent, Sorkin gambled and lost in the stock market more than $1 million in earnings of more than fifty hockey and basketball players. Investigations revealed that Sorkin bet as much as $100,000 per week on horses, baseball, and football.[68] The district attorney found that Sorkin lost $626,000 gambling and $271,000 in the stock market. Other missing funds could not be traced or otherwise accounted for.[69] Following a guilty plea to seven counts of grand larceny, Sorkin was sentenced to three years in prison.[70]

Civil Suits

Players also invoke the civil process in their attempts to hold agents legally accountable and to recover money lost as a result of financial mismanagement. For example, Mookie Wilson won a judgment against James Brown and Marion Jones, the principals of Summit Management Group.[71] Wilson alleged that Summit and its principals "failed to make mortgage, car and credit card payments" for him. He also asserted that Summit "used his credit card and power of attorney for personal gain."[72] A judge awarded Wilson damages of $450,000 that consisted of "$360,000 for money lost, $50,000 for punitive damages and $40,000 for lawyer's fees."[73] Wilson's attorney doubts that his client will recover much, if any, of the money the court awarded him.[74]

In a much-celebrated case in the early 1990s, former baseball player Bill Madlock filed a malpractice and fraud action against his former agent and attorney Steve Greenberg, stemming from unsuccessful investments made on Madlock's behalf.[75] The arbitrator who heard the case "cleared Greenberg and his law firm of all charges with the exception of two counts of negligence."[76] Because the statute of limitations had expired, Greenberg, who characterized these findings of negligence as technical glitches, was not required to pay any damages.[77]

In a case involving both bad investment and breach of an agent's duty to avoid conflicts of interest, former NBA star Scottie Pippen won a $11.8 million judgment against Robert Lum, a financial adviser. Pippen had alleged that more than $7 million of $17 million that Pippen had entrusted to Lum was channeled into real estate ventures with a developer with whom the adviser had a close relationship. As is often the case, however, Pippen's ability to recover any of the judgment is questionable.[78]

A common form of mismanagement involves players' allegations that agents or financial advisers persuaded them to enter into investments with promises that the players would reap tax-related benefits. When the IRS informs the players that they have a tax deficiency, players may seek recourse against their agents or financial advisers. Such was the case when former baseball star Keith Hernandez filed a suit in which he asserted numerous claims, including breach of contract, fraud, and breach of fiduciary duty. The gist of Hernandez's lawsuit was that his sports agent, who at one time handled virtually all of his financial affairs, improperly established an investment that failed as a tax shelter.[79]

In pursuing civil actions, athletes are most likely to assert claims of fraud, negligence, breach of fiduciary duty, and breach of contract. A lawsuit filed in 2000 by football players Ike Hilliard and Fred Taylor against Tank Black and several other individuals and entities is representative. The plaintiffs asserted that they were "'unsophisticated with respect to business and financial matters' and that they 'relied completely on the advice and expertise of Defendants Black, Franklin, and PMI' who 'exercised substantial if not complete control and authority over the financial decisions of Plaintiffs and others.'"[80] The plaintiffs generally alleged that the defendants, among other things, improperly lured them to invest several million dollars into investment schemes and that defendants engaged in conduct in violation of securities laws. Finally, the athletes asserted causes of action sounding in breach of fiduciary duty, breach of contract, conversion, negligence, and civil conspiracy relating to the investment schemes.[81]

In *Williams v. CWI, Inc.*, NBA player Reginald Williams and his wife sought to recover $50,000 that they had entrusted with Waymon Hunt, a financial adviser.[82] Rather than invest the money, Hunt diverted it for his own purposes.[83] The federal district court judge who heard the matter ruled that Hunt was liable to the plaintiffs under either a breach of contract or fraud theory. A noteworthy aspect of this case is the court's perspective as to why players appear particularly susceptible to financial abuse by agents and other financial advisers.

Like many young professional athletes, Mr. Williams was earning a considerable salary but had no experience in making investments or managing money. He needed reliable expert advice and did not find any readily available.

Because Mr. Williams' predicament appears to be a recurring problem for basketball players and other athletes who suddenly receive large disposable incomes, it seems that it would be appropriate for either the NBA, or the player's team, or the players' association to develop a three-pronged program to assist these young people. First, they could offer at least rudimentary education in business and finance. Second, they could assemble a package of low risk blue-chip investments for young players that will provide for their futures as well as a system for referring them to wise and ethical professionals who can advise them on managing money. Third, they might offer a financial incentive for players to place a portion of their funds in a deferred investment program. Perhaps the League and the players' association could even establish their own high-grade, low-risk investment fund. In this way, young athletes would be protected from highly speculative ventures like the one involved in this case.[84]

One of the most widely reported earlier cases of income mismanagement was that of retired Los Angeles Lakers basketball star Kareem Abdul-Jabbar, who sued agent Tom Collins. Abdul-Jabbar alleged that Collins had mismanaged his basketball earnings by placing them in questionable investments, including a rib restaurant in Texas, a hotel in Alabama, two hotels and a restaurant in California, an exercise rope, a sports club, a limousine service, a commodities brokerage firm, and a cattle-feed business. Abdul-Jabbar also claimed he had been defrauded. He sought damages of a reported $59 million in his 1986 lawsuit.[85] The case was settled in early 1990, but the settlement terms were not publicly disclosed.[86]

Other notable cases in which athletes have filed lawsuits relating to alleged mismanagement of their financial affairs by agents and financial managers include the following:

An action alleging fraud, breach of contract, negligence, and breach of fiduciary duty in which a court awarded damages in the amount of about $868,000 to former NBA player Bill Willoughby against his agent, Jerry A. Davis[87]

An arbitration case in which an athlete alleged his agent made unsuitable investment recommendations and misrepresentations relating to the sale of securities[88]

Kendricks v. Grant Thornton International,[89] in which 127 investors, many of whom were professional athletes, filed a lawsuit against an accounting firm alleging, among other claims, fraud, aiding and abetting fraud, breach of contract, breach of fiduciary duty, negligence, negligent misrepresentation, and securities law violations

Baseball player Charles ("Walt") Terrell's lawsuit against an agency firm that allegedly mismanaged his funds and defrauded him[90]

An arbitrator's award of $204,886 to football player John Farley for damages arising out of investment advice[91]

In responding to such a panoply of allegations, agents and financial managers not only deny that they acted incompetently but also assert that it was the athlete who squandered his or her resources. A lawsuit filed by former football player Vincent Clark against his financial manager is illustrative. Clark asserted that his financial adviser performed services including "paying Clark's bills, providing Clark with spending money, investing the balance, managing the investments, and procuring and maintaining appropriate insurance."[92] After suffering a career-ending football injury and the realization that his financial resources were not what he believed they should have been, Clark sued Weisberg, alleging various forms of improper financial management. According to the court, Weisberg responded as follows: "Weisberg claims that like many professional athletes, Clark spent almost all of the money he earned. Weisberg believes that Clark failed to acknowledge that 'he now has insufficient funds because he wasted his assets by making exorbitant purchases, transferring large sums of money to his family members and friends, and refusing to save for the future or consider the consequences if he were injured or unable to continue playing football, and not because of any action taken by Weisberg.'"[93] In another lawsuit involving Vincent Clark, *Clark v. Robert W. Baird Co., Inc.*, the defendants successfully obtained the dismissal of certain claims, including allegations of RICO violations and fraud.[94]

The stories of abuse described above should not make us forget that there are legitimate financial success stories. *Sports Illustrated* reported that former major league outfielder Gary Maddox paid IMG $12,000 a year to manage his investments and was very successful. Similarly, major league pitcher Orel Hershiser, a former business major, worked with his agent to invest $1 million per year for an annual expected yield of $300,000 during his retirement.[95] Even boxer Oscar De La Hoya, in an industry riddled with financial failures, seems to be doing admirably. The number of success stories probably rivals the disasters, but it is the latter that receive the most extensive press coverage.

Excessive Fees

In 1983, agent Bob Woolf negotiated a five-year, $800,000 contract for hockey player Andrew Brown.[96] Woolf contracted with Brown to receive a fee of $40,000, or 5 percent of Brown's projected $800,000 salary. The team for which Brown played—the Indianapolis Racers of the fledgling World Hockey Association (WHA)—suffered financial difficulties. Consequently, Brown received only $185,000 of the anticipated $800,000 when the Racers went bankrupt.[97] Nevertheless, the Racers agreed to pay Woolf his $40,000 fee calculated on the basis of the full $800,000 player/team contract. The fee received by Woolf approximated 20 percent of the total compensation actually paid by the team to Brown rather than the 5 percent that was contemplated. Brown sued Woolf, alleging misrepresentation and breach of fiduciary duty.[98] The Woolf case illustrates one problem associated with agent fees: the receipt of the entire fee "up front" from the athlete's signing bonus or first few paychecks.

Issues relating to the timing of fee payments to agents and excessive fees charged by agents have become less problematic due to actions taken primarily by players' associations. These actions include limits on the amount of fees that an agent is permitted to charge for negotiating a contract on a player's behalf and restrictions on when agent fees are payable.

The current *NFLPA Regulations Governing Contract Advisors* address both of these issues. Section 4(B)(1) of those regulations imposes a 3 percent maximum on fees for contract negotiation–related services. "The maximum fee which may be charged or collected by a Contract Advisor shall be three percent of the 'compensation' . . . received by the player in each playing season covered by the contract negotiated by the Contract Advisor."[99] Another section of the regulations defines "compensation" so as to "include only salaries, signing bonuses, reporting bonuses, roster bonuses, and any performance incentives earned by the player during the term of the contract (including option year) negotiated by the Contact Advisor."[100] The 3 percent represents a decrease from earlier NFLPA regulations. Prior to 1988, the NFLPA allowed agents to charge for contract negotiation services up to 5 percent of "a player's compensation in excess of the minimum salary for the first three years of the contract."[101] This decrease is not particularly significant given that in all of the major professional leagues the average fee for contract negotiations alone is around 3 percent of the value of the contract negotiated.

The NFLPA's regulations also address when agent fees are payable. As a general proposition, the regulations mandate that an agent or "Contract Advisor," as stated in the regulations, is "prohibited from receiving any fee for his/her services until and unless the player receives the compensation upon which the fee is based."[102] The player's receipt of compensation for athletic services is a condition to the payment of fees to an agent. The regulations allow an exception in cases of deferred compensation to be received by a player. They recognize that a player may desire to pay an agent in advance with respect to deferred compensation. Under such circumstances, the advance payment of fees is collectible by the agent only after the player has performed the services "necessary under his contract [with his team] to entitle him to deferred compensation."[103]

In 2005, the NFLPA considered amending its regulations to reduce the maximum fee from 3 percent to 2 percent. In 2006, the NFLPA decided to retain its existing fee structure. The NFLPA stated that its rejection of the proposed amendment was based, in part, on increased agent expenses with regard to mandatory malpractice insurance and on heightened educational and other regulatory requirements. The NFLPA adopted a considerably more modest plan that reduces maximum fees that agents can charge for contract negotation services for franchise and transition players. Such reductions seem warranted for veteran players with salaries within a certain range.[104]

Regulations promulgated by the NBPA contain limitations similar to those imposed by the NFLPA. NBPA regulations impose a 4 percent maximum on the fees agents can charge for contract negotiations. Moreover, a ceiling of 2 percent is imposed on the fees that an agent can charge NBA players who sign for the league minimum with their teams.

Interestingly, the Major League Baseball Players Association (MLBPA) imposes no universal maximum limit on the fees that an agent can charge as a percentage of player compensation. MLBPA counsel Gene Orza maintains that the market will regulate itself. He argues that because of the athletes' knowledge of the market, agents charging too much will soon be out of business. This being said, *MLBPA Regulations Governing Player Agents* (MLBPA regulations) include provisions intended to protect players signed to minimum salary contracts. The MLPBA regulations state, "No Player Agent shall charge a Player any fee for negotiating that Player's individual salary unless the salary negotiated exceeds the minimum salary for that year established by the Basic Agreement."[105]

Conclusion

Broadly these are among the legal issues frequently being grappled with in the sports agent business. As you will note, they are largely focused on athlete earnings in terms of wealth management. The next chapter will focus on ethical and qualification issues that go beyond monetary concerns.

Chapter 6

Conflicts of Interest

Factual scenarios involving financial mismanagement potentially implicate several of the obligations identified in Chapter 1 that agents owe to their principals. These obligations include the duty of an agent to comply with all applicable laws and the agent's duty to notify the principal of all matters that may affect the principal's interests.[1] Allegations of financial mismanagement also implicate agent obligations related to conflicts of interest—the subject explored in this chapter.

Agents have been under the microscope for engaging in practices in which conflicts of interest may be present. As discussed in Chapter 1, critical features of the agent/athlete relationship are the agent's obligation of undivided loyalty and the duty to act in good faith at all times.[2] These duties preclude an agent from acting on behalf of parties adverse to his or her principal.[3] A conflict of interest occurs when a duty owed to one party is compromised by a separate interest or agreement with a third party. As revealed below, agents are likely to confront numerous situations in which they must act with care to avoid violating the basic duties of undivided loyalty and good faith that they owe to their athlete clients.

Agent Self-Interest: Undisclosed Financial Interests

Historically, the conflict of interest scenario involving the athlete/agent relationship that has been most problematic is one involving nondisclosure by an agent of a financial interest that conflicts with that of the athlete client. One such notable instance involved the late NFL Hall of Famer Reggie White and his former agent Patrick Forte. White alleged that while Forte was negotiating with the Eagles regarding White's player contract, Forte was also negotiating a contract for himself to be an assistant to the president of that NFL franchise. In a suit filed in U.S. District Court in Philadelphia, White maintained that this constituted a conflict of interest and affected Forte's performance in his player-contract negotiation.[4] The suit was eventually settled, and both parties were prohibited from commenting on the settlement terms.[5]

Similar issues were present in *Detroit Lions, Inc. v. Argovitz*,[6] which pitted agent Jerry Argovitz against former Detroit Lions running back Billy Sims. Argovitz was negotiating on behalf of Sims with both the NFL's Detroit Lions and the then-competing United States Football League's (USFL) Houston Gamblers. During the course of his negotiations with the Lions on behalf of Sims, Argovitz informed the athlete that he had applied for the Houston franchise. Sims, however, was unaware of the extent of his agent's interest in the USFL franchise. After Argovitz's ownership application for the Gamblers' franchise was assured, Argovitz reduced his offer on behalf of Sims to the Lions and dropped prior demands for so-called skills guarantees that had the potential to provide Sims with even greater income. While these negotiations continued, Argovitz also decided to seek an offer from the Gamblers and provided one of his partners with information regarding the offer Sims had received from the Lions. Based on the information about the progress of Argovitz's negotiations with the Lions, Sims believed that the Lions were not negotiating in good faith and were not interested in his services. Therefore, he did not urge Argovitz to seek a final offer from the Lions even though that team was willing to provide him with the guarantees that Sims had sought from it.

Sims agreed to join the Gamblers on the terms of the team's offer and signed a contract with the team on July 1, 1983. Argovitz did not contact the Lions and request a final offer so that both offers could be presented to Sims. After the true nature of the Lions' interest in him was revealed, Sims signed a contract with the Lions on December 16, 1983. Subsequently, he and the Lions went to court requesting that the contract with the Gamblers be invalidated because it was a product of fraud and because of the conflict of interest by Sims's agent, Argovitz.

The court ruled in favor of Sims. In so ruling, it concluded that Argovitz had breached his duty to contact the Lions and receive and present its final offer alongside that of the Gamblers to Sims. It also concluded that to deny rescission of Sims's contract with the Gamblers would be unconscionable in view of Argovitz's egregious and pronounced breach of his fiduciary duty to Sims during negotiations on behalf of Sims with the Lions.

Finally, the court found that Sims's knowledge of Argovitz's application for the franchise or approval of the franchise did not absolve the agent of his duties to Sims. The court found that Argovitz could not have expected Sims to understand the extent to which his agent's interest and position as president of the team undermined Argovitz's efforts as an unbiased third-party negotiator. The court pointed out, "Argovitz's conflict of interest and self-dealing put him in the position where he would not even use the wedge he now had to negotiate with the Lions, a wedge that is the dream of every agent."[7] This "wedge" was the offer from a franchise in a rival league. Argovitz knew that if he called the Lions, the Lions would offer Sims a contract and Sims would not be available to the Gamblers, of which Argovitz was an owner. Moreover, Argovitz improperly had Sims sign a waiver of any claims Sims might have against him without telling Sims to obtain advice independently; arranged a $500,000 loan from the Gamblers to Sims at 1 percent above prime, out of which he knew his $100,000 fee would be paid; and did not demand benefits for Sims, a proven NFL talent, comparable to those that Jim Kelly, another player, obtained from the Gamblers.[8]

Argovitz violated the agent's basic duties of undivided loyalty, good faith, and honest and fair dealing in several ways. Without obtaining appropriate consent, Argovitz represented a third party in a transaction in which his client was involved, possessed direct interest in the transaction that was antagonistic to his client's interest, and failed to disclose all information relevant to the principal's interests.[9] This conduct amounted to an extreme failure to adhere to the fiduciary relationship that existed between him and Sims.

Conflict of interest concerns have also arisen when leaders of players' unions represent individual union members in their contract negotiations with their respective teams. The argument against such representation is that the union leader's primary responsibility is to safeguard the rights of all union members; and circumstances may exist in which an act may be advantageous to the union leader's client but not to the union as a whole or in which an act could be advantageous to the union but not to the individual athlete.

The late Larry Fleischer, former head of the NBPA, represented individual athletes while he was the union's leader. Similarly, former National Hockey League Players' Association (NHLPA) chief Alan Eagleson represented individual athletes in that league. Eagleson's conflicts in representation and other areas became so extreme that the members of the union initiated an independent investigation of his interests in 1989.[10]

MULTIPLE REPRESENTATION AND OTHER POTENTIAL CONFLICTS

Agent representation of athletes presents conflicts in addition to those described above. In examining the following scenarios, consider whether a conflict exists and, if so, what steps an agent might take to avoid the conflict. Also consider what, if any, additional variables become relevant if the agent is also an attorney. These additional "complications" will be examined in the following chapter.

1. An agent represents players from different teams in the same sport. Does either a potential or a real conflict of interest exist? Is

it inevitable that the agent will consciously or unconsciously favor the interests of one client over another?

2. Is the potential for a conflict of interest enhanced when the athletes play at the same position? Does the following situation present a conflict of interest? Former professional quarterback Warren Moon left the Canadian Football League (CFL) and sought a position in the NFL. Moon's agent, Leigh Steinberg, shopped Moon to numerous teams including the New York Giants, the team for which another one of Steinberg's clients, Scott Brunner, played quarterback.[11]

3. Suppose an agent represents multiple players on the same team. Should this be permissible? Does it create a potential or an actual conflict of interest? Consider the following factual scenario: The same agent represented two Kansas City Royals baseball players, Hal McRae and Frank White. Allegedly, the agent refused to finalize a contract on behalf of White until the team had extended McRae's contract.

In such a scenario is the conflict real or potential? What, if anything, can the agent do to avoid a conflict?[12] Is the players' consent to dual representation necessary to avoid a conflict of interest?

4. In the NBA, NHL, and NFL, each team has a salary cap that limits the amount of money a team may allocate for player salaries. Suppose an agent represents multiple players on one team and the players are seeking remuneration from a limited fund. Does this situation present a potential or a real conflict of interest?

If so, what is the nature of the conflict? Does it lie in the fact that the athletes expect their agent to seek the greatest amount of compensation possible from this limited fund for each of them?[13] Is a conflict unavoidable because a negotiation leading to increased compensation for one player will lead to decreased compensation for the other player?[14]

5. Does the gravity of the scenario described above intensify if the athletes play the same position, or is this irrelevant?

6. Agents are compensated based upon a percentage of the compensation received by athletes. Compensation includes the salary to be earned under the contract as well as certain bonuses such as a signing bonus. Standard athlete/agent contracts provided by the major professional players' associations restrict agents from collecting fees until the player has received compensation, or in cases of deferred compensation, until the athlete has performed the services on which the compensation is based.

Suppose an agent encourages a young player to sign a long-term contract that includes a large signing bonus, "modest annual salaries and substantial deferred compensation" rather than a "short term contract with a modest signing bonus, substantial annual salaries and little or no deferred compensation."[15] Given that agents are typically compensated based upon a percentage of an athlete's compensation, does this advice represent a conflict of interest? What steps, if any, can an agent engage in to avoid a conflict of interest?

7. Suppose an agent represents numerous clients. Does multiple representation undermine the agent's obligation to represent his or her client zealously, given the substantial time demands placed on agents engaged in contract negotiations and the short period of time in which negotiations must occur? Is it relevant whether the agent is a member of one of the larger athlete representation agencies such as CAA, Octagon, or WMG ? Is a member of a small athlete agent firm? Is solely responsible for representing his or her clients?

8. Suppose an agent encourages an athlete to endorse a product that may not be in the athlete's best interest. Does a conflict exist given that the agent will receive a percentage of the endorsement contract that the player signs? How can a conflict be avoided?

9. Does a conflict exist when an agent represents multiple players who may be suitable for an endorsement contract? Is the conflict resolved if an agent recommends both players for the contract? As noted by one commentator, "is there the possibility that, had the clients retained independent counsel, their interests could have been more vigorously represented?"[16]

10. Changes in the sports industry have caused coaches increasingly to seek representation by agents or attorneys in their contract negotiations with teams. Does a conflict exist when an agent represents a player and a coach on the same team? If so, what is the basis for the conflict? Does it reside in the fact that the dual representation may result in the agent advocating a position that favors the team/coach to the disadvantage of the athlete client? Assume that a goal of a coach is to have players arrive at training camp and begin preparations for the start of the playing season as early as possible. Might an agent who represents both a player and a coach on the same team unconsciously encourage a player to sign early and facilitate an early arrival? Would doing so constitute a conflict of interest? What level of coach involvement in contract negotiations on behalf of a team creates a conflict when the agent represents the coach and the athlete?

11. Is there a conflict of interest if a player represents fellow players on the same team? This situation arose for a short period of time

when Percy Miller, popularly known as Master P, represented NBA players during a period when he failed two NBA tryout attempts.

The foregoing scenarios demonstrate the complexity of the conflicting issues that may arise in the sports agency industry. The discussions that immediately follow and that appear in Chapter 7 are not intended to provide definitive answers to the previous questions. They may, however, provide information that proves helpful in attempts to resolve conflicting issues that arise out of the agent/athlete relationship.

Standards Governing Conflicts

As was noted at the beginning of this chapter, the agent's fiduciary obligation to his or her athlete client imposes upon the former a duty to act in his or her client's best interest. As stated in the Restatement (Second) of Agency, "Unless otherwise agreed, an agent is subject to a duty to his principal to act solely for the benefit of the principal in all matters connected with his agency."[17] Under agency law principles, the fiduciary nature of the relationship along with duties of loyalty, good faith, and honest and fair dealings impose an obligation on agents to avoid conflicts of interest.

Player Union Regulations

Regulations promulgated by players' associations that govern agents recognize the agent's duty not to engage in conduct amounting to conflicts of interest. For example, the *National Basketball Players Association Regulations Governing Player Agents* include general provisions exhorting agents to avoid conflicts of interest, as well as specific provisions that prohibit agents from representing management and from holding financial interest in certain business ventures. These provisions provide:

To further effectuate the objectives of these Regulations players agents are prohibited from:

(e) Holding or seeking to hold, either directly or indirectly, a financial interest in any professional basketball team or in any other business venture that would create an actual conflict of interest or the appearance of a conflict of interest between the individual player and his agent;

(f) Representing the General Manager or coach of any NBA team (or any other management representative who participates in the team's deliberations or decisions concerning what compensation is to be offered individual players) in matters pertaining to his employment or any other matters in which he has any financial stake by or association with any NBA team;

(g) Engaging in any other activity which creates actual or potential conflicts of interest with the effective representation of NBA players; provided that the representation of two or more players on any one club shall not itself be deemed to be prohibited by this provision;

(h) Soliciting or accepting money or anything of value from any NBA club in circumstances where to do so would create a conflict or an apparent conflict with the interests of any player he represents . . . ;

(k) Concealing material facts from any player whom the agent is representing which relate to the subject of the individual's contract negotiation.[18]

Sanctions for violating these regulations may include suspension or revocation of the agent's certification to be involved in individual contract negotiations on behalf of NBA players. Similarly, *NHLPA Regulations Governing Agent Certification* threaten the suspension or revocation of a player agent's certification if he or she engages in enumerated conduct that creates an actual or potential conflict of interest. According to such regulations, holding a financial stake in any professional hockey club, the Canadian Major Junior Hockey Club, or other financial venture creates an actual or potential conflict of interest, or more generally creates an actual or potential conflict of interest in the agent's effective representation of a player.[19] Agent regulations of the NFLPA and MLBPA also contain such prohibitions.

Players' unions have relied upon these regulations in several prominent recent situations involving possible conflicts of interest on the part of agents. In 2001, IMG terminated a sponsorship sales agreement with the NHL after the NHLPA complained that the arrangement constituted a violation by IMG of rules that prohibit agents from representing both players and management.[20] The complaint lodged against IMG by the NHLPA is illustrative of an emerging approach by players' unions to prevent potential conflicts. A year prior to this complaint, IMG Hockey President Mike Barnett was forced by the union to terminate a twenty-year business relationship with Wayne Gretzky after the former player joined a group of investors seeking to purchase the NHL's Phoenix Coyotes.

Pressure by the NHLPA and MLBPA resulted in a restructuring of SFX. These players' unions raised concerns of potential conflicts of interest by SFX following its acquisition by the conglomerate Clear Channel Communications. A then major shareholder of Clear Channel was Tom Hicks, who owned MLB's Texas Rangers and the NHL's Dallas

Stars. On January 1, 2001, "attempting to shield itself from conflict issues and appease the NHLPA and MLB Players Association . . . SFX Entertainment Inc. separated its athlete representation division into a semi-autonomous business unit."[21] Later in the year, SFX divided the division into individual agencies that are devoted to particular sports.[22] The following discussion of the baseball group aptly described the nature of the restructuring that was put into effect at the time:

> Under the new structure, SFX Baseball Group is owned by Clear Channel, but Clear Channel has no ability to interfere in the business of the group. Even David Falk, head of SFX Sports, has no authority over the baseball agents in the group. . . . The group is run by the baseball agents whose businesses were acquired by SFX over the past few years. . . . [Randall Hendricks, a longtime baseball agent who is CEO of the new company] compare[s] the structure of the new company to a blind trust. "They own the stock, but we have an agreement with Clear Channel and our new company. . . . They cannot remove any officers or directors. They don't have the powers of normal shareholders. . . . We can take a position in the interest of our clients even if it's adverse to [Clear Channel]."[23]

Apparently, the new structure came too late to satisfy agents Jim Bronner and Robert Gilhooley, who filed suit against SFX arguing that the conflict presented by Clear Channel's ownership indirectly resulted in their losing baseball player Juan Gonzalez as a client.[24] Bronner and Gilhooley, who were fired by SFX after they filed suit, also alleged that SFX fraudulently withheld information regarding the takeover by Clear Channel when they sold their company to SFX in February 2000.[25]

Another interesting potential conflict arose during Michael Jordan's tenure in a management and ownership role with the NBA's Washington Wizards. Jordan's longtime agent and business adviser David Falk represented players on that team as well as players who might join that team. The issue was raised regarding Jordan's ability to avoid preferential dealings with his own business manager.[26] Jordan, Falk, and the league all asserted that there was no conflict. Some critics argue, however, that on the surface the relationship appeared to run afoul of NBPA regulations that prohibit agents from representing management representatives who participate "in the team's deliberations or decisions concerning what compensation is to be offered individual players in matters pertaining to his employment or any other matters in which he has any financial stake by or association with any NBA team."[27]

Unrelated to the Jordan conflict, agent David Falk notes that it is not the existence of a conflict alone that is a problem: "The question is whether you have a debilitating conflict." Falk and others maintain that because of the limited number of agents with actual expertise in sports business issues, most successful agents are bound to have conflicts:

"Invariably you're going to have conflicts even if you only have two clients." Falk makes a valid point. If an endorsement deal is offered to an agent to give to either of his two clients, only one can be given the deal and necessarily the other is shortchanged.

Conclusion

In summary, all agents are subject to the duty to avoid conflicts of interest that grows generally out of the law of agency. In addition, all agents are governed by regulations promulgated by the players' associations. Whether agents are subject to additional proscriptions often depends on the existence of state-enacted agent regulations or whether the agent is also an attorney. Discussion of state-enacted agent regulations is reserved for Chapter 11. We turn in the next chapter to a discussion of conflicts of interest and other complex issues that are present when an agent is also an attorney.

Chapter 7

Ethics
Attorney Versus Nonattorney Agents

The sports agent industry has evolved such that licensed attorneys comprise a significant percentage of the agents who represent athletes. The intersection of the legal profession and the agent profession is often an uneasy fit. Rules governing the practice of law do not seem particularly well equipped to handle the unique nature of the sports agent profession. Law professor Walter Champion notes that "[the] ethical code of a well-established profession . . . may not perfectly fit to the emerging, evolving and dynamic relationships that are inherent in the sports arena."[1] This uneasy fit creates a myriad of issues, including the following:

1. What standards govern the determination and management of conflicts of interest when an agent is also an attorney?
2. Is the attorney who represents an athlete as an agent bound solely by generally applicable principles of agency law such as the duty of loyalty that proscribes conflicts of interest and regulations of players' unions?
3. In order to avoid standards and regulations attendant to their professional status, under what circumstances may a licensed attorney disclaim his or her status as an attorney when representing athletes?
4. Under what circumstances do nonattorney agents, and attorney agents negotiating contracts and engaging in other activities on behalf of clients in jurisdictions in which they are not licensed, violate prohibitions against the unauthorized practice of law?

Standards Governing Attorney Agents: Conflicts of Interest

As it relates to most matters, there is not much difference between the standards to which the lawyer and nonlawyer agent will be bound. General agency law principles, as well as those that govern the practice of law, impose duties on both attorney agents and nonattorney agents. Examples of such duties include requirements that services be rendered competently and that clients be represented with the utmost loyalty and good faith.[2]

Whereas a nonlawyer agent is subject to general agency law principles and league and players' union regulations, the attorney agent will also be held accountable to the code of ethics for lawyers. Failure to adhere to this code may result in disciplinary action, including a fine, reprimand, suspension, or even disbarment. Such sanctions are in addition to any that might be imposed for the agent's failure to adhere to general agency law principles or union regulations.[3] Various state supreme courts impose the professional ethics requirements on attorneys. These ethical standards are set forth in the Model Rules of Professional Conduct, formulated by the American Bar Association (ABA). Many states have adopted these standards. The disciplinary rules of the ABA apply when a breach of these rules occurs in the lawyer-client relationship.[4]

The code of ethics that governs attorneys with respect to conflicts of interest illustrates the additional standards that apply to the attorney agent. Rule 1.7 of the Model Rules of Professional Conduct generally addresses conflicts of interest. It also provides guidance with respect to the circumstances under which conflicting representations can be undertaken[5] and supplies "a general standard for lawyers analyzing the propriety of representing multiple clients with adverse interests."[6] Model Rule 2.2 specifically focuses on multiple representations—"the common representation of two or more clients in a single transaction or several related transactions."[7] As the hypotheticals in Chapter 6 suggest, the sports attorney may "frequently encounter representations where the conflicts associated with multiple-client representations are subtle and appear insignificant when representation is first considered. In reality, sports transactions are often complex and involve clients occupying disparate positions."[8]

Chapter 6 described various situations in which agents or attorney agents represent multiple players, such as when an agent represents players who seek compensation from a limited fund. Ethics rules governing attorneys deliver some guidance in regard to a potential conflict resulting from multiple representation. These rules provide that the fact of a potential conflict does not automatically preclude multiple representation.[9] According to Rule 1.7, "an attorney may proceed with conflicting representations only after obtaining the client's consent and only if she 'reasonably believes' that none of the clients' interests is likely to be compromised by the representations."[10] Model Rule 2.2 instructs attorneys in situations involving multiple representation to take the same precautions: consultation and consent. The model rules define consultation as the "communication of information reasonably sufficient to permit the client to appreciate the significance of the matter in question."[11] Allowing for multiple representation where proper precautions are taken is premised on notions of freedom of contract. It is also based on the belief that a person should be allowed to select the lawyer that he or she wants to represent his or her interests.[12]

Leagues and players' unions recognize the reality of multiple representations of players by agents and perhaps the premise on which the above-described ethical rule is based. For example, NBPA agent regulations expressly state that an agent who represents one or more players on the same team has not automatically violated its proscriptions against conflicts of interest.[13]

In summary, if the lawyer makes a good faith determination, from the perspective of a "disinterested lawyer," that he or she can adequately represent the interests of multiple clients, the lawyer can do so, but only if the consent of all clients is obtained.[14] The question of whether appropriate consent has been given carries its own risk for the agent. Notes one author discussing general conflict of interest concerns that arise from multiple representation:

> Although the athlete-clients may have given their consent to the potential conflicts of interest, there should be concern as to whether the consent was informed consent. This involves the question of whether the athletes understand the amount of time and effort which is necessary to negotiate their contract and undertake other areas of their representation, in order to adequately discern a possible lack of attention from their attorney due to other clients' demands on the attorney's time. Furthermore, it is difficult to draw a line between the point when the conflict of interest is merely potential and the point where the time and resource demands upon the individual attorney make the conflict an actual conflict.[15]

Similarly, Professor John Walton states that

> According to Rules 1.7 and 2.2, an attorney may proceed with conflicting representations or intermediations only after obtaining the clients' consent and only if she "reasonably believes" that none of the clients' interests is likely to be compromised by the representation. However, the admonition in the Rules is misleading simply because it essentially ignores the possibility that the attorney's judgment may be clouded when evaluating the clients' conflicting interests. Moreover, it provides no hint of how complex the consent to conflict process can be.[16]

As also discussed in Chapter 6, the court in *Detroit Lions, Inc. v. Argovitz*,[17] which involved a dentist acting as an agent, provided a very strict standard in determining when adequate consent has been given. In that case the court held that an agent must fully inform the client of all relevant facts and obtain the principal's consent: "the agent must show that his principal had full knowledge, not only of the fact that the agent was interested, but also of every material fact known to the agent which might affect the principal and that having such knowledge the principal freely consented to the transaction."[18] On the question of consent, the court stated consent will be deemed to be freely given under circumstances where the agent "inform[s] the principal of all facts that come to his knowledge that are or may be material or which might affect his principal's rights or interests or influence the action he takes."[19] The rule enunciated in *Argovitz* suggests that consent will be deemed proper only when the disclosure made by the agent "include[s] not only a specification of the extent of the agent's financial interest, but a disclosure of significant risks that the player confronts in the conflicting relations and important alternative courses of action that are available."[20] Note two commentators, the "impression is left that the court requires a level of disclosure so exacting that it is difficult to imagine a reasonable person continuing to be represented by the agent with the conflict."[21] Yet, *Argovitz* can also be interpreted as giving agents the flexibility to engage in multiple representations so long as proper disclosures are made to the clients.

Attorney, Agent, or Both?

Given that attorneys must comply with state-imposed professional codes of conduct, the violation of which may result in disciplinary action, it is not surprising that some attorney agents have claimed that the representation of athlete clients does not involve legal work. Thus, they argue that they should not be subject to professional codes with respect to such services. Attorney agents, attempting to disavow their attorney status in this context, find justification in the fact that nonattorney agents who provide competent services on behalf of their athlete clients are not subject to the same requirements. Most fundamentally, these attorney agents argue that it is unfair to impose standards on them to which nonattorney agents are not bound. As captured by one analyst: "some sports lawyers argue that based on the nature of the representation industry, . . . if they enter the industry and hold out themselves as a sports agent, they avoid application of the ethical rules of the legal profession."[22]

One problem with this argument lies in the nature of the services provided by agents. A principal service provided by the athlete agent is the negotiation of the athlete's contract with his or her team. As pointed out by one commentator, "There can be little doubt that the general service of negotiation is an area of traditional legal representation."[23] On the other hand, athlete agents provide services that do not fall within the scope of what is typically considered legal representation.

Many of these services relate to the athlete's business affairs for which legal training is not required, such as advice on personal and financial matters. Indeed, it has been suggested that changes in the industry make agent expertise in accounting and business planning as relevant as legal training, if not more so.

Only a few courts and administrative bodies have addressed the issue of whether an attorney agent is subject to the ethical rules that govern attorneys. Therefore, it would be unwise to draw any definitive conclusions regarding how a particular court or administrative body might resolve the issue. Nevertheless, these rulings provide some indication of judicial thinking in this regard.

An advisory opinion of the Illinois State Bar Association directly addressed whether attorney agents are governed by the Illinois Code of Professional Responsibility that regulates attorney conduct.[24] The panel considered whether "the representation of athletes is actually the practice of law in that it may include a wide range of business counseling, as well as contract negotiations. This doubt could be prompted by the fact that nonlawyers frequently engage in these activities." The panel concluded that "when an attorney engaged in the private practice of law represents a client in contract negotiations and general business counseling, these activities constitute the practice of law."

In another matter, *Cuyahoga County Bar Association v. Glenn*,[25] an attorney agent represented Richard Dent in contract negotiations with the Chicago Bears. The attorney's mishandling of Dent's funds amounted to violations of state disciplinary rules governing the conduct of attorneys. The Ohio Supreme Court assumed, without discussion, that the attorney was subject to such rules in upholding sanctions imposed by a state bar disciplinary panel.

The Georgia Supreme Court also upheld a state bar's discipline of an attorney agent who violated professional standards governing attorneys. As in *Cuyahoga*, the court in *In the Matter of Fredrick J. Henley, Jr.* assumed without discussion that the attorney who represented a professional football player was governed by standards regulating attorneys.[26]

One commentator endorses the view suggested by these cases:

The fact that a person is believed to be a member of a profession is certainly a reason for the selection of the agent by the client. The client's interests are thus best protected by continuing the obligation of the profession beyond the scope of the practice. It may also be argued that the activities of a sports agent or an attorney may be indistinguishable, for which reason it is appropriate to adopt a policy which supports the application of the ethical code regardless of form. From the [foregoing], it appears the better rule is that the ethical codes of any regulated profession should apply to the activities of that professional while acting in the capacity of a sports agent.[27]

The perspective expressed above may be premised, in part, on protecting the public's reliance interest. Attorney status carries with it assumptions made by the public as to the training, competence, ethics, and accountability of attorneys. In the case of the attorney agent, he or she also may profit from such assumptions in that they may result in a recruiting advantage.

Cases outside of the agent context seem to support the position taken above. *In re Dwight* is illustrative.[28] There an attorney provided accounting and investment services, in addition to legal services. In the transaction at issue, the attorney provided financial advice to a client. In responding to a complaint filed by the client with the Arizona Bar, the attorney contended that when he provided the financial advice he was not acting in his capacity as an attorney, but rather as a financial adviser. The court rejected his defense: "As long as a lawyer is engaged in the practice of law, he is bound by ethical requirements of that profession, and he may not defend his actions by contending that he was engaged in some other kind of professional activity."[29] In articulating a rationale for its ruling, the Arizona Supreme Court stated, "only in this way can full protection be afforded to the public."[30]

The California Supreme Court reached the same result in *Kelly v. State Bar of California*.[31] In that case, an attorney who had represented a client in various legal matters participated in a business transaction—the sale of an airplane—that did not involve practicing law. Nevertheless, the court concluded this action would not insulate him from attorney discipline. Making reference to previous cases, the court stated, "We have held that when an attorney serves a single client both as an attorney and as one who renders nonlegal services, he or she must conform to the Rules of Professional Conduct in the provision of all services."[32] Similarly, in a case decided prior to *Kelly*, the California Supreme Court concluded as follows: "[W]here an attorney occupies a dual capacity, performing, for a single client or in a single matter, along with legal services, services that might otherwise be performed by laymen, the services that he renders in the dual capacity all involve the practice of law, and he must conform to the Rules of Professional Conduct in the provision of all of them."[33]

An Arizona court pointed to the difficulty in differentiating between legal and nonlegal work as a rationale for holding attorneys, who perform both legal and nonlegal work for clients, to the code of professional ethics. It stated:

> The duties of a lawyer who also holds other professional licenses cannot be circumscribed by the fine distinctions that we might draw between the nature of the services performed under a particular license. How is one to tell whether, in advising the Petersons about the tax consequence of the condemnation settlement,

respondent acted as an accountant or a lawyer? Respondent could have given the same advice as a lawyer without having been licensed as an accountant. He might have given the same advice under his accountant's license, even though he had never been admitted to the bar. More importantly, how is any client to know when a lawyer *cum* accountant *cum* investment adviser removes one hat and puts on another? Respondent admitted the distinctions between attorney, accountant, and tax adviser are far from clear.[34]

The court concluded that an attorney will be viewed as an attorney whenever he enters into a relationship to provide services that the client might reasonably believe are law related.

Disavowing Attorney Status, Unauthorized Practice, and Other Issues

The cases discussed in the preceding section strongly suggest that an attorney agent who engages in dual representation—providing legal and nonlegal advice to a client—will be subject to the appropriate state professional standard. But this conclusion does not end our inquiry. Other questions arise both within and outside of the dual representation context. These questions include:

1. Is an agent who is a licensed attorney, but who makes no representations or otherwise holds him- or herself out as an attorney, subject to professional rules governing attorneys? Stated somewhat differently, is an attorney agent who effectively withholds information of his or her attorney status from clients subject to professional standards of responsibility?
2. Is client knowledge or lack of knowledge of an agent's status as an attorney irrelevant so long as the attorney agent is licensed and performs legal and nonlegal work on behalf of the client? In other words, in cases of dual representation, is the attorney agent bound by professional standards of conduct regardless of whether the client is aware that the agent is an attorney?
3. Should an attorney who acts as an agent on a full-time basis and does not otherwise practice law be subject to the professional code of conduct that governs attorneys? Some commentators have suggested that an attorney agent who relinquishes his or her law practice may not be subject to attorney codes of professional conduct.[35] This view seems premised on the notion that the attorney agent who does not hold himself out as an attorney does not implicate the reliance interest of clients.
4. What other steps, aside from not having a legal practice, might an attorney agent take so as to effectively disavow attorney status and

thus be subject to general fiduciary principles of agency law rather
than ethical mandates of state bar associations?

5. What of the agent who graduated from a law school program but
never became licensed and does not hold him- or herself out as
practicing law? Does this constitute an effective means of "disavow-
ing ties to the legal profession" so as to effectively avoid application
of its code of conduct?[36]

6. Has the nonattorney agent who provides services that include those
traditionally considered to involve the practice of law (for example,
contract review and negotiation) engaged in the unauthorized
practice of law? Does the fact that services typically provided by
agents are performed competently by nonattorneys take such services outside of the parameters of what constitutes practicing law?

7. Has the attorney agent who provides services for clients in states
other than those in which the attorney is licensed to practice law
run afoul of rules prohibiting the unauthorized practice of law?
Will an attorney agent who provides such services be precluded
from recovering his or her fee if the athlete refuses to pay?

The above issues defy easy resolution. The answer to several of these
issues, however, may hinge on determining whether the attorney agent
who renders services, such as contract negotiation on behalf of athletes,
is engaged in the "practice of law." There are no appellate court rulings
that address this question as it relates to the services provided by sports
agents. Guidance may, nevertheless, be found in appellate court decisions in which courts attempt to define what constitutes the practice of
law. For example, the New Jersey Supreme Court in addressing whether
a lawyer, unlicensed in New Jersey, had engaged in the unauthorized
practice of law recognized that the issue is often difficult to determine.
"Often issues related to the unauthorized practice of law involve exercises in line drawing between the proper realm of another profession or
business activity and the practice of law."[37] The court went on to articu-
late the general standard that "one is engaged in the practice of law
whenever legal knowledge, training, skill, and ability are required."[38] In
examining the facts of the case before it, the court determined that
unauthorized practice of law had occurred.

The California Supreme Court addressed the "unauthorized to practice issue" in what has come to be viewed as a leading case on the subject,
*Birbrower, Montalbano, Condon & Frank, P.C. v. The Supreme Court of Santa
Clara County.*[39] Birbrower, a New York law firm, represented ESQ, a California corporation, and its affiliated entity. Attorneys for Birbrower
performed substantial work for ESQ. This work included the negotiation
of an agreement between ESQ and another company, giving advice in a

dispute regarding the agreement, making recommendations regarding settlement of the dispute, and initiating and interviewing arbitrators for an arbitration proceeding. However, neither the attorneys who performed these services nor any other attorney of Birbrower was licensed to practice in California. ESQ brought a malpractice claim against Birbrower. The law firm counterclaimed to recover its attorneys' fees. ESQ claimed that the fee agreement was unenforceable because Birbrower had engaged in the unauthorized practice of law in California.

The relevant California statute provided that "No person shall practice law in California unless the person is an active member of the State Bar." The statute did not define "practice of law" or "in California." Because the statute failed to define "practice of law," the court looked to case law for guidance. It approvingly cited a case in which practice was defined broadly to include "the doing or performing of services in a court of justice, in any matter depending therein, throughout its various stages, and in conformity to the adopted rules of procedure. . . . Included in [this] definition [is] legal advice and legal instrument and contract preparation, whether or not these subjects were rendered in the course of litigation." The court added that a lawyer need not be physically present within the state in order to be practicing law in California. The court concluded that a lawyer could violate the unauthorized practice statute "by advising a California client on California law in connection with a California legal dispute by telephone, fax, computer, or other modern technological means. Conversely . . . we . . . reject the notion that a person automatically practices law 'in California' whenever that person practices California law anywhere, or 'virtually' enters the state by telephone, fax, e-mail or satellite. . . . We must decide each case on its individual facts."[40] The court concluded that the facts clearly established that Birbrower had practiced law in California. Consequently, Birbrower was unable to recover compensation for services performed because it ran afoul of a statute that prohibits compensation for work rendered when the attorney was not a member of the State Bar.

Readers are also reminded of the advisory opinion of the Illinois State Bar Association discussed above. In that matter, the attorney represented athletes and coaches in contract negotiations and practiced law. Although this fact pattern appears to involve dual representation, the Bar Association's definition of practicing law is relevant. The Bar Association concluded that "when an attorney engaged in the private practice of law represents a client in contract negotiations and general business counseling, these activities constitute the practice of law."[41]

A final area worthy of noting is the topic of solicitation. The heart of this issue is the same as the ethical concerns discussed above—the business advantage potentially gained by the nonattorney agent by virtue of being subject to fewer operational constraints. Attorney ethical rules against client solicitation highlight the relative difficulty attorney agents face in recruiting athlete clients as compared to the nonattorney agent. Long-standing rules exist against solicitation of business by attorneys. The primary basis for antisolicitation rules is to prevent overreaching by attorneys against the public.

As discussed in Chapter 4, recruitment of athlete clients is inherently difficult. But the rules against attorney solicitation generally provide that "A lawyer shall not by in-person or live telephone contact solicit professional employment from a prospective client with whom the lawyer has no family or prior professional relationship when a significant motive for the lawyer's doing so is the lawyer's pecuniary gain."[42] Such is certainly the case when the agent seeks to contact the college or even high school athlete with whom he or she has had no previous contact. In the end, the possibility of legal action by appropriate governing bodies or by clients exists to avoid the contracts or to withhold fees against the attorney agent, whereas no such consequence is present for the nonattorney.

Conclusion

As the last section highlights, the dichotomy that has been created in seeking to hold attorneys to high ethical standards is one that arguably provides a business advantage to nonattorney agents over attorneys. This dilemma adds to the complicated nature of the sports agent business. The argument is not that attorneys necessarily make "better" agents than nonattorney agents, but that they should not be disadvantaged by rules that hold them to higher ethical standards. Many of the ethical rules discussed herein, some would argue, should be applied to all agents. In fact, agency law principles impose standards on all agents that narrow the differences in the ethical obligations imposed on attorney and nonattorney agents.

Chapter 8

Agent Wars

Agents Against Athletes

Sometimes agents breach obligations they owe to their athlete clients. In many instances, however, athletes engage in conduct that runs contrary to the obligations that agency law imposes upon them. Although an athlete, unlike an agent, is not a fiduciary with respect to his or her agent, the athlete possesses certain obligations vis-à-vis his or her agent. Athletes are required to reimburse agents for reasonable expenses incurred on their behalf, to indemnify agents for any loss that agents incur in properly carrying out duties on behalf of their athlete clients, and to afford the agent a reasonable opportunity to perform his or her duties.[1]

A successful lawsuit by decertified agent Tank Black against NBA player Vince Carter illustrates the basic obligation that athletes owe to agents. The imprisoned Black sought to recover $9 million in commissions that Carter allegedly owed to Black's firm, PMI, for endorsement and marketing contracts the agency had secured on the athlete's behalf and $5 million for breach of contract. Carter asserted a counterclaim seeking, among other things, $15.9 million that Carter allegedly lost when the athlete was sued by footwear company Puma in connection with an unsuccessful shoe deal. In late 2004, a jury awarded Black approximately $4.7 million in damages for lost commissions and damages. Carter was awarded $800,000 for Black's violation of fiduciary duties involving two loans the athlete made to the former agent. Even though the jury found that Black and his firm negligently handled Carter's contract with Puma, their negligence did not result in financial harm to Carter. Following the jury verdict, Carter and his attorneys stated they would file an appeal.[2]

Another fundamental obligation that agency law imposes upon an athlete is the duty to reasonably compensate agents for the services that they properly perform.[3] Not surprisingly, most claims by agents that an athlete has breached the relationship revolve around pay disputes. A 1998 *New York Times* article reported that the arbitrator who (at the time) handled agent/player disputes stated he "has handled 88 cases in the last two years.... Most of the disputes ... involve disagreements over fees."[4] Illustrative is the federal lawsuit filed in the mid-1990s by agent Mark Gandler, who alleged that hockey player Andrei Nazarov failed to pay for services that the agent had performed pursuant to a representation agreement between the two.[5] The NFLPA, for example, regularly works through these types of issues via its arbitration system.

Agency principles provide that if a "principal wrongfully terminates the agency contract, he is liable to his agent for damages for breach of contract in addition to reasonable compensation for services rendered up to the date of termination."[6] This principle was applied in *Total Economic Athletic Management of America, Inc. v. Pickens*.[7] Football player Bruce Pickens contracted for Total Economic d/b/a Team America to advise him in negotiating his NFL player contract. Before Team America began negotiations, Pickens retained agent Tom Condon, who negotiated Pickens's contract with the Atlanta Falcons. Pickens and Howard Misle of Team America gave different accounts of the circumstances leading up to the player signing an undated representation agreement with the agency. The five one-year contracts negotiated by Condon resulted in total compensation to the athlete, including various bonuses, of $4,100,000.

A jury awarded Team America $20,000 in damages. On appeal, a Missouri court rejected Pickens's defense that the contract was unenforceable due to illegality. Pickens asserted that Team America engaged in illegal conduct when it gave a car to him as an inducement to sign a representation agreement. NFLPA rules preclude agents from giving items of value to athletes to induce them to sign representation agreements. The court concluded the resulting contract was not illegal under Missouri or Nebraska law simply because the alleged inducements would violate NCAA and NFLPA rules.

As for Team America's contention that the jury award of $20,000 was too low, the court sided with Pickens. It enunciated the following standard for determining the amount to which a terminated agent is entitled: "the player's breach of an agency agreement does not necessarily entitle the agent to commission. . . . the agent is entitled to his commission only if he can show that, had he been permitted to continue performance, he would have been able to consummate the contracts upon which he claims commission. Contrary to Team America's assertions, it was not entitled to commissions based solely on the contract negotiated by others."[8] The court concluded that the evidence supported the jury's damage award.

Often, an athlete who has been sued by an agent based on the athlete's failure to pay will defend his position by asserting that the agent engaged in improper conduct. This conduct includes providing substandard services, breaching other basic obligations that agents owe to principals, or engaging in illegal conduct (such as Pickens alleged). For instance, an agent assumes a duty that he or she "possesses a degree of skill commensurate with the job to be done and that he will use such skill with diligence."[9] An agent commits a breach when he or she fails to act with the care and skill employed by a reasonable person under the same circumstances.[10] If such a failure is established, an athlete possesses a defense that, at a minimum, may entitle him or her to offset losses against any fees owed when the losses resulted from the agent's failure to exercise due care.

The paradigmatic illustration of this scenario remains the dispute in the early 1980s between agent Leo Zinn and football player Lemar Parrish.[11] Zinn sued Parrish to recover agent fees due to him under a representation agreement according to which the agent was obligated to "use 'reasonable efforts' to procure pro-football employment for Parrish, and at Parrish's request to 'act' in furtherance of Parrish's interest by: a) negotiating job contracts; b) furnishing advice on business investments; c) securing professional tax advice at no added costs; and d) obtaining endorsement contracts. . . . Zinn's services would include . . . efforts to secure for [Parrish] off-season employment."[12]

Between 1971 and 1974, Zinn negotiated contracts on Parrish's behalf with the Cincinnati Bengals. In 1974, Zinn negotiated a series of contracts with the Bengals that included substantially better terms than previous contracts. After Parrish signed this series of contracts, he informed Zinn that he "no longer needed his services."[13] Parrish also informed Zinn of his intention not to pay Zinn a 10 percent commission on these contracts, which Zinn claimed totaled at least $304,500, including bonus and performance clauses. Zinn sued to recover the commission owed to him.

In addition to negotiating Parrish's contracts with the Bengals, Zinn performed other services including negotiating an endorsement deal (for which he received a commission), assisting Parrish in the purchase of an apartment building, forwarding to Parrish the stock purchase recommendations of other individuals (after having screened them), and arranging for the preparation of Parrish's taxes. Zinn was unsuccessful in securing other endorsements for Parrish or securing off-season employment for Parrish.

Parrish defended his case by arguing that the representation agreement with Zinn was void because the agent had not been registered as an investment adviser as required by a federal statute. The court concluded that the nature of the investment services Zinn provided did not subject him to the registration requirements of the statute: "isolated transactions with a client as an incident to the main purpose of his management contract to negotiate football contracts do not constitute engaging in the business of advising others on investment securities."[14]

Parrish also argued that he was relieved of his obligation to pay Zinn because the agent inadequately performed services relating to procuring employment, endorsements, and off-season employment, and providing substantial tax and investment advice to Parrish. Applying a reasonable efforts standard, the court rejected Parrish's defense. With respect to the other services that Zinn agreed to provide, the court found that Zinn "was subject to an implied promise to make 'good faith' efforts to obtain what he sought."[15] Providing a word of caution that success with good faith efforts should not be confused with undertaking good faith efforts (the latter being the appropriate standard), the court found that Zinn had fulfilled his obligations to Parrish.

A 1999 opinion outlines the suit against former football player Matt Millen by Athletes and Artists (A&A), a sports management firm. They had agreed contractually that A&A would "represent Millen in his negotiations as a professional football broadcaster and that they would undertake the management of Millen's broadcasting career."[16] A&A sought to recover 8 percent of $255,000 and $155,000 contracts that Millen had entered into with CBS Television and CBS Radio, respectively. Millen sent A&A a check in the amount of $10,000, which he claimed represented payment for all past and future services A&A provided or might provide. Thereafter, it appears that A&A represented Millen in exploring broadcast opportunities with NBC and Fox television networks. Ultimately Millen terminated A&A's services and obtained another person to assist in finalizing his deal with Fox, the company for which he agreed to work.

A&A sued to recover compensation for services it had rendered in connection with its representation of Millen. In addition to asserting technical legal defenses, Millen contended that A&A was not entitled to compensation because it played no role in the negotiations with Fox, and that A&A engaged in "unauthorized actions and made misrepresentations concerning negotiations with NBC."[17] The court ruled that A&A's breach of contract claims were barred by the statute of frauds because there was no writing that contained all of the essential terms of the agreement. The court, however, allowed A&A to take its *quantum meruit claim* to trial. It noted that A&A was entitled to compensation for services rendered to Millen. The value of such services had to be determined at trial because it might be no more than the $10,000 Millen had already paid or a much greater sum.[18]

Agent Versus Agent: The Quest for Clients

The term or duration of the agency relationship is determined by the terms of the contract. For example, the NFLPA's Standard Representation Agreement allows either the athlete or the agent to terminate the relationship with five days' written notice.[19] This contract further provides that in the event that the termination occurs subsequent to when the player has signed an NFL contract that was negotiated by the agent, the latter is entitled to the fee the parties agreed upon. If termination occurs prior, the agent is entitled to reasonable compensation for the services he or she provided.[20] The ease with which athletes can terminate their relationship with agents, the fierce competition by agents for clients, and the significant amounts in fees that are often at stake erupt into considerable conflict when one agent accuses another agent of stealing clients.

An illustrative case involves football player Patrick Worley. Worley ended up being sued by agent Gary Wichard and his firm, with whom he had entered into a representation agreement. Worley initially signed with an agent on January 3, 1989. Thereafter, on January 18, 1989, he signed an exclusive representation agreement with Wichard's firm. A few months later on April 17, 1989, Worley signed an exclusive representation agreement with another firm to negotiate a rookie contract that eventually would come to $3,050,000. In the reported case, a default judgment for agent fees that was originally entered in Wichard's favor was overturned.[21]

In 2005, successful agent Drew Rosenhaus was the target of a lawsuit filed by Ken Sarnoff. The suit alleged that Rosenhaus improperly induced NFL player Anquan Boldin to terminate a marketing contract with Sarnoff's firm. Sarnoff also filed a grievance with the NFLPA, as required by the union's agent regulations, asserting that Rosenhaus improperly solicited his client. Boldin was one of approximately thirty football players who terminated their relationships with their former agents to enter into representation agreements with Rosenhaus during 2004.[22] With respect to the claim of interference with the marketing contract, Rosenhaus sought to compel arbitration. A Florida court ruled that the dispute regarding the marketing agreement was subject to arbitration under the NFLPA agent regulations.[23]

A case involving baseball star Ivan Rodriguez further demonstrates how factors, such as the ease in terminating agency agreements and competition, converge to create conflict.[24] Rodriguez signed a series of terminable at-will one-year agency contracts with Speakers of Sport. In an effort to expand its representation of baseball players, ProServ approached Rodriguez. It stated that it "would get him between $2 and $4 million in endorsements if he signed with ProServ—which he did."[25] As a consequence of his agreement with ProServ, Rodriguez terminated his contract with Speakers. A year after he contracted to have ProServ act as his agent, Rodriguez signed with another agent when ProServ failed to secure the endorsements. Subsequently, Speakers filed suit alleging that ProServ improperly interfered with its contractual relationship with Rodriguez.[26]

A federal appellate court upheld the trial court's grant of summary judgment dismissing Speakers' lawsuit. In reaching this conclusion, the court recognized that the competitive nature of the athlete agent business is reflective of our business system. Proceeding from this premise, the court adopted an approach that affords a broad range of acceptable activity when it comes to attempts by one agent to recruit another agent's client. "There is in general nothing wrong with one sports agent trying to take a client from another if this can be done without precipitating a breach of contract. That is the process known as competition, which though painful, fierce, frequently ruthless, sometimes Darwinian in its pitilessness, is the cornerstone of our highly successful economic system. Competition is not a tort . . . , but on the contrary provides a defense (the 'competitor's privilege') to the tort of improper interference."[27] Despite its recognition of the competitive nature of the business, the court noted an important limitation: the competitor's privilege does not validate inducing clients by way of fraud.

A similar standard was adopted by a court in a case involving baseball superstar Barry Bonds.[28] The court found that to establish interference with prospective economic advantage, Bonds's former agent, Roderic Wright, would have to show that his then-new agent, Beverly Hills Sports Council (BHSC), engaged in some wrongful conduct beyond "mere interference." The court noted that evidence—showing that BHSC hid the fact that it had contacted Bonds and that BHSC had a history of contacting athletes under contract with other agents—would not establish an interference claim. One commentator observed that although these cases "appear legally accurate, they provide a broad spectrum of competition that borders on interference thereby tolerating unfair and corrupt dealing."[29] Following its successful defense against Wright's claims, BHSC filed a malicious prosecution action against Wright and the attorneys who represented him in the underlying action against BHSC. BHSC's lawsuit was dismissed because it was unable to establish that either Wright or his attorneys acted with malice when they pursued the underlying action against BHSC.[30]

Agents on occasion have sued teams alleging that they interfered with the former's relationship with an athlete. Such an instance that resulted in litigation involved a lawsuit by agent John Manton against the Los Angeles Lakers. Manton claimed that in 1979 he entered into a contract pursuant to which he agreed to represent Earvin "Magic" Johnson. According to Manton, the Lakers improperly induced Johnson to breach the representation agreement so that the team could negotiate directly with Johnson and get him to sign for a lesser sum than Manton could have procured.[31]

Although two recent disputes defy easy characterization, they demonstrate the range of conflicts that occur in the industry. In early 2007, a financial adviser with several NBA clients sued the firm hired by the NBPA to provide financial audits for NBA players. The suit accused the auditing firm of soliciting players as clients. The auditing firm denied the allegations.[32] In another matter, agent Hadley Engelhard sued his runner, Safarrah Lawson, alleging that Lawson solicited Engelhard's clients on behalf of other agents. Lawson denied soliciting the clients and subsequently asserted a counterclaim asserting Engelhard "used the NFL Players Association to keep him out of the representation business."[33]

A dispute that falls within none of the typical categories of conflicts between agents and athletes is nevertheless worth noting. Former NFL quarterback Jim Kelly authored an autobiography in which he expressed his contempt for certain of his former mentors, including his former agent A. J. Faigin. In the book, Kelly stated in part:

> I learned my lesson the hard way about whom to trust and whom not to trust in business. I had had complete faith in my first agents, Greg Lustig and A. J. Faigin. . . .
>
> Then Danny and the Trevino brothers started taking a closer look at my business affairs. And the more they looked, the more they didn't like what they found.
>
> Finally, I saw the light. In 1988, I fired Lustig and Faigin and put my brother [Danny] and the Trevinos in charge of all my business dealings. Then I filed a major lawsuit against my former agents, as well as the former owners of the Gamblers for defaulting on the payment of my signing bonus.[34]

As adroitly stated by the court, Faigin "took umbrage [with these comments] and sued both Kelly and Vic Carucci, the journalist who assisted Kelly in writing the book."[35] In his libel action, Faigin argued that the relevant statements "falsely implied that he was dismissed for unlawful conduct, thus damaging his reputation and jeopardizing his career."[36] A jury found the language at issue to be defamatory in that it tended to harm Faigin's reputation, but also concluded that Faigin failed to prove the falsity of the language. Consequently, the jury rendered a decision favorable to the defendants. The jury's verdict was upheld on appeal.

Acrimony Among Agents

Disputes may also erupt when agents who worked together decide to end their relationship. Intervention by an arbitrator or a court is often necessary when former associates cannot decide on their own how to divide fees and clients. For example, a dispute resulting in litigation arose between agents Steve Weinberg and Howard Silber over how to divide up clients and fees after a joint venture agreement, including one involving professional football players, turned acrimonious.[37] After they filed lawsuits against each other, Weinberg and Silber agreed to arbitration. Following the arbitration hearing, but before the arbitrator rendered a decision, Weinberg negotiated a nine-year, multimillion-dollar contract for Washington Redskins running back Stephen Davis. The arbitrator ordered that Weinberg pay $2,079,495 to Silber for fees earned from representation of Davis. The arbitrator also ruled that each party should take nothing with respect to their dispute regarding other athlete clients.

In court, Weinberg requested that the arbitrator's ruling be vacated. Silber requested that the decision be confirmed. Relying on the considerable deference given by courts to arbitration decisions and the extremely narrow scope of review of such awards, the court rejected Weinberg's request to set aside the judgment. In so doing, the court rejected Weinberg's arguments that the arbitration agreement between him and Silber was void and unenforceable, that the evidence failed to support the arbitrator's decision, and that the arbitrator was biased.

Often former business associates, after a relationship has soured, must turn to courts to determine who is entitled to fees earned from representing athletes. The relationship between sports agents Lawrence Jacobs, Robert Bond, and Dan St. John, who formed ProSports Management, ended up in court when the agents could not decide upon a division of fees and clients. The relationship between the three agents, which began in late 1992, began to unravel in 1996. Bond and St. John accused Jacobs of breach of fiduciary duty to ProSports, conversion, larceny, and embezzlement with respect to conduct by Jacobs revolving around commission fees he received from football player Kevin Carter. Jacobs argued in defense that the funds were rightfully payable only to him and not to ProSports. Finding that the evidence supported the contention that he had committed embezzlement, conversion, and larceny, the court concluded that ProSports was "the owner of the commissions and Jacobs was required to turn over all funds to the corporation."[38]

The definitive case in this area may now be the dispute involving allegations of client stealing between Leigh Steinberg and David Dunn. Dunn, a partner in the former firm of Steinberg, Moorad & Dunn (a one-time division of Assante), left the partnership to begin his own firm, Athletes First. He reportedly started Athletes First with as many as eighteen clients who had previously been represented by Steinberg, Moorad & Dunn. Athletes including Kerry Collins, Rob Johnson, Drew Bledsoe, Ryan Leaf, Amani Toomer, and John Lynch terminated their relationships with

Steinberg & Moorad as a prelude to signing representation agreements with Athletes First.[39]

The dispute reached new levels of intensity and acrimony when Steinberg and Moorad filed a lawsuit against Dunn in the California Superior Court in Los Angeles in May 2001. In August 2001, the state court action was withdrawn, and a lawsuit was initiated in federal district court. Allegations of improperly taking clients and the legal ramifications thereof were set forth in the complaint. The key goal of Leigh Steinberg (who in 2003 purchased what remained of his firm from Assante and began a new agency) and then remaining partner Jeff Moorad (who eventually left for a management position with the Arizona Diamondbacks) was to gain an injunction against Dunn, which would stop him from representing the players. In addition to allegations that Dunn improperly signed clients of Steinberg & Moorad, plaintiffs asserted that Dunn had breached a five-year employment contract and violated the provisions of a covenant not to compete.[40] In arguing his client's position, Dunn's attorney stated that "Dunn left because he didn't feel that athletes were being taken care of properly and because promises made to him were not honored."[41]

This case raises several interesting questions, including whether athletes have the right to be represented by the sports agent of their choice, even if that representative has "stolen" them from their previous firm and even if a noncompete agreement exists. The importance of the dispute was signaled when the NFLPA spoke in support of this athlete right.[42] The NFLPA filed a brief seeking to intervene in the lawsuit between the agents. According to NFLPA general counsel Richard Berthelsen, "By doing this, we are not taking the side of either Leigh Steinberg or David Dunn, we are instead taking the side of the player who wishes to have an agent of their choice to represent them." Acknowledging the possible ramifications of the NFLPA's position on future acquisitions, Berthelsen stated, "[It] certainly would impact covenants not to compete . . . , which I guess would be important for companies considering [acquisitions]."[43]

In August 2001, a federal district court judge issued a temporary restraining order against David Dunn and Athletes First. The order prohibited the defendants from "soliciting former or current clients of Steinberg, Moorad and Dunn." It also prohibited Athletes First "from arranging, facilitating or promoting any further terminations by former SMD clients."[44] In a show of support for Dunn and Athletes First, twenty-one players signed a declaration indicating that they wanted Dunn and Athletes First to represent them.[45]

A jury found Dunn had breached his contract with the Steinberg firm, engaged in unfair competition, and acted fraudulently. Based on these findings, the jury awarded Steinberg $44.66 million in damages. In 2005, however, a California appellate court vacated the $44.66 million jury award.[46] Among the several grounds on which the appellate court reversed was the trial court's improper instruction regarding the covenant not to compete. The court pointed to a state statute, which it interpreted as "establishing that non-competition clauses in an employment agreement are unenforceable to the extent that they limit the employee's ability to compete after leaving, whether or not the employee is at-will and whether or not his term of employment has ended."[47]

In response to the $44 million judgment, Dunn filed for personal Chapter 11 bankruptcy. His bankrupcty filing suspended the NFLPA's disciplinary action against him. (In 2003, the NFLPA had suspended Dunn for two years based on evidence revealed during the trial.) On March 1, 2006, a federal district court judge agreed with the NFLPA's argument that Dunn lost the right to retain his certification without the union's permission after he entered bankruptcy.[48] The court also ruled, however, it was within the jurisdiction of the bankruptcy court judge to determine whether and when to lift the stay so as to allow the NFLPA to proceed with disciplinary action against Dunn.[49] In 2006, the NFLPA and Dunn reached a settlement that allowed the union to proceed with disciplinary action against him.[50] In November 2006, Dunn and the NFLPA reached a settlement pursuant to which Dunn agreed to an eighteen-month suspension. Dunn admitted to no wrongdoing in reaching the settlement with the NFLPA.[51]

Conclusion

The final case is illustrative of the continuing battles and the role the law may play in resolving agent disputes. None of the parties involved in athlete/agent relationships or in competition for those relationships is beyond suing or being sued. Starting with an examination of amateurism, the final chapters examine the rules and laws that attempt to control the wide-ranging issues in this business.

Chapter 9
The Last Amateurs on Earth
Amateurism and Opportunity

"Ancient amateurism is a myth."[1]
—*David C. Young*

Chapters 10 and 11 will explore private and public efforts to address the problems associated with the athlete agent industry. The major impetus behind such efforts, particularly state-enacted agent legislation, is to protect the interests of institutions of higher education that may be jeopardized by student athlete and agent interactions that violate NCAA rules and regulations. The NCAA has established a complex set of rules and regulations that govern all aspects of intercollegiate sports. Included within this regulatory structure are rules that circumscribe the student athlete/agent relationship. These and other rules within the NCAA's regulatory regime are premised on several notions, including the amateurism ideal. Consequently, a predicate to understanding the NCAA regulatory scheme and state agent statutes that are sensitive to this regime is exploring the controversial notion of amateurism. If not for the dominant desire to preserve amateurism, the web of NCAA regulations would be much less complex. As is true of any regulatory structure, those willing to violate the rules may gain an advantage. That advantage may be maintained unless they are caught. There is an old saying, "the catching comes before the hanging."

Much of the controversy surrounding the amateurism issue revolves around how the term "amateur" should be defined. In simplest terms, an amateur is whatever the organization regulating the particular athletic event or organization says it is.[2] This definition generally appears in the organization's constitution or bylaws. For example, the NCAA describes the amateur principle as follows: "Student-athletes shall be amateurs in an intercollegiate sport, and their participation should be motivated primarily by education and by the physical, mental and social benefits to be derived. Student participation in intercollegiate athletics is an avocation, and student-athletes should be protected from exploitation by professionals and commercial enterprises."[3] Other NCAA provisions specifically delineate how amateur status can be lost.[4]

Consistent with the NCAA amateurism principle, an amateur has been popularly defined as someone who participates, and always has participated, in sports solely for pleasure and for physical, mental, or social benefits. The amateur receives no financial gain of any kind (or the minimum amount allowed), direct or indirect, for his or her athletic prowess.

The payment of any money to amateur athletes has traditionally been viewed as contradicting the true meaning of amateurism.[5] Questions of amateurism most often arise when compensation of some sort is given to student athletes. Current NCAA rules prohibit such payments. Pursuant to NCAA rules, amateur status is lost when a student athlete: "(a) Uses his or her athletics skills (directly or indirectly) for pay in any form in" the particular sport in which the individual competes, or "(b) Accepts a promise of pay."[6] Often "boosters," alumni, and educational institutions "cheat," however, by making payments to student athletes when it is advantageous for them to do so. Cheating appears sometimes in the form of a monetary payment or sometimes in the transfer of goods or services. Athlete agents, seeking an advantage, also cheat by engaging in conduct that ranges from directly paying student athletes to bestowing gifts upon an athlete's friends and relatives.

Payments by agents to student athletes are particularly successful in recruiting student athletes from economically disadvantaged families. Ironically, if these student athletes cannot find time to earn money from working within the framework of NCAA rules, they are forced to ask their families for extra money in order to pay for things that range from clothes, to expenses for a date, to a stereo system like the one possessed by the student in the dorm room next door. If an athlete's family cannot afford the expenditure, the athlete may be tempted to look elsewhere. Often a willing donor is the athlete agent, booster, or alumnus. Such payments violate NCAA rules, most state athlete agent statutes, and players' union regulations.

Coupled with the issue of money is a generally held view that, unlike their professional counterparts, amateur athletes participate in sports for the glory of the sport alone. Both the pay and the motive issues are commonly viewed as having originated in ancient Greek athletics. However, we shall see that this interpretation is questionable at best: as David Young has remarked, "Ancient amateurism is a myth." The next sections examine the origin of rules against giving compensation to amateur athletes.

Origin of Rules Against Compensation

THE ANCIENT GREEKS

The amateurism ideal in sports is commonly posited on the long-standing Olympic model, which in turn is assumed to be derived from ancient Greek athletics. The "myth" of ancient amateurism is that a society existed, presumably the Greeks, in which athletes participated in sport solely for the glory thereof and received no compensation for their participation or winning. This view is reflected in one of the most extensive studies of the relationship of college athletics to the colleges and universities, which was conducted by the Carnegie Foundation in 1929 and published in *American College Athletics* by Howard J. Savage.[7] Adopting this view, Savage writes, "The essential differences between the amateur and the professional in athletics were clearly understood among the ancient Greeks."[8] Classicist David C. Young, however, in his book *The Olympic Myth of Greek Amateur Athletics*, writes that he "can find no mention of amateurism in Greek sources, no reference to amateur athletes—no evidence that the concept 'amateurism' was even known in antiquity. The truth is that 'amateur' is one thing for which the ancient Greeks never even had a word."[9] In fact, Young examines various levels of compensation that were received in ancient times and uncovers a prize in one event that was equal to ten years' wages.[10]

The absence of compensation was not an essential element of Greek athletics.[11] As another classicist notes, the ancient Greeks "had no known restrictions on granting awards to athletes."[12] Many athletes were generously rewarded; according to Young, the only real disagreement among classical scholars is when these payments or awards to athletes began.[13]

The myth regarding ancient Greek athletics was apparently developed and perpetuated by individuals who profited in various ways from the development of such a system.[14] Young examines the work of scholars who are most often cited for espousing this view of Greek amateurism. He cites an article written by classical scholar Paul Shorey in *The Forum* as one of the first misstatements of the actual history:

And here lies the chief, if somewhat obvious, lesson that our modern athletes have to learn from Olympia, if they would not remain barbarians in spirit. . . . They must *strive*, like the young heroes of Pindar, *only* for the complete development of their manhood, and their sole prizes must be the conscious delight in the exercise . . . and some simple symbol of honor. They must not prostitute the vigor of their youth for gold, directly or indirectly. [T]he commercial spirit . . . is fatal, as the Greeks learned in their *degenerate* days. . . . Where money is the stake men will inevitably tend to rate the end above the means, or rather to misconceive the true end . . . the professional will *usurp the place of the amateur*. [Emphasis Young's][15]

This passage was written prior to 1896, when the first modern Olympiad was held in Athens, and was directed at potential Olympians. Young points out that Shorey writes about "the Greek record for the high jump" although there was no high jump at the time,[16] that the statements attributed to Pindar throughout the text do not exist,[17] that dates are off by five hundred years,[18] and that Shorey actually knew very little about Greek athletics.[19] Young goes on to identify other scholars who made the same erroneous statements and shows how the myth was perpetuated because these scholars inevitably cited each other for authority.[20] One scholar, Harold Harris, in his *Greek Athletes and Athletics*, actually created an account of an ancient Greek athlete with detailed dates that Young concludes is a "sham" and "outright historical fiction"[21] and was probably designed to serve as "a moral lesson to modern man."[22]

The "modern man" for whom the lesson was apparently designed seems to have been the gentleman amateur athlete of Victorian England:

Harris' bogus Greek athlete and Shorey's false history of ancient athletics are not isolated cases nor mere instances of sloppy scholarship. They are representative examples of a far-flung and amazingly successful deception, a kind of historical hoax, in which scholar joined hands with sportsman and administrator so as to mislead the public and influence modern sporting life. We shall never know whether these men performed their deception consciously or unconsciously, nor does it much matter now. But the deception itself is still with us, and we need to inquire into its results and its causes.[23]

In simplest terms, Harris, Shorey, and other early scholars of Greek "amateurism" were part of a process that sought to justify an elite British athletic system that was to find its way into American collegiate athletics. The fact that scholars were promulgating these definitions of amateurism meant that nonscholars would inevitably do so. Probably the leading voice in the United States in favor of segregating pay and amateurism was Avery Brundage, former president of the United States Olympic Committee and the International Olympic Committee. Brundage was one of the main opponents to Jim Thorpe's efforts to recover his Olympic medals, which were taken away because Thorpe had played semiprofessional baseball. One of the ironies of Thorpe's losing his medals was his statement that "I did not play for the money there was in it, but because I liked to play ball."[24] Other athletes assumed false names while playing semiprofessional baseball; Thorpe did not even realize he was jeopardizing his eligibility.[25] Similarly, during Brundage's reign, Olympic hurdler Lee Calhoun lost his amateur status because he received wedding gifts as part of his appearance on the television show *Bride and Groom*.[26]

Brundage's view of Olympic amateurism was published in an article entitled "Why the Olympic Games?":

> The ancient Olympic Games . . . were strictly amateur . . . and for many centuries, as long as they continued amateur, they grew in importance and significance. . . . Gradually, however, abuses and excesses developed. . . . Cities tried to demonstrate their superiority . . . by establishing special training camps . . . , by recruiting athletes from other communities, and by subsidizing competitors. Special prizes and awards and all sorts of inducements were offered and winners were even given pensions for life. What was originally fun, recreation, a diversion, and a pastime became a business. . . . The Games degenerated, lost their purity and high idealism, and were finally abolished. . . . [S]port must be for sport's sake.[27]

Brundage firmly opposed amateurs receiving any compensation whatsoever related to participation in sports and used the Greek amateur athletic story to justify his position.

ENGLAND

Young and other scholars contend that it was not the Greeks who developed the current collegiate ethic of amateurism. Rather it was scholars such as Savage and Harris as well as the Avery Brundages of the day and the practices that developed in Victorian England. In fact, the first published definition of the term "amateur" by a sports organization was made by the Amateur Athletic Club of England in 1866.[28] That definition described an amateur as "Any gentleman who has never competed in an open competition, or for public money, or for admission money, or with professionals for a prize, public money or admission money, and who has never at any period of his life taught or assisted in the pursuit of athletic exercises as a means of livelihood; nor is a mechanic, artisan, or labourer."[29]

The purpose of the Amateur Athletic Club was to provide English gentlemen with the opportunity to compete against each other without having to compete against professionals.[30] The development of concepts of amateurism in Britain was largely based on class distinctions. The distinctions were forced by the use of so-called "mechanics clauses" in amateur definitions, such as the one quoted above, which maintained that mechanics, artisans, and laborers could not participate in sports as amateurs.[31] According to Ronald A. Smith in his book *Sports and Freedom*, the British Amateur Rowing Association included such a clause in its eligibility rules in 1870.[32] It was from these rules that the modern eligibility rules of the NCAA evolved. In fact, any negative connotations that remain today regarding professionalism probably evolved from this distinction.

Interestingly, part of the reason for the "mechanics clause" was that those who used their muscles as part of their employment in fact had a competitive advantage.[33]

UNITED STATES

Smith describes the profound amateur/professional dilemma that confronts American universities in this way: "If a college has truly amateur sport, it will lose prestige as it loses contests; if a college acknowledges outright professional sport, the college will lose respectability as a middle-class or upper-class institution. The unsatisfactory solution to the dilemma has been to claim amateurism to the world, while in fact accepting a professional mode of operation."[34]

The first two sports to face these questions of professionalism versus amateurism in the United States were baseball and rowing. Initially, the norm in sports in this country was professionalism. Baseball was played at the semiprofessional level as early as 1860; and the first professional team, the Cincinnati Red Stockings, was formed in 1868,[35] the same year in which the New York Athletic Club, the first amateur organization in the United States, was created.[36]

"Professionalism" in college sports abounded. For example, in the 1850s Harvard University students rowed in a meet that had a $100 first prize purse, and in the 1860s they raced for as much as $500.[37] Smith maintains that amateurism, as historically conceived, was largely absent from college sports at the beginning of the twentieth century:

> By the early twentieth century, there was probably no college in America which was able to preserve amateurism in men's sport, as competition for money and non-money prizes, contests against professionals, collection of gate receipts, support for training tables, provision for athletic tutors, recruitment and payment of athletes, and the hiring of professional coaches pervaded the intercollegiate athletic scene. Professionalism had invaded college sports and had defeated amateurism as it was understood in the nineteenth century.[38]

One of the more graphic illustrations of the benefits students received, even in the early 1900s, involved 1904 Yale football team captain James Hogan. After the final game in his career, Yale rewarded Hogan by sending him to Havana on vacation.[39]

One reason that college sports developed beyond amateurism in the United States, as opposed to its British counterpart, was the sheer number of competing institutions.[40] In England, upper-level education meant Oxford or Cambridge. With only two institutions, the odds of stepping outside the established bounds of amateurism were not that high. In the United States, on the other hand, the Ivy League and other private and public colleges and universities vigorously competed against one another in sports. Even if Harvard and Yale wanted to be the athletic and intellectual elite of the United States, as Oxford and Cambridge were in England, they could not do so. As Smith notes, with the Wesleyans and Cornells developing athletically, refusing to compete against them would cause Harvard and Yale to lose their athletic "esteem and prestige."[41] According to scholars such as Smith and Daniel L. Boorstin, the English system of amateurism, loosely derived from the Greeks, simply did not have a chance of surviving in the United States.

Competition among a larger community of institutions was a major element in the weakening of Victorian notions of amateurism. Another factor is what Smith refers to as a difference in egalitarian beliefs: "The English amateur system, based upon participation by the social and economic elite and rejection of those beneath them from participating, would never gain a foothold in American college athletics. There was too much competition, too strong a belief in merit over heredity, too abundant an ideology of freedom of opportunity for the amateur ideal to succeed. . . . It may be that amateur athletics at a high level of expertise can only exist in a society dominated by upper-class elitists."[42] Even with this sort of ideological conflict, the NCAA's early years were heavily burdened by attempts to enforce various amateur standards.

In spite of this tradition, or perhaps because of it, in 1909 the NCAA, through its committee on amateur law, recommended and later adopted the following amateur/professional distinction:

1. An amateur in athletics is one who enters and takes part in athletic contests purely in obedience to the play impulses or for the satisfaction of purely play motives and for the exercise, training, and social pleasure derived. The natural or primary attitude of mind in play determines amateurism.
2. A professional in athletics is one who enters or takes part in any athletic contest from any other motive than the satisfaction of pure play impulses, or for the exercise, training or social pleasures derived, or one who desires and secures from his skill or who accepts of spectators, partisans or other interests, any material or economic advantage or reward.[43]

With this, Victorian England's amateur/professional distinction was incorporated into American collegiate athletics.

The first NCAA eligibility code sought to ensure that the athletes who participated in collegiate sports were in fact full-time registered students who had not been and were not being paid for their participation in athletics. The 1906 NCAA Eligibility Code provided:

> The following rules . . . are suggested as a minimum:
>
> 1. No student shall represent a college or university in any intercollegiate game or contest, who is not taking a full schedule of work as prescribed in the catalogue of the institution.
> 2. No student shall represent a college or university . . . who has at any time received, either directly or indirectly, money, or any other consideration, to play on any team, or . . . who has competed for a money prize or portion of gate money in any contest, or who has competed for any prize against a professional.
> 3. No student shall represent a college or university . . . who is paid or received, directly or indirectly, any money, or financial concession, or emolument as past or present compensation for, or as prior consideration or inducement to play in, or enter any athletic contest, whether the said remuneration be received from, or paid by, or at the instance of any organization, committee or faculty of such college or university, or any individual whatever.
> 4. No student shall represent a college or university . . . who has participated in intercollegiate games or contests during four previous years.
> 5. No student who has been registered as a member of any other college or university shall participate in any intercollegiate game or contest until he shall have been a student of the institution which he represents at least one college year.
> 6. Candidates for positions on athletic teams shall be required to fill out cards, which shall be placed on file, giving a full statement of their previous athletic records.[44]

During the years subsequent to the establishment of this code, the NCAA has sought further to define its views on amateurism. One notable effort involved the formal incorporation of the Amateur Code into the NCAA constitution.[45] This step, said Palmer E. Pierce, former president of the NCAA, was intended "to enunciate more clearly [the NCAA's] purposes; to incorporate the amateur definition and principles of amateur spirit; [and] to widen the scope of government."[46]

The amateurism ideal undergirds several current NCAA rules. These rules reflect the extent to which the amateurism and the anticompensation principles have historically permeated the NCAA regulatory structure and influenced views held of intercollegiate athletics. One illustration of the impact of perceptions of college athletics is the pervasiveness of the influence of the amateurism ideal in judicial decision making. Many courts have adopted the NCAA's amateurism ideal. Illustrative of judicial recognition of the amateurism myth are the court's comments in *Walters and Bloom v. Fullwood and Kickliter*.[47] Although

Fullwood involved a question regarding which entity possessed jurisdiction or the power to decide the dispute between the parties, Chief Judge Charles L. Brieant found it appropriate to state his views on amateurism. In his conclusion, referring to what must appropriately be called a stereotypical view of amateurism, Brieant wrote, "All parties to this action should recognize that they are the beneficiaries of a system built on the trust of millions of people who, with stubborn innocence, adhere to the Olympic ideal, viewing amateur sports as a commitment to competition for its own sake."[48] In his opinion, Brieant cited scholars who disagreed with Young's view and maintained that Greek tradition excluded compensation.[49]

The United States Supreme Court recognized the amateur ideal in *NCAA v. Board of Regents*.[50] Therein the Court stated that the "NCAA plays a critical role in the maintenance of the *revered tradition of amateurism* in college sports."[51] Similarly in *Gaines v. NCAA*, the court's decision was influenced by the revered amateurism ideal.[52] The court noted that the "overriding purpose of [NCAA] eligibility rules, thus, is not to provide the NCAA with commercial advantage, but rather the opposite extreme—to prevent commercializing influences from destroying the unique 'product' of NCAA college football. Even in the increasingly commercial modern world, this Court believes there is still validity to the *Athenian concept* of a complete education derived from fostering full growth of both mind and body."[53] Finally, in *Banks v. NCAA*, a student athlete challenged the legality of the NCAA's no-draft and no-agent rules.[54] In upholding the validity of the restrictions, the court concluded that the "no-agent and no-draft rules are vital and must work in conjunction with other eligibility requirements to preserve the *amateur status* of college athletics, and prevent the sports agents from further intruding into the collegiate educational system."[55] The court relied in part on the amateurism principle in rejecting a student athlete's challenge of no-draft and no-agent rules. The court stated that "the NCAA's second primary goal is preserving amateurism as an integral part of the educational process."[56]

The ultimate decisions reached in *Fullwood, Gaines, Banks*, and other cases may have been sound notwithstanding judicial reliance on the amateurism ideal. What is problematic, however, is the extent to which an inaccurate belief in the amateurism ideal has influenced judicial resolution of legal disputes in intercollegiate athletics. In fact, Young would probably maintain that certain of these decisions are doctrinally incorrect and unfair. Young said that he wrote his book on amateurism because he "couldn't stand to see all these problems associated with amateurism blamed on all those poor dead Greeks."

NCAA Pay Restrictions

As briefly mentioned above, an individual loses amateur status and will be rendered ineligible to compete in intercollegiate competition in a particular sport through the receipt of "pay" related to his or her athletic skills.[57] "Pay" includes "any direct or indirect salary, gratuity or comparable compensation."[58] Amateur status will also be lost if an athlete or his or her relatives or friends accept benefits from a prospective agent.[59] Moreover, amateur status will be lost if a student athlete enters into "an agreement with an agent."[60]

NCAA restrictions on payments to student athletes related to their athletic abilities also extend to outside employment.[61] Until recently, NCAA rules limited the time an athlete on full athletic scholarship could work during the school year or at any time that class was in session or, in the case of football, after practice had begun.[62] The NCAA imposed this limitation through bylaw 15.02.4, which limited the amount of financial aid a student could receive to "tuition and fees, room and board, and required course-related books."[63] The bylaws specifically included as a source of funds that must be considered in this amount "employment during semester or term time."[64] The NCAA's employment rule presented a perfect "opportunity" for boosters, alumni, agents, or prospective agents to fill the financial gap for student athletes.

In 1997 the NCAA rules were revised, effective 1998, to allow student athletes to earn up to $2,000 per year from employment during the school term. These earnings will not be included when calculating financial aid. The irony of this rule modification is that few student athletes seem to be taking advantage of this opportunity. One possible reason for the lack of utilization of this rule change is the tremendous demand that is already placed on their time. The limited amounts that a student athlete might earn from employment might not seem to be worth the time expended given other demands on his time.[65] The 1997 revision was subsequently modified to provide greater flexibility for student athletes. The $2,000 limit on compensation from employment was eliminated. Moreover, employment income is exempt and is not to be "counted in determining a student-athlete's cost of attendance or in the institution's financial aid limitations."[66] The primary restrictions on student athlete employment income is that the student athlete be compensated only for work actually performed and that employment income not be earned as a consequence of "the publicity, reputation, fame or personal following [the student athlete] has obtained because of athletics ability."[67]

The student athlete on full athletic scholarship may not be paid for athletic prowess nor does he or she apparently have time to work for additional spending money. The throwback to the aristocratic idea of the amateur is clear here. If the student athlete has adequate funds for the activities of student life, the ideal situation is not to work. This scenario clearly provides more time to concentrate on studies. However, if the athlete does not have the funds (from family or elsewhere) and may only work to a limited extent under the rules, what happens when the limited earnings are gone, or, if the athlete desires to make a larger purchase, such as an automobile? This window of opportunity is often seized by boosters, alumni, or sports agents. Indeed, some view payments in violation of NCAA rules as synonymous with other "victimless crimes." The athlete needs the money and no one is hurt in the transaction; the payment just happens to violate NCAA rules. Moreover, such payments are likely to run afoul of athlete agent legislation enacted by state legislatures and may be prosecuted under federal racketeering laws.

Conclusion

The societal desire to retain the oldest forms of amateurism is one of the strongest impediments to cleaning up the sports agent business. Improvement should come, particularly on the recruiting side of the business, as meaningful amateurism reforms take place. The chapter that follows begins the discussion of private and public efforts to regulate the athlete agent.

Part III
Solutions

Chapter 10

Knights of Columbus Rules?
Private Sports Agent Regulations

With the growth of problems in the sports agent industry, many concerned parties have sought regulatory solutions. Historically, the key entities involved in attempting to formulate legislation as the panacea for the problems that afflict the agent industry have been the NCAA, NCAA member institutions, players' unions, state and federal law enforcement and legislative entities, and, of course, professional athletes, student athletes, and sports agents themselves. This chapter examines the legislative efforts of private entities, and Chapters 11 and 12 explore public entities' efforts to regulate agents. The discussion below describes the private entities that have attempted to regulate sports agents and evaluates the relative effectiveness of their efforts to control the activities of sports agents.

National Collegiate Athletic Association

INDIRECT REGULATORY EFFORTS

The NCAA is the oldest and most powerful governing body in college sports. The NCAA developed as the result of a meeting in 1905 (of thirteen colleges) to discuss safety reforms in intercollegiate athletics. The meeting was convened at the urging of President Theodore Roosevelt following deaths and other serious injuries that resulted from the violent brand of football that was played at the time.[1] Currently, the association has more than 1,000 members, commonly referred to as member institutions.

Although the NCAA sometimes appears to be a monolith, its actions represent the joint decision making of its member institutions. A former executive director defines the organization's basic premise as "institutional control of intercollegiate athletics."[2] In other words, each institution is ultimately responsible for the governance of its intercollegiate athletics program. Notwithstanding the notion of institutional control, the NCAA, through its promulgation of rules and regulations, sets national standards for the governance of intercollegiate athletics. These bylaw provisions, rules, and regulations, as revised from time to time, are published annually in the *NCAA Manual* that is produced for each of the divisions—I, II, and III—of the organization.

Among the provisions contained in the *NCAA Manual* are those that establish specific guidelines for governing the relationship between a student athlete and a sports agent. A student athlete who fails to comply with these provisions may lose his or her eligibility. Section 12.3.1 of the NCAA's *Division I Manual* articulates the NCAA's general rule concerning agents: "An individual shall be ineligible for participation in an intercollegiate sport if he or she ever has agreed (orally or in writing) to be represented by an agent for the purpose of marketing his or her athletics ability or reputation in that sport. Further, an agency contract not specifically limited in writing to a sport or particular sports shall be deemed applicable to all sports and the individual shall be ineligible to participate in any sport."[3] This provision precludes student athletes from engaging in a contractual relationship with agents. A student athlete who violates this provision will be deemed ineligible to compete in intercollegiate athletics for his or her college or university.

A student athlete may also lose his or her eligibility by accepting benefits from agents. Sections 12.3.1.2 (a) and (b) render an athlete ineligible if he or she (or relatives or friends) accepts benefits from "[a]ny person who represents any individual in the marketing of his or her athletics ability" or an agent even if the agent has no "interest in representing the student athlete."[4] For example, payment by an agent of expenses related to sending a prospective student athlete to a summer camp would constitute an extra benefit, in addition to gifts of money, cars, and other items from agents to student athletes. Acceptance of such benefits runs afoul of NCAA rules that prohibit athletes from accepting "extra benefits" that are "not available to the student body in general." Such conduct by agents and athletes is also likely to violate state statutes regulating agents, which are discussed in Chapters 11 and 12.

NCAA rules do not prohibit a student athlete from obtaining advice from lawyers regarding a proposed professional contract. The lawyer may not, however, represent the "student-athlete in negotiations for such a contract."

Despite the huge domain the NCAA is chartered to regulate, the association lacks authority to directly impose sanctions against all of the actors that may be involved in a violation of its rules and regulations. The NCAA has the power to impose sanctions against a member institution for violations of association rules by student athletes and athletic personnel of a college or university. Consistent with the NCAA's notion of institutional control, member institutions—not the NCAA—take action against student athletes and other athletics personnel who violate NCAA rules. The failure by an institution to take action may result in the imposition of sanctions by the NCAA. Sanctions take various forms, but they can include barring a member institution from television appearances and postseason play, which may generate considerable profits for a college sports program. This authority provides the NCAA with the strength to govern, because schools hesitate to jeopardize participation in such revenue-laden opportunities as the NCAA basketball national championship tournament, which can yield a school millions of dollars. Ultimately, the authority that the NCAA wields is primarily economic.

One of the most stunning examples of the NCAA's power is the so-called "death penalty." Use of this penalty bars a member institution not only from championship competition but also from playing altogether. The first and only Division I school's athletic program to receive this sanction, due to extensive recruiting and other violations, was Southern Methodist University (SMU). In 1987, SMU received a one-year version of the penalty for paying thirteen players a total of $61,000 from a slush fund. The payments were approved by the SMU athletic department. When the sanction was imposed, SMU's football players were allowed to transfer to other schools. The experts' projections at the time held that it would take at least five to six years to rebuild SMU's football program following the death penalty.[5]

Lesser penalties such as probation can be devastating as well. In 1989 the University of Kentucky's basketball program was placed on a three-year probation for recruiting and other violations. The *Sports Industry News* estimated that the school would lose $1.8 million over the three years. Kentucky's initial losses due to the NCAA sanction were $350,000 from the 1988 NCAA basketball tournament, $250,000 from its share of its conference's television syndication package, and $1,100,000 from its conference tournament.[6]

Thus NCAA rules and regulations indirectly impact agents by discouraging student athletes from entering into relationships with agents that run afoul of NCAA rules and regulations. These rules may also encourage institutions to take preventive action to avoid improper conduct between student athletes and agents. Moreover, as discussed in Chapter 11, an agent who violates an NCAA rule risks having run afoul of state laws that govern the student athlete/agent relationship.

DIRECT REGULATORY EFFORTS

In contrast to the considerable economic power that the NCAA possesses in relation to its member institutions, its power over sports agents is severely limited. According to former NCAA Executive Director Richard

Schultz, sports agent improprieties are "really one of the knottiest problems we have because there is not a lot we can do about it. All we can do is penalize the institution or the athlete."[7] This lack of regulatory authority combines with other factors to create opportunities for sports agent improprieties.

One failed NCAA attempt at direct regulation was a voluntary sports agent registration system.[8] Under the system, sports agents were required to complete a form, return it to the NCAA, and agree that they would not contact a student athlete or coach without first contacting the athletic director at that member institution. An NCAA memorandum that accompanied the registration form explained that the NCAA made available to the student athlete and others a list of the individuals who had registered under this program.

The NCAA's agent registration system was *voluntary*. In the memorandum that accompanied the registration form, the NCAA acknowledged that the system operated without the force of law behind it. Former sports agent Mike Trope succinctly described the ineffectiveness of NCAA rules and regulations in his book *Necessary Roughness* when he wrote, "The NCAA rules are not the laws of the United States. They're simply a bunch of hypocritical and unworkable rules set up by the NCAA. I would no sooner abide by the rules and regulations of the NCAA than I would the Ku Klux Klan."[9] Similarly, athlete agent Norby Walters told a *Sports Illustrated* reporter, in reference to an NCAA rule forbidding student athletes to contract with sports agents before their eligibility was exhausted, "I'll sign anyone I want. The NCAA can't enforce [its rules]. I'll sign a sophomore if I want."[10] Much like Trope, Walters told *USA Today* that breaking NCAA rules is "like saying we bent the Knights of Columbus rules."[11] In a recent article, two commentators accurately describe the inherent limitations on the NCAA's authority to directly regulate athlete agents as follows:

Only the federal government and the individual states possess the power to regulate agents; the NCAA simply lacks jurisdiction to regulate athlete agents. The NCAA is merely a voluntary organization with jurisdiction only over its member constituents (i.e., the colleges and universities that elect to join the NCAA). It does not even have jurisdiction over its athletes, and it must instead enforce its rules against its member institutions. In other words, if an athlete violates an NCAA rule or regulation, the NCAA will mandate that the member university not allow the athlete to participate further in intercollegiate sports.[12]

In 1989, some NCAA members began to acknowledge that it was possible that the voluntary agent registration system might have been doing more harm than good. Agents who registered could then tell prospective student athlete clients that they had a registration "validation" from the NCAA. In fact, all the registration validated was that the agent had taken the time to complete a form. Former NCAA Executive Director Richard Schultz referred to the system as "meaningless," and at the end of 1989 it was abolished.[13]

Players' Associations

Players' associations, which constitute trade unions for the athletes in the major professional sports, also regulate athlete/agent relationships. These unions operate under the guidelines of the National Labor Relations Act (NLRA).[14] The first players' union agent regulation program was instituted in 1983 by the NFLPA. The creation of the NFLPA program was followed by the NBPA and later by Major League Baseball's counterpart, the MLBPA, and hockey's counterpart, the NHLPA. In varying forms, these unions require sports agents to register with them and to receive "certification" before representing members of their unions.[15]

The sports unions' power to regulate and certify agents represents a departure from the ways in which employees' unions typically operate. In most industries, unions (pursuant to collective bargaining agreements with employers) negotiate terms and conditions of employment as well as all union member salaries. Professional sports leagues, also pursuant to collective bargaining agreements, possess the exclusive authority to negotiate individual player salaries and other terms and conditions of employment such as minimum salaries, pension benefits, health insurance, playing conditions, travel accommodations, the ability of a player to move from one team to another, medical treatment, and grievance and arbitration procedures.[16] Unlike other unions, however, sports unions have delegated their exclusive authority to negotiate individual player salaries. Thus, players are free to select representatives to negotiate the individual terms of their contract compensation packages within the framework established by the collective bargaining agreements.[17]

In 1983, the NFLPA asserted that it possessed the inherent authority to regulate agents who represented football players in contract negotiations with teams. Pursuant to its asserted authority, the NFLPA mandated that those agents who desired to represent its members be certified by the union. Similarly, in 1986, in response to complaints by players of abuse by agents, the NBPA established a comprehensive system of agent certification. One court described the abuses that prompted union regulation of agents:

> players complained that the agents imposed high and non-uniform fees for negotiation services, insisted on execution of open-ended powers of attorney giving the agents broad powers over players' professional and financial decisions,

failed to keep players apprised of the status of negotiations with NBA teams, failed to submit itemized bills for fees and services, and, in some cases had conflicts of interest arising out of representing coaches and/or general managers of NBA teams as well as players. Many players believed that they were bound by contract not to dismiss their agents regardless of dissatisfaction with their services and fees, because the agents had insisted on the execution of long-term agreements. Some agents offered money and other inducements to players, their families, and coaches to obtain player clients.[18]

The NBPA established a comprehensive system of regulation and certification that attempted to address most, if not all, of the abuses cited above.

The regulatory systems developed by the players' associations address two broad areas of concern: matters relating to fair competition, and competence and ethics. As they relate to fair competition, anti-tampering provisions prohibit agents from initiating communications with an athlete in an agency agreement with another agent with respect to matters involving agent representation or the player's contract with his team. Agent regulations include provisions that prohibit improper solicitation and inducements.

Included among provisions relating to competence and ethics are those that restrict contract negotiations on behalf of players to persons certified by the players' associations. With respect to certification, players' association regulations provide processes pursuant to which persons can become certified agents. The requirements differ. By way of example, the NFLPA and NBPA require that agents comply with certain educational requirements. The MLBPA and NHLPA agent regulations impose no such requirement. In 2005, the NFLPA heightened its educational requirement. A prospective agent must possess a postgraduate degree in order to be certified unless he or she can demonstrate sufficient negotiation experience.[19] The NBPA process requires the completion of a form, attendance at a seminar, and payment of a fee. The NFLPA requires a prospective agent to pass an exam related to this representation. The MLBPA does not allow a sports agent to register until he or she actually agrees to represent a client.[20] The sanctions for noncompliance with the rules set forth by unions include "decertification."[21]

The players' associations for the major team sports, the NBA, the NFL, MLB, and the NHL, restrict representation of athletes for contract negotiation to union-certified agents.[22] The MLBPA asserts its authority in the MLBPA regulations by citing to the NLRA that the MLBPA is "the exclusive representative for all the employees in such unit."[23] It then cites its collective bargaining agreement with management, noting that players may negotiate contracts with teams "in accordance with the provisions set forth in this Agreement."[24] The certification requirement also appears in the Major League Baseball Collective Bargaining Agreement (effective December 20, 2006), which states that a player may use an agent for negotiations "provided such agent has been certified to the Clubs by the Association [MLBPA] as authorized to act as a Player's Agent for such purposes."[25]

Courts have upheld the authority of players' associations to regulate agents. In *Collins v. National Basketball Players Association*, an appellate court upheld a federal district court ruling that recognized the authority of players' associations to establish agent regulations and to certify agents.[26] "The integrity of a prospective negotiating agent is well within the NBPA's legitimate interest in maintaining the wage scale and working conditions of its members."[27]

The authority of players' unions to impose sanctions against agents was recognized in *Black v. National Football League Players Association*.[28] Former agent Tank Black sought dismissal of disciplinary proceedings initiated against him by the NFLPA. Black asserted that the NFLPA's proceeding and a proposed ruling that revoked his contract adviser certification were the products of an antitrust conspiracy, the product of an arbitration system established pursuant to NFLPA regulations that violated the Federal Arbitration Act, and interfered with his business relations. The court rejected his claims. In *White v. National Football League*, agents Leigh Steinberg, Jeffrey Moorad, and Gary Wichard argued that they were not subject to discovery in a proceeding in which the National Football League Management Council alleged that the agents and the San Francisco 49ers entered into undisclosed agreements concerning player compensation.[29] The agents argued that they were not subject to discovery in the proceeding because they were not signatories to certain agreements, including the NFL Collective Bargaining Agreement, and because they were not subject to the penalty scheme provided for in these agreements. In rejecting the agents' arguments, the court cited approvingly to *Collins v. NBPA* and the notion that players' unions can regulate sports agents.

Players' associations' agent regulations also include dispute resolution mechanisms. Among the more important of such provisions are those that allow a players' association to sanction agents who commit violations of the agent regulations. Sanctions for proscribed agent conduct range from invalidating agency contracts with athletes to reprimands, fines, supsensions, and decertification.

Unions have on occasion used their authority to discipline agents. The first NFLPA suspension occurred in 1996 when agent Robert Caron was fined $5,000 and suspended for a year for conduct involving the University of Southern California (see discussion in Chapter 11).[30] Other suspensions have included Jimmy Gould for two years and a fine of $15,000 and those of Jeffrey S. Nalley and Joel Segal.[31] Also, as discussed in

Chapter 5, the NFLPA revoked the license of Dunyasha Yetts,[32] and Tank Black was decertified by the NFLPA in 1999.[33] In 2005, the NFLPA suspended agent Jerome Stanley for failing to "give notice to the Cleveland Browns that his client . . . was eligible for free agency."[34] The NFLPA disciplined agent Neil Cornrich for working as an expert witness for a defendant, General Motors, in a lawsuit filed by the estate of deceased NFL player Derrick Thomas.[35] Players' associations also use their authority and the threat of suspension to influence an agent to voluntarily relinquish certification. This situation occurred recently when long-time agent Sal DeFazio resigned as a certified player representative. His resignation came in the aftermath of charges by the NBPA accusing him of improperly withdrawing more than a million dollars from players' accounts.[36]

As suggested above, the NFLPA has been the most aggressive of the players' associations in taking disciplinary action against agents. The NFLPA suspensions of prominent agents David Dunn and Carl Poston in recent years are indicative of its increasing willingness to aggressively assert its authority in this regard. In November 2006, agent David Dunn agreed with the NFLPA to accept an eighteen-month supension.[37] The deal came amid a protracted battle between the agent and the players' association that initially arose from a dispute in which Leigh Steinberg filed a lawsuit accusing Dunn, formerly a member of Steinberg's agency, of stealing clients. Based in part on evidence presented during the trial, the NFLPA suspended Dunn for two years. Dunn appealed to an arbitrator. The settlement between Dunn and the NFLPA occurred just before Dunn's appeal was to be heard by the arbitrator.[38] In a related matter, Joby Branion, an agent who had previously worked for Steinberg and then joined Dunn at the Athletes First agency, was suspended in early 2007 based on evidence disclosed in the Steinberg/Dunn lawsuit. The NFLPA accused Branion of violating NFLPA regulations that prohibit an agent from interfering in the contractual relationship between a player and his agent. Another agent, Zeke Sandhu, was also suspended for interfering with Branion in the same relationship.[39] At the time this book went to press, an attorney for Branion expressed his client's intent to appeal the suspensions.[40]

As the Dunn appeal indicates, agents will go to great lengths to challenge a union's disciplinary action. In March 2006, the NFLPA's Committee on Agent Regulation voted to suspend NFL certified agent Carl Poston for "allegedly signing an important contract for a client without fully reading it first."[41] Poston negotiated a contract between NFL player LaVar Arrington and the Washington Redskins that allegedly failed to include an important bonus term to which the team and player had orally agreed. Rather than proceed through the NFLPA's dispute resolution mechanism and appeal, Poston filed a lawsuit seeking to overturn the NFLPA's complaint and suspension. In his lawsuit, Poston alleged, among other things, that he was denied adequate due process in part because he did not have the opportunity to have his appeal heard by a neutral arbitrator.

In contrast to the other unions, the NFLPA has exhibited a greater willingness to amend its agent regulations to respond to emerging problems. In response to financial mismanagement by agents, the NFLPA imposed a requirement that agents obtain malpractice insurance beginning in 2005.[42] Also, the NFLPA has adopted what it calls the one-in-three rule. Under this rule, NFLPA certified agents who fail to negotiate at least one contract during a three-year period must reapply for certification. An intended consequence of the insurance and one-in-three requirements is a likely decrease in the number of NFLPA certified agents. In 2005, it was estimated that perhaps as many as 150 NFLPA certified agents may have been decertified as a result of the one-in-three rule.[43] It was subsequently estimated that the combined effect of the two rules was a reduction in the number of NFLPA certified agents by approximately 240.[44] In 2004, the NFLPA amended its regulations to require that agents list their runners.[45] This amendment was in response to revelations that agent David Dunn had agreed to pay an nfl.com writer, Pat Kirwan, 40 percent of the fee Dunn earned from negotiating the contract of former NFL number-one draft pick Carson Palmer.[46]

Whereas some support the NFLPA's actions in disciplining agents as demonstrating, unlike other players' associations, a willingness to aggressively enforce its agent regulations, others have reservations about the NFLPA's fairness. One commentator questions whether the NFLPA enforces its agent regulations in an unreasonable and arbitrary manner and whether accused agents are afforded sufficient due process, particularly as it relates to the ability to select a neutral arbitrator. To critics, the NFLPA's actions against Cornrich, Dunn, and Poston illustrate these concerns.[47]

In 2007, the NFLPA adopted regulations that focus on recruitment, discipline, and conflicts of interest. One rule prohibits suspended agents from directly or indirectly recruiting players during the period of their suspension.[48] This amendment responded to agent complaints that agent David Dunn, who was suspended for eighteen months in November 2006, recruited clients during his suspension. Responding to the complaints by college coaches that agents were placing the intercollegiate eligibility of student athletes in jeopardy and encouraging juniors to jump to the NFL before they were ready, the NFLPA in 2007 enacted a no-contact rule that prohibits agents from communicating with college football players prior to their senior year.[49] Also in 2007, the

NFLPA passed a new regulation requiring that agents disclose to players those coaches, including college coaches, the agents represent.[50]

Initially, a key flaw in the NFLPA system was that the union did not represent student athletes until they signed a professional contract.[51] Thus the relationship with the recent graduate, where the greatest problems were occurring, was not covered by the regulation. The NFLPA now asserts its authority over the interests of the rookie athlete as well.[52] This circumstance contrasts with the NBPA, in which student athletes drafted by the league have been considered to be members of the union since the creation of its agent regulatory rules.[53]

Interestingly, the MLBPA's primary goal is education as opposed to punishing the shady agents. According to Gene Orza, chief operating officer of the association, "we do not think that agents are bad. We believe players should have more information at their disposal when they go about choosing an agent."[54] The MLBPA system strives to make this information available.

Players' association certification obviously carries more force than the NCAA program did. The strength in the union certification programs lies in the ability of the players' associations to decertify or even to deny initial certification of an agent. The NCAA had no similar power. However, union regulations run the same risk as the NCAA system of "validating" an agent without a thorough evaluation. Some agents do not want to register. Orza notes that one attorney maintained, "I am not an agent, I am an attorney," and fought the registration requirement on that basis.

NFLPA Financial Adviser Regulations

In early 2002, the NFLPA became the first sports union to adopt regulations governing the financial advisers of its members. The *NFLPA Regulations and Code of Conduct Governing Registered Player Financial Advisors* represent the union's response to an increasing number of incidents in which football players have been victimized by financial advisers. The stated goal of the regulations is to promote "the integrity of those who represent NFL players in financial matters."[55] Financial advisers are requested to voluntarily participate in the program. According to the regulations, participants in the program will be afforded "unique access and information on NFL players, their benefits, and compensation structure."[56] Perhaps more important, participating financial advisers will be viewed as having received the union's blessing as "qualified" and "pre-selected financial advisers."[57] The regulations include disclaimer language stating that the NFLPA does not endorse any Registered Player Financial Advisor. Nevertheless, registered status will obviously provide a competitive advantage to participants over financial advisers who elect not to participate or whose application for registration is denied.

The regulations contain definitions of key terms such as "financial advisor," which is defined as "any person who, for compensation in any form, gives any financial advice with respect to a Player's funds, property and/or investments of any kind."[58] The regulations contain definitions of numerous other terms, including "alternative investment," "broker," "control," "financial planner," and "investment advisor."

In addition to the definitions section, the regulations include provisions that delineate the criteria for determining an individual's and a firm's eligibility for certification as a Registered Player Financial Advisor. Other provisions delineate minimum education, training, and experience requirements. Applicants must have graduated from an accredited four-year college or university.[59] An applicant must also have had a minimum of three years' relevant work experience and graduate training in his or her area of financial expertise (e.g., a master's degree in business administration) or a professional designation (e.g., certified financial planner). Establishing an area or areas of financial expertise is critical for the applicant, given that the regulations prohibit registered financial advisers from providing financial advice to NFL players outside of the area(s) of financial expertise for which the union has granted registration.[60]

Several bases exist pursuant to which an applicant can be deemed ineligible for union registration as a Player Financial Advisor. For example, if an area of financial expertise requires registration or licensure with governmental entities such as the SEC, the applicant who has not duly complied is ineligible for registration as a Player Financial Advisor.[61] Other grounds for ineligibility include conviction, guilty pleas, or indictments for a felony or misdemeanor offense under state or federal law relating to matters involving finances and breach of trust, such as investments, fraud, breach of fiduciary duty, bribery, and theft.[62] Relatedly, an applicant must not have had a final civil judgment rendered against him, her, or it (in the case of firms) for matters such as fraud, conversion, misappropriation of funds, professional malpractice, or breach of fiduciary duty.[63] An applicant is ineligible if he or she has been disciplined by a regulatory agency such as the Securities and Exchange Commission, a self-regulatory organization (SRO) such as the National Association of Securities Dealers, Inc. (NASD), or a professional association for matters that generally call into question the trust that can be placed in an applicant and his or her competence. Finally, an applicant will be deemed ineligible for failure or inability to pay debts and for seeking protection of bankruptcy laws within seven years prior to the time of application.

Affirmative obligations are imposed upon applicants who become registered financial advisers. Illustrations of such duties include periodically informing players of the investments made on the players' behalf and the economic status of such investments, periodically providing players with itemized statements of fees charged, and notifying of any change in the adviser's professional status.[64] Advisers must also retain for at least three years "promotional, solicitation, and advertising materials provided to any Player."[65]

The regulations create a fiduciary relationship between advisers and player clients. They provide that "[a] Registered Player Financial Advisor shall have the duty to act in the best interests of his/her Player-clients."[66] Consistent with this fiduciary obligation, advisers are required to assess the suitability of particular investments for their player clients by taking into consideration factors such as the player's assets and liquidity, risk tolerance, and short- and long-term liabilities.

Certain conduct is expressly prohibited by the regulations. Not surprisingly, "any device, scheme, or artifice to defraud a Player" is included in the prohibited conduct, as is "soliciting or obtaining any general power of attorney from a Player over his assets or investments."[67] Other prohibited conduct includes commingling the player's funds or property with the adviser's and, more generally, engaging in unlawful conduct or conduct involving breach of trust such as fraud, deceit, and dishonesty. Advisers are prohibited from engaging in any activity that "creates an actual or potential conflict of interest with the effective representation of a Player."[68]

The regulations provide arbitration and disciplinary procedures that constitute the exclusive methods for resolving disputes arising from denial of registration and violation of the regulations. The NFLPA's president or executive director is authorized to appoint a three-person panel to hear complaints regarding the denial of registration and to prosecute violations of the regulations. Appeals of adverse action proposed or taken by the panel can be made to an outside arbitrator to be selected by the NFLPA.

Financial advisers who wish to participate in the program must complete an application and pay a $1,500 fee. (In 2007, the annual fee for NFLPA certified contract advisers—agents—was $1,200 if an agent represented fewer than ten active players and $1,700 if an agent represented ten or more active players). The application requests information that presumably will allow the union to assess the qualifications and integrity of applicants. In addition, the applicant must be covered by a fidelity bonding and/or professional liability insurance.[69]

The NFLPA is currently engaged in litigation involving its Financial Advisory Program. In 2006, several current and former NFL players, including Steve Atwater and Ray Crockett, sued the NFLPA, alleging that it had negligently operated the program. They also sued the NFL, alleging that it had negligently performed background checks on certain financial advisers. The lawsuit grew out of the actions, previously discussed in Chapters 4 and 5, of Kirk Wright, who reportedly defrauded investors, including NFL players, of $115 million to $185 million. The plaintiffs alleged that in "reliance upon the NFL's and NFLPA's purported check and clearance of Wright and Nelson Bond, and the NFLPA's registration of them in the Financial Advisors Program, plaintiffs collectively invested approximately $20 million in a hedge fund managed by International Management Associates," the company with which Wright and Bond were principals.[70] The NFL and NFLPA sought to dismiss the players' complaint. In early March 2007, a federal district court denied their respective motions to dismiss and ruled that the lawsuit could proceed. Of particular interest in this regard was the court's refusal, in the early stages of the lawsuit, to dismiss plaintiffs' claims notwithstanding exculpatory language in the Financial Advisor Regulations stating that the NFLPA did not endorse any registered adviser and disclaimed responsibility and liability for the acts or omissions of registered financial advisers.

Association of Representatives of Professional Athletes

The agents themselves at one time had a set of self-regulating rules established through the Association of Representatives of Professional Athletes (ARPA).[71] This organization, composed of approximately 120 members at its peak, was a self-regulatory agency formed by agents to reform their industry. Membership in the organization was voluntary, as was compliance with the organization's rules. Although ARPA had its own code of ethics, there was no entity that mandated its enforcement. It received high praise from some circles; however, ARPA had virtually no power to implement its enforcement. The authors made several calls and it appears that ARPA is no longer in existence.

Conclusion

This chapter has provided an overview of private sector attempts to regulate agent conduct. An equally important and more widely discussed area is government regulation. The next chapter examines state and federal law attempts at legislation affecting the sports agent.

Chapter 11

The Laws

In a recruiting pitch to an athlete, Norby Walters said, "The normal sports agent . . . he's not gonna shake white America. I have been shaking those people for years in that music side of entertainment. Now it's time to shake 'em hard in the sports side of entertainment."[1] The "shaking" needs to come from the regulators of the sports agent industry. This chapter examines public attempts to regulate sports agents. In examining the problems that may restrict the effectiveness of existing public regulatory schemes, it looks at changes, such as the Uniform Athlete Agents Act, that may ameliorate certain of the impediments to effectively using existing laws to hold sports agents accountable to their clients and other persons and entities (the following chapter fully explores that act). It also considers the need for more rigorous enforcement of existing regulations and looks at the necessity for a uniform sports agent law.

With varying degrees of success, individual states attempted to arrest the athlete/agent problems for decades. This chapter briefly describes state legislative efforts and addresses the issues that arise out of such legislation. A uniform law that regulates athlete agents at the state level has been promulgated and adopted by the majority of state legislatures.[2] As discussed in Chapter 12, uniform legislation addresses some of the problems that imbue pre-uniform state agent acts.

Federal Regulation

Although sports topics tend to generate a great deal of public and political interest, federal legislative intervention into the sports realm is rare. Examples of such legislation include the Amateur Sports Act and the Curt Flood Act. Prior to 2004, no federal legislation had been promulgated that specifically addressed the athlete agent industry. Nevertheless, federal law played an important, albeit sporadic, role in regulating agents. As previously discussed in Chapter 4, federal mail fraud and tax statutes were used in the successful 2001 prosecution of Myron Piggie. Federal charges of mismanagement of funds, fraud, and racketeering were made in the Walters-Bloom trial. The prosecuting tool used in that trial was the Racketeer Influenced and Corrupt Organizations Act, commonly referred to as RICO,[3] which is especially noted for the broad range of factual contexts in which it has been asserted by prosecutors.

RICO was initially designed to attack organized crime and to stymie political corruption. Since its enactment in 1970, RICO's scope has expanded significantly beyond those factual contexts. Indeed, RICO's applicability to agent/athlete contracts surprised commentators and agents. Lonn Trost, then head of the sports department at the national law firm of Shea & Gould, testified at the Walters-Bloom trial that he had informed agents that signing student athletes to contracts before their eligibility expired did not violate any criminal statutes.[4] Walters, Bloom, and Trost all turned out to be incorrect.

RICO created three criminal offenses. If a party violates two or more from a list of approximately thirty criminal statutes over a period of ten years, he or she may be found guilty of acquiring, controlling, or operating an "enterprise" through "a pattern of racketeering activity." If the party is convicted, the penalty for the RICO violation alone is seizure and forfeiture of the assets from the illegal enterprise and a fine of up to $25,000. In addition, under RICO, not only can the government bring an action but also the civil provisions allow private citizens to bring actions and give them the right to recover three times their actual damages and reasonable attorneys' fees.

The most notorious case involving the application of the federal RICO statutes to sanction agents was the Norby Walters matter. In *U.S. v. Walters-Bloom*, criminal application of the RICO Act was deemed appropriate by the jury. In that case, the "pattern of racketeering" was the mail fraud perpetrated against the NCAA when the student athletes, paid by Walters and Bloom, had letters sent to the NCAA by their schools proclaiming that they were eligible to compete under NCAA rules when, in fact, they were not. *U.S. v. Walters-Bloom* also involved a reputed organized crime figure, Michael Franzese, who allegedly helped finance Walters and Bloom's venture into the sports agent business in exchange for a 25 percent share.[5] It does not seem, however, that Franzese's involvement was an essential element in the jury's determination. Thus, as is the case with many RICO actions to date, the organized-crime component need not be present; all that apparently must occur is for an agent to induce two athletes to violate an NCAA regulation and for those athletes to proclaim to their institutions and the NCAA that they are eligible.

As detailed in Chapter 5, the Summit Management case also provides an excellent illustration of the use of non-sports-specific federal laws to prosecute alleged wrongful conduct by those who represent athletes. The violations alleged in the federal grand jury's indictment against the principals of Summit Management Group arose from alleged schemes to perpetrate fraud on several of the company's athlete clients. Central to the government's case were allegations of mail fraud stemming from the alleged improper transfer of funds from athletes' banking accounts to Summit's account that ultimately wrongfully deprived the athletes of their property. The indictment also alleged that the principals of Summit violated federal statutes that criminalize money laundering and bank fraud.

Successful legal actions may also be asserted against student athletes who participate in the fraud as well. Minnesota Vikings wide receiver Cris Carter was fined $15,000 and ordered to perform 600 hours of community service for failing to cooperate with federal authorities when they were investigating Walters and Bloom. Carter failed to reveal that he had received a $5,000 signing incentive from agent David Lueddeke.[6]

Federal and state civil RICO actions have also been asserted by private parties seeking compensation for alleged improper conduct by persons involved in sports. Football player Vincent Clark sued his brokerage company, Robert W. Baird Co., Inc., and agent, Kenneth Fox. In addition to asserting fraud, breach of contract, and fiduciary duty claims, Clark asserted civil violations of RICO. As in *Walters-Bloom*, the alleged RICO violation revolved around allegations of mail fraud. Although the court in *Clark* acknowledged the applicability of civil RICO actions to this context, it concluded that the plaintiff had failed to plead facts sufficient to support a civil RICO action and granted the defendants' motion to dismiss the claim.[7] In a state civil RICO action, *Jones v. Childers*, the plaintiffs met with more success.[8] Looking to the United States Supreme Court's standards for guidance in determining whether defendants had engaged in conduct that amounted to a violation of Florida's state RICO statute, the Eleventh Circuit Court of Appeals held that "[t]he number of occasions on which Childers and TSI fraudulently induced the professional athletes to invest in a number of Israeli securities, the relationship between the fraud with respect to Jones and the fraud perpetrated against the other investors, the similarity of all victims—all professional athletes— and the similarity of the acts, taken collectively, demonstrate[d] a pattern of racketeering activity which constitute[d] proof of a RICO violation."[9]

Another source of federal regulatory activity is the federal Securities and Exchange Commission (SEC). The SEC has exerted regulatory authority in the athlete agent industry. This agency has "reprimanded" some of the larger sports management firms for violating existing investment advisory laws.[10] As discussed in Chapter 5, the agency initiated legal proceedings against several agents including John W. Gillette, Jr., Farrion Newton, Donald Lukens, and Dunyasha Yetts.

Prior to 2004, many commentators maintained that aggressive federal legislation providing appropriate sanctions would be the best way to deter agent misconduct. Commentators in search of a more direct federal vehicle to regulate athlete agents proposed various types of sports agent–specific legislation ranging from a federal version of state legislation to a model based on federal securities law. Federal legislation would certainly provide the uniformity that heretofore has been absent and go a long way toward resolving problems associated with a lack of uniformity—such as conflict of law issues and commerce clause problems. Lloyd Shefsky, former president of the Sports Lawyers Association (SLA) and a veteran of a three-year lobbying effort for sports agent legislation, cited three reasons for the lack of success in passing such legislation: "The first was it was not as important as current events like the arms race; second, the former jocks like [New Jersey Senator Bill] Bradley and [New York Representative Jack] Kemp did not want to be associated with sports; and third, and this is the best of all, they said, 'You want us to protect millionaires?'"[11]

These and other barriers to a federal solution were overcome in 2004, when the Sports Agent Responsibility and Trust Act (SPARTA) was enacted.[12] Modeled after the Uniform Athlete Agents Act, which is examined in Chapter 12, SPARTA is designed principally to protect colleges and universities and, to a lesser extent, student athletes from improper recruitment activities of agents. Its primary emphasis is to deter agents from recruiting student athletes through the use of incorrect inducements and the provision of misleading information. SPARTA includes provisions also intended to discourage student athletes from taking improper benefits from agents.

SPARTA delineates what constitutes illegal conduct by athlete agents. In addition to proscribing certain conduct, SPARTA imposes affirmative obligations on agents, including notice and disclosure requirements such as those imposed by the UAAA. Violations of SPARTA constitute deceptive trade practices acts under the Federal Trade Commission Act. The Federal Trade Commission (FTC) is granted authority to enforce SPARTA. In addition, state attorneys general are authorized to pursue civil actions in federal court if a violation of SPARTA adversely affects a state's residents.

Although it provides uniformity, SPARTA does not represent the far-reaching regulatory statute that advocates of federal legislation had sought. Even if SPARTA's scope were broader, it would not be a panacea for all the problems confronting the industry. There is clear evidence that in other professions in which legislation exists to control professional ethics (for example, securities brokers), fraud and unethical activities persist within the industry. Ivan Boesky and Michael Milken were both aware of the rules against insider trading, but because of the potential for huge profits, they took the risk of breaking the laws and getting caught.[13]

State Regulation

Two tiers of state regulation are potentially applicable to athlete agents. The first level consists of generally applicable civil and criminal laws that might apply to improprieties committed by agents in negotiating and drafting contracts, and improprieties that constitute violations of agents' fiduciary responsibilities to their athlete clients. The prosecution of Richard Sorkin under New York State criminal laws in 1977 is one of the earliest examples of the prosecution of a sports agent under generally applicable state laws. Later, in 1989, prosecutors in Florida filed fraud and conspiracy charges against a Florida sports management firm. Former Atlanta agent Jim Abernethy was found guilty under a state statute covering tampering with a sporting event as well as commercial bribery and violation of deceptive trade law. The trial of the sports agent who represented Kevin Porter, a former Auburn University football star, led to a successful prosecution under state law in an Alabama county circuit court.[14] That conviction, however, was later reversed on appeal. Florida and federal authorities have pursued actions against agent Tank Black.[15]

The second level consists of sports agent–specific statutes designed to regulate athlete agents. As of January 1, 2001, twenty-eight states had enacted agent-specific legislation.[16] Interestingly, the state of Washington had enacted agent legislation but repealed it in 1999.[17] Until the Uniform Athlete Agents Act (UAAA) is adopted in states with existing agent statutes, however, these statutes will remain the governing law. For example, Mississippi's agent statute was repealed in order to be replaced by the UAAA, which the state adopted effective July 1, 2001.[18] Other states that displaced existing agent-specific statutes with the UAAA include Alabama, Texas, Connecticut, and Arkansas. As of February 27, 2007, five states—California, Colorado, Iowa, Michigan, and Ohio—had existing non-UAAA agent-specific regulations. Due to the likelihood that most of the states with existing non-UAAA agent statutes and those without agent-specific statutes will adopt the Uniform Athlete Agents Act, the discussion that follows provides only an overview of agent statutes that preceded the UAAA.

Athlete Agent Statutes

As discussed in Chapter 10, NCAA rules and regulations that seek to protect the amateurism ideal have provided the major impetus for agent-specific regulation. Premised on the authority of state governments to protect the public interest, athlete agent legislation prior to the UAAA sought principally to protect the financial interests of universities and colleges that might be undermined when the relationships between agents and student athletes violated NCAA amateurism and agent-related provisions. For example, a successful football program at a public or private Division I college could potentially lose millions that might be derived from television and postseason competition if it were sanctioned by the NCAA due to improper conduct between an agent and a student athlete. A clear example of the financial harm caused by a student athlete's dealings with a sports agent involved the University of Alabama. The NCAA required the school to forfeit $253,477 for using two ineligible players in the 1987 NCAA basketball tournament.[19] The players were declared ineligible because of their dealings with sports agents. Many feel that schools should have to forfeit their funds or have players rendered ineligible because of interference by sports agents. This sentiment was captured, in part, in pre-UAAA agent statutes that granted an educational institution a statutory private cause of action to seek damages that reflected losses resulting from agent misconduct.[20] Marcus Camby's interactions with agents resulted in the deletion of the University of Massachusetts' record of performance in the 1996 postseason NCAA men's basketball tournament and its forefeiture of $151,617 because Camby was retroactively declared ineligible.[21] Similar sanctions were imposed on the University of Connecticut when two of its basketball players, Kirk King and Ricky Moore, received benefits from agents in violation of NCAA rules.[22]

Another interest that pre-UAAA agent statutes sought to protect was that of the student athlete who might unknowingly be drawn into committing violations of NCAA rules by athlete agents. The desire to protect these interests was expressly recognized in Alabama's pre-UAAA agent statute, which stated, "The Legislature finds that dishonest or unscrupulous practices by agents who solicit representation of student-athletes can cause significant harm to student-athletes and the academic institutions for which they play. It is the intent of the Legislature to protect the interests of student-athletes and academic institutions by regulating the activities of athlete agents."[23]

Although pre-UAAA athlete agent legislation varied among states, common characteristics emerged from these statutes.[24] For example, individuals were required to register, pay registration fees, and post surety bonds in order to act as agents. Certain of these statutes also required that agents notify educational institutions should an agent enter into a contract with a student athlete. Likewise, a student athlete was required to inform his institution if the athlete entered into an agent representation contract. Over two-thirds of pre-UAAA agent statutes required an agent to notify a student athlete of the consequences of violating the NCAA's agent regulations. Other common features of pre-UAAA legislation were the prohibition against postdated contracts and the imposition of a range of criminal, civil, and administrative sanctions on agents who engaged in prohibited conduct.

IMPACT OF AGENT STATUTES

The impact of pre-UAAA agent-specific legislation varied. Many sports agents, including prominent agents, ignored registration and certification requirements. One explanation for this situation is the pervasive lack of enforcement in some states. In 1989, San Francisco attorney Edward King maintained that "one of the most famous football agents in California has not registered as an agent."[25] Apathy toward the lack of registration by popular sports agents provided little incentive for the novice agent to seek certification.

An additional explanation for the lack of sports agent registration was the existence in many pre-UAAA agent statutes of language that completely or partially exempted attorneys licensed to practice from the provisions of the statute.[26] It should be noted that other statutes either provided no such exemption or included an attorney within the purview of agent statutes when he or she negotiated a contract on behalf of an athlete.[27] Requiring all athlete representatives to register, including licensed attorneys, would increase the number of registrants as well as the state's ability to enforce the provisions of the statute effectively.

At one time, the state of Texas seemed to take the most aggressive stance with respect to enforcement of its agent statute. In 1989, the state levied a $10,000 fine against an agent and a firm, each for violations of its agent law.[28] Former Heisman Trophy winner Johnny Rodgers and Total Economic Management of America, Inc. were accused of contacting 1989 Heisman Trophy winner Andre Ware of the University of Houston. In addition to the improper contact violation, the alleged violations included offering gifts, cash, and other inducements to Ware's mother.[29]

The $10,000 fine levied against Rodgers and his firm was surpassed a few years later. Agent Jeffrey Newport was fined $16,500 by the Texas Secretary of State.[30] He was also suspended from operating as a sports agent in Texas for two years. These penalties resulted from Newport's violation of provisions of the Texas athlete agent statute that prohibited agents from offering anything of value in attempting to procure athletes as clients. Newport provided a college football player with $5,100 in cash and other improper benefits, including $1,400 toward the purchase of a disability insurance policy.

During the 1990s, the state of Florida took an aggressive stance in enforcing its pre-UAAA agent regulation statute. In 1994, agent Nate Cebrun, who participated in making improper payments to a Florida State University football player, received thirty days in jail and was assessed $2,255 in fines after pleading no contest to the felony charge of refusing to register with the state as a sports agent.[31] Two other individuals who took part in making the improper payments were charged and sentenced for violating Florida's agent registration law statute.[32] In 1999, Florida state authorities charged agents Wesley Carroll and James Ferraro with having contact with a student athlete at the University of Miami, which violated Florida's athlete agent statute. Both agents settled the charges out of court.[33] Also in 1999, Florida authorities charged sports agent Sean Alfortish with funneling money to University of Florida football players in violation of Florida's agent law and practicing sports agency without a license.[34] Alfortish was sentenced to one year of unsupervised probation following a guilty plea to a misdemeanor charge of "attempting to conduct business in Florida without an agent's license."[35] He was also ordered to leave the state of Florida and reimburse the University of Florida's police department the $30,000 it had spent on its investigation of his activities.[36]

ACTION BY EDUCATIONAL INSTITUTIONS

Institutions of higher education may be the entities most harmed by sports agent improprieties. As discussed above, colleges and universities may receive stiff sanctions from the NCAA if a player is found to have a relationship with a sports agent in violation of NCAA rules. Because the NCAA has no direct contractual relationship with student athletes, it enforces its regulations by taking action against its member institutions. The NCAA's member institutions generally do not promulgate rules regarding sports agents. Doing so would be futile because, like the NCAA, educational institutions do not have the force of law to implement any regulations they might institute. Thus, institutions are left to rely on private causes of action such as the tort of interference with a contractual relationship. Such a theory would appear promising given that courts have overwhelmingly recognized the relationship between the student athlete and his or her college as contractual in nature.[37]

In 1995, the University of Southern California (USC) filed an unprecedented lawsuit seeking monetary damages against an athlete agent.[38] USC's suit alleged that agent Robert Caron gave money and other benefits to three of the school's football players. This conduct allegedly violated California's agent statute, which at the time required an agent to be registered and post a $25,000 surety bond.[39] USC also alleged that Caron interfered with the university's contracts with its student athletes by inducing them to engage in conduct that violated NCAA rules. Caron, who denied USC's allegations, agreed to pay the school $50,000 and to a permanent injunction that prohibited him from conferring benefits to amateur USC athletes.[40]

Certain universities have taken a more proactive approach by becoming involved in the agent selection process. Some have ad hoc systems whereby coaches or administrators assist student athletes in selecting an agent. Some institutions, such as Temple University, have developed professional sports advisory panels. As they relate to agents, these NCAA-authorized advisory panels are permitted to "assist the student-athlete in the selection of an agent by participating with the student-athlete in interviews of agents, by reviewing written information player agents send to the student-athlete and by having direct communications with those individuals who can comment about the abilities of an agent (e.g., other agents, a professional league's players' association); and . . . visit with player agents or representatives of professional athletics teams to assist the student-athlete in determining his or her market value (e.g., potential salary, draft status)."[41] Although the effectiveness of such panels in ending the corruption of agents in college sports is limited, they hold the potential to provide valuable information to student athletes regarding agents' qualifications.[42]

Problems with Pre-UAAA Athlete Agent Legislation

Several significant issues—jurisdiction, vagueness, commerce clause, freedom of speech, conflicts of interest, and excessive fees—impacted the legal viability of many pre-UAAA athlete agent statutes. Certain other weaknesses also characterized many of these statutes.

JURISDICTION

The first major problem that confronted pre-UAAA athlete agent statutes related to the jurisdictional authority of states to apply and enforce their laws. This issue arose from the national character of college athletics. For example, may California enforce its registration requirements against an Ohio resident who attempts to represent a student athlete from a California school? Should Ohio's athlete agent law govern the activities of this same agent while he or she "recruits" a client in California? Can a state's athlete agent law be enforced against an agent who has no contact with that state? Two commentators provide the following illustration of Ohio's statute (the described statute remains in effect because, as of July 2007, Ohio had not replaced its existing agent statute with the UAAA).

The Ohio statute provides that "a court may exercise personal jurisdiction over the athlete agent who resides or engages in business outside [Ohio] as to a cause of action arising from the athlete agent entering into an agent contract with a student-athlete *outside* [Ohio] without complying with section 4771.02 of the Revised Code." A reading of this one sentence from Ohio's statute demonstrates its obvious unconstitutional stretch of jurisdictional power, attempting to reach athlete agents who have had absolutely no contact with the forum state (i.e., Ohio).[43]

The foregoing questions and illustrations point to a crucial issue: whether and to what extent a state possesses personal jurisdiction over an athlete agent who is not a resident of that state. Thus far, courts have not provided answers to this question.

VAGUENESS

Non-UAAA athlete agent statutes were criticized for failing to adequately define the conduct that would result in a violation of the statutes. Constitutional law dictates that statutes that suffer from this flaw are unenforceable due to the vagueness doctrine. The notion that underlies the vagueness doctrine is that "[v]ague laws serve as a trap for innocent people by failing to provide them with fair warning. In other words: statutes that are insufficiently clear are void for three reasons: (1) to avoid punishing people for behavior that they could not have known was illegal; (2) to avoid subjective enforcement of the laws based on 'arbitrary and discriminatory enforcement' by government officers; and (3) to avoid any chilling effect on the exercise of First Amendment freedoms."[44] Several provisions of pre-UAAA athlete agent statutes were viewed as opening the door for an agent to invoke the vagueness doctrine as a defense. These include unclear definitions (for example, of "athlete agent" and "athlete") and provisions that failed to specifically define prohibited conduct.[45]

COMMERCE CLAUSE

Another problem with pre-UAAA agent-specific regulations was the possibility that the commerce clause of the United States Constitution might bar their enforcement.[46] The commerce clause prohibits states from regulating affairs of interstate commerce—that is, issues that affect more than one state. Railroads and airlines are two common examples of entities that are regulated by the federal government rather than by individual states. Rather than allowing states to regulate what types of railroad car coupling must be used and thus run the risk of having to change couplings each time a state border is passed, the federal government establishes guidelines for all interstate commerce.

There is precedent for the successful assertion of the commerce clause in barring state regulation of athlete agents based upon judicial decisions involving other sports issues. In *City of Oakland v. Oakland Raiders*, the city of Oakland, California, was barred by the courts from exercising eminent domain rights over a sports franchise because such an action would interfere with interstate commerce.[47] That case was one of several pieces of litigation in the saga of the Raiders NFL franchise in its move from Oakland to Los Angeles. The city of Oakland instituted an action that sought to "condemn" the sports franchise, much in the way municipalities condemn and take homes and other property to construct freeways, parks, or airports. The taking of a sports franchise under this eminent domain principle was a novel idea that looked like it might prove to be successful. However, instead of reaching its decision on the facts of the case—whether this was the type of property a city could condemn and keep in the city for the public interest—the court ruled that the commerce clause barred the city from taking such an action. The court reasoned that the sport is an interstate affair and that only the federal government should be able to regulate those activities. It was believed that a similar defense could be asserted by an athlete agent if a state attempted to prosecute him or her under an athlete agent statute.

FREEDOM OF SPEECH

Pre-UAAA athlete agent statutes were also criticized for potentially violating the First Amendment. Provisions that were subjected to this criticism included those that prohibited contact (including the dissemination of written information) without first notifying certain individuals, such as a university's athletic director. The argument was made that no law should interfere with the constitutional right to free speech.

CONFLICTS OF INTEREST AND EXCESSIVE FEES

Two further areas that any new statute should address are the conflict of interest and excessive fee issues. These matters are discussed in detail in Chapters 5 and 6. Attorneys who represent athletes must conform to a canon of ethics that guards against trying to represent the interests of two clients that might conflict without disclosing the conflict to the respective clients. The scenarios in Chapter 2 wherein agents represent conflicting interests would properly have to be disclosed by attorneys to their clients. Nonattorneys have no similar requirement, absent legislation. Although some states are mindful of this, others have neglected to include an appropriate provision.

Another concern about pre-UAAA state regulations were the excessive fees that sports agents had to pay to comply with registration in a number of states in which they might conduct business. Not only did agents have to pay registration fees in these states but also many states required them to post a bond. If all fifty states had a statute requiring this, the cost of entering the sports agent business could be tens of thousands of dollars. Sports agent Craig Fenech maintained that he could not find an entity that would provide him with a bond for his business. If his experience were typical, such requirements would effectively restrict the number of people to a select category of the well financed. Those excluded would undoubtedly include many talented and conscientious individuals; those admitted might be able to raise enough money for fees but might not make as meaningful a contribution. Moreover, the need for thousands of dollars might in itself be a corrupting factor for agents without enough money who would have to seek financial support from other backers. These "silent partners" might be of questionable integrity.

Vigorous Enforcement of Existing Laws?

That non-sports-agent-specific regulations can be used effectively is illustrated by the pursuit of Tank Black and of Norby Walters and Lloyd Bloom, as well as the state prosecutions of the same parties and, earlier, of Richard Sorkin. As discussed in detail in Chapter 5, fraud or income mismanagement issues can be attacked by utilizing these laws.

But conviction is not necessarily deterrence. In one case, even after conviction, all charges against agent Norby Walters in Alabama were dropped when he paid the University of Alabama a settlement of $200,000.[48] Similarly, Walters's associate Lloyd Bloom received a sentence that required him to serve one week of a one-year sentence washing state trooper cars while staying at the hotel of his choice.[49] Finally, all charges against agent Jim Abernethy were thrown out at the appellate level.[50] The sentences against Bloom and Walters in their federal trial were overturned as well.

Conclusion

The focus of sports agent regulation should be on enforcing these existing laws and not on incorporating outdated concepts of amateurism into new regulations. The emphasis should be on illegal activities that occur while agents recruit athletes and on any violations once an agreement is entered into. These are the types of activities, as with any industry, that public entities should expend their limited resources on, not in seeking to regulate activities that harm no one. Law enforcement should focus on the issues addressed in the *Sorkin, Abernethy*, and *Walters and Bloom* cases. Individuals with private causes of action must assert their rights as well. For some activities, a private civil suit may be the only manner of regulating the activity. The next chapter focuses on the Uniform Athlete Agents Act.

Chapter 12

A Uniform Approach
The Uniform Athlete Agents Act

The Process of Developing a Uniform Athlete Agents Act

Somewhat anticlimactically, a uniform law regulating sports agents became official in the first year of the new millennium. The full impact of the uniform law is still not yet clear. This chapter describes the process undertaken to develop the Uniform Athlete Agents Act, discusses the basic elements of the final product, and provides some analysis of its likely long-term impact.

On August 3, 2000, the National Conference of Commissioners on Uniform State Law (NCCUSL) completed a process begun in 1996 when it passed the long-awaited Uniform Athlete Agents Act (UAAA).[1] The press release issued by NCCUSL identified the purpose of the act as protecting the interests of student athletes and academic institutions by regulating the activities of athlete agents. The promulgation of uniform laws such as the UAAA is not novel.[2] Three familiar examples of the 250 uniform laws drafted by NCCUSL are the Model Penal Code, the Uniform Probate Code, and the Uniform Commercial Code. Before examining the UAAA, we briefly discuss NCCUSL and its function.[3]

The primary function of the NCCUSL is to promote "uniformity in state law on all subjects where uniformity is desirable and practicable."[4] (This purpose certainly brings to mind the sports agent–related dilemmas discussed herein.) The NCCUSL consists of 340 commissioners who are appointed by the governors of the 50 states, the District of Columbia, and Puerto Rico. The process by which commissioners are appointed differs from state to state;[5] however, commissioners most typically are "lawyers, judges, legislators and law school professors."[6]

The process that led to promulgation of the UAAA began when NCCUSL's Committee on Scope and Program, by a narrow three-to-two vote, recommended to the organization's Executive Committee that a drafting committee be established to "draft an act to govern the relationship among sports agents, student athletes and educational institutions."[7] The Executive Committee assigned the UAAA to the Study

Committee on Athlete Agents, which it created in 1996.[8] The purpose of the Study Committee was articulated as follows: "The committee was created to study the problem of sports agents contacting college athletes prematurely and affecting their eligibility, in order to determine whether a uniform act should and could be created consistent with National Conference policy, and if so, whether outside funding would be available for the drafting effort."[9]

Thus, early on, the focus of the uniform legislation was on issues relating to recruitment, not sports agent quality control. In July 1996, NCCUSL's Executive Committee approved the creation of a Drafting Committee by a narrow six-to-five vote. The close vote was a manifestation of low support for the proposed act due to "a heavy Conference agenda and concern that drafting a Uniform Athlete Agents Act would have less impact on a national basis than many other topics on the agenda or to be proposed."[10] Following the creation of the Drafting Committee, a search to find funding for the project was successful when the NCAA agreed to "allocate $50,000 for the drafting of an act relating to sports agents."[11] NCAA support seems appropriate considering the legislation's narrow focus on sports agents' recruitment of student athletes. This is a prime concern of the NCAA, and not as urgent a concern for other stakeholders in sports, including the professional leagues and unions. Securing funding and "including the interests of student-athletes in the drafting process" were conditions imposed by the Executive Committee when it approved the establishment of a Drafting Committee.[12] After funding was obtained, the Drafting Committee proceeded with the development of the UAAA.

At the end of a three-year drafting process—which allowed comments by various interested parties including athlete agents; coaches; individuals responsible for administering existing acts; representatives of the players' associations of the NFL, the NHL, and Major League Baseball; and the NCAA—NCCUSL approved the UAAA during its annual meeting on August 3, 2000.[13] Once a uniform act is passed by the conference and endorsed by the American Bar Association, NCCUSL urges state legislatures to adopt the proposed uniform act.

Although a state legislature may adopt a uniform act as proposed by NCCUSL, it may also vary the provisions of the act. As a result, absolute uniformity may not exist even if all fifty states adopt a particular uniform act. In reality, however, a lack of uniformity may not present a significant problem. A clear majority of the states that have adopted the UAAA have done so without making any substantively significant variations to it.

A final note is that a uniform act developed by NCCUSL does not displace all existing law that might be relevant to the subject matter of the uniform act. For example, principles of law and equity will supplement the provisions of the UAAA. Consequently, legal principles such as fraud, intentional interference with contractual relations, and embezzlement remain readily available tools for addressing agent misconduct.

THE UNIFORM ATHLETE AGENTS ACT

The UAAA was perceived as the means of resolving problems caused by differences among individual state athlete agent statutes. The *Prefatory Note* to the UAAA identifies certain problems resulting from a lack of uniformity and indirectly articulates the rationale for the UAAA:

> At least twenty-eight States have enacted legislation regulating athlete or sports agents. The statutes differ greatly. About two-thirds of the statutes impose registration requirements. There are substantial differences in the registration procedures, disclosure required, and requirements relating to record maintenance, reporting, renewal, notice, warning and security. The term of the registration is one year in thirteen States, two years in four States, and two States do not specify a term. Most States require notification to States or educational institutions and athletes of certain matters, but the matters vary widely. Conscientious agents operating in more than a single State must have nightmares caused by the lack of uniformity in the existing statutes, the difficulty in compliance and the severity of penalties which may be imposed for violations.[14]

In attempting to maintain the ability to address the problems that nonuniform state legislation sought to regulate, the NCCUSL included within the UAAA many of the key provisions of existing state athlete agent legislation. For example, the UAAA adopts the position of most statutes by requiring registration of athlete agents.[15] Other key provisions include the following:

1. *Definitions*: The act provides definitions of key terms such as "agency contract," "athlete agent," and "student athlete." For example, athlete agent is defined to mean "an individual who enters into an agency contract with a student-athlete or, directly or indirectly, recruits or solicits a student-athlete to enter into an agency contract."[16] The comment to Section 2 of the UAAA specifically identifies "runners" as falling within the definition of an athlete agent. The comment also points out that corporations are not defined as persons and are not required to register, but individuals working within corporations will be required to register. Finally, attorneys are not excluded from the act if they perform the services of an athlete agent.
2. *Registration*: Agents are required to register before they initiate contact with a student athlete if the purpose of the contact is to

induce a student athlete to sign an agency contract. The UAAA further provides that "if the student-athlete initiates contact with an athlete agent, the athlete agent must apply for registration within seven days after commencing any effort to induce the student-athlete to enter into an agency contract."[17]

"Athlete agents are also required to make specific disclosure as a part of their application for registration."[18] Applications, which are deemed public records, require disclosure, inter alia, of a description of formal training as an athlete agent; practical experience as an agent; educational background relevant to athlete agent services; references; the name of each person for whom the applicant acted as an agent during the five years prior to submission of the application; criminal convictions involving acts of moral turpitude and felonies; administrative or judicial determinations regarding fraudulent acts; any conduct of the applicant that led to a sanction imposed on a student athlete; and any denial, suspension, or revocation of a registration or licensure to act as an athlete agent.[19] State authorities responsible for registration decisions are directed to a list of factors to "consider in determining whether to issue a certificate of registration or suspend, revoke or refuse to renew a registration."[20]

Consistent with state athlete agent legislation that preceded the act, it does not develop minimum educational or certification requirements for athlete agents. It was believed that such a task is best left to players' associations.[21]

Finally, the act allows for each state to determine the amount of registration and renewal fees.[22] The comment to the relevant section, however, urges states to adopt reasonable fee structures to avoid discouraging compliance. It adds that "the wide range of registration fees imposed by states with existing athlete agent laws has likely contributed to low registration totals in many jurisdictions."[23]

3. *Reciprocity of Registration*: The Secretary of State of the state in which an applicant has submitted an application is required to grant reciprocity of registration if the applicant is licensed in another state. The applicant may submit the application and certificate of registration from the other state in which the applicant is registered if certain conditions are met.[24]

4. *Void Contracts*: Section 4(c) provides that any agency contract made in derogation of the registration requirements set forth in the Section is deemed void and the athlete agent is required to "return any consideration received under the contract."[25]

5. *Contract Terms*: The substantive content of agency contracts is also regulated by the act, which specifies terms that must be included

in such contracts.[26] Required terms include provisions relating to the method for calculating the fee to be paid by the student athlete, a warning to the student athlete that signing the contract will result in a loss of any remaining intercollegiate athletic eligibility,[27] and notice that the contract can be canceled within fourteen days after the student athlete signs it.[28]

6. *Notification Requirements*: As was true of some pre-UAAA state athlete agent laws, the act imposes obligations on agents and student athletes to notify educational institutions after an agency contract has been consummated.[29] In this regard, athlete agents and student athletes are required to notify the athletic director of the educational institution in which the student athlete is enrolled that they have entered into an agency contract. Notice must be given within seventy-two hours after entering into an agency contract or before the next scheduled athletic event, whichever occurs first.[30]

7. *Record Keeping*: Athlete agents must maintain certain records for a minimum of five years.[31] Records include those relating to identities of individuals represented by the athlete agent and the costs incurred by the athlete agent in soliciting and recruiting a student athlete to enter into an agency contract.[32]

8. *Prohibited Conduct*: The act specifies improper conduct by agents. Prohibited conduct includes furnishing anything of value to a student athlete as an inducement to sign an agency contract, failing to register as required by the act, and intentionally initiating conduct with a student athlete while unregistered.[33]

9. *Criminal Penalties*: The act provides that an athlete agent who engages in the conduct prohibited by Section 14 of the UAAA may be guilty of a misdemeanor or a felony. Each state is left to determine the extent of criminal penalties for violations of the act.[34]

10. *Civil Penalties*: With respect to civil penalties, the act grants colleges and universities civil remedies against both athlete agents and former student athletes for damages resulting from a violation of the act.[35] Even though institutions are granted a right to proceed against a student athlete, the comment to Section 16 recognizes that this is likely to occur in only the most egregious cases.

It is assumed that educational institutions will be very reluctant to bring an action against a former student athlete. Public opinion and the desire to be successful in future recruiting of athletes should cause educational institutions to carefully consider whether to exercise the right established by subsection (a) in most situations. There are, however, known instances of extremely egregious conduct by student-athletes who receive lucrative professional contracts that caused serious damage to educational institutions.

Subsection (a) keeps open the possibility of a civil action against those individuals.[36]

11. *Administrative Penalty*: The Secretary of State of each state may assess a penalty against an athlete agent not to exceed $25,000 for violations of the act.[37]

Conclusion

The UAAA was drafted and promulgated without attempting to tackle issues beyond the recruitment of athletes by agents at the preprofessional level. Without question, had NCCUSL attempted to grapple with the full range of concerns beyond recruitment that negatively impact the sports agent business (for example, agent competency, conflicts of interest, fraud, and solicitation), the ensuing controversy would have delayed or perhaps even precluded the promulgation of the act. Notwithstanding the limitations of its mission, the UAAA "embodies most of the principles of the 'aggressive' sports legislation already in existence" in that it adopts the approach of existing statutes with the broadest scope and jurisdictional reach.[38]

The UAAA provides a foundational basis for uniformity. Drawing from a complex and confusing web of existing state legislation, the UAAA standardizes registration, notice, and disclosure requirements. Standardization of these and other requirements provides a level of uniformity that hopefully will encourage agents to comply with the law in each state without incurring financial hardship and without having to understand the often confusing matrix of laws that currently exist. Thus the UAAA's uniform registration and reciprocity provisions are key in effectuating the UAAA's implicit goal of encouraging voluntary agent compliance with its requirements.[39]

NCCUSL seeks to deliver two additional messages by virtue of its approach. The first is that quality control is someone else's responsibility. That someone else is the respective players' union for each league. The other regulator will be the market: as "bad" agents are exposed, prospective customers will get the word from disgruntled customers. The other message is that existing civil law concepts and criminal legislation are sufficient to address agent misconduct that adversely affects the interests of their athlete clients. All that has been lacking is rigorous enforcement.

The first UAAA-based indictment was filed in Louisiana. On October 13, 2006, a grand jury in Baton Rouge, Louisiana, charged Charles Taplin with two counts of violating Louisiana's athlete agent statute, which is the UAAA. Taplin allegedly violated the UAAA's registration and notification provisions when he sent text messages to two Louisiana

State University (LSU) football players on behalf of an agent. At the time, Taplin was not a registered agent and allegedly failed to notify LSU within seven days of contacting the players.[40] In the process of investigating Taplin, information was allegedly uncovered that led to the arrest of Travelle Gaines, who at the time was an assistant strength coach at LSU. Gaines was booked on a felony count of engaging in activities prohibited by Louisiana's UAAA. Gaines allegedly invited players to his home where they came into contact with a California-based agent, C. J. Laboy.[41] Gaines's attorney denied that his client had done anything illegal.

The UAAA and SPARTA have been applauded and criticized.

Critics assert the legislation protects the NCAA's and colleges' interests more than those of student-athletes. Others assert that the statutes fall short of providing the types of sanctions and penalities that will deter agents from engaging in improper conduct. . . . Others argue that the UAAA and SPARTA fall short in not providing student-athletes with a cause of action for harm caused to them by the conduct of agents. . . . The statutes have been viewed as erecting barriers to entry that will advantage agents in larger firms and/or those agents with substantial numbers of clients. In this regard, the UAAA has been criticized as detrimental to independent agents who, notwithstanding cross-registration, must still pay registration fees in any state in which they plan to solicit and sign athlete-clients. . . . Finally, the legislation has been characterized as a band-aid that fails to get to the root cause of the problems in the agent industry—a system of entitlement that corrupts athletes from the time that they are in their early teenage years.

On the other hand, the UAAA and SPARTA have been applauded as representing steps in the right direction toward attempting to level the playing field with respect to agent competition for clients. The statutes' disclosure requirements have been commended for providing information that assists athletes and their families in making informed decisions. In response to those critics who assert that the UAAA does not go far enough, proponents point out that the UAAA was not designed to address every problem confronting the agent industry. Proponents of the statutes also assert that the problems in the industry are as much about greed and morality as anything else. Ultimately, as morality cannot be legislated, mechanisms must be implemented that have some deterrent effect and the UAAA and SPARTA represent such mechanisms.[42]

The UAAA is an important step forward. At a minimum, "the act will establish uniformity and provide for reciprocity among the States adopting it."[43] And while the UAAA or any other legislation is incapable of eradicating all of the problems associated with athlete agents, it will make compliance easier and encourage compliance by providing for reciprocal registration and renewal.[44] The UAAA goes a long way in addressing many of the operational issues that confront the athlete agent who is attempting to comply with the law of each individual state. Uniformity makes it easier for those agents who desire to comply to do so. Note two commentators, "The UAAA provides some welcomed relief in that, as a uniform law, it is intended for adoption in all states so that consistent obligations and results can be achieved in any state in which an athlete agent conducts business. Further, its provisions, with . . . [a] few exceptions . . . serve the states well by being relatively straightforward and uncluttered. However, to accept the UAAA as a good thing for states to adopt, one must first believe that athlete agents should be regulated in the first place."[45] As agent Bill Strickland maintains, "conceptually, it is a step in the right direction."

The UAAA and SPARTA represent the statutory layers of a web of complementary mechanisms that attempt to address specific problems in the athlete agent industry. The others layers include non-agent-specific federal and state statutes, players' associations' agent regulations, NCAA regulations, and common law principles (e.g., breach of contract and fraud). One critical factor to the effectiveness of the UAAA and SPARTA layers of agent regulatory strategies may lie in the willingness of the states and the FTC to devote the resources required to aggressively implement the statutes' provisions. Another key variable was described as follows:

Agents profess that they want a level playing field. Similarly, athletes and their families claim that they do not want to be bothered by overly aggressive sports agents. Yet athletes remain conspicuously silent when called upon to participate in the enforcement processes intended to prevent and provide relief from improper agent behavior. In short, the success of agent legislation in ameliorating the industry's problems will depend to a large extent on the willlingness of the two principal actors in the agent industry—agents and players—to play an active role in these regulatory schemes.[46]

Even with a uniform law in place, wrongdoing will continue. After the long wait for a uniform attempt to deal with sports agent issues, it took the UAAA and SPARTA to crystallize the obvious—that there is no panacea.

Chapter 13
Conclusion
The Absence of a Panacea

This book has presented an overview of the background and the current state of the sports agent business along with the legal principles that impact the industry. In addition, it has touched on efforts undertaken by diverse parties to address the problems that confront the business. For example, the discussion in Chapter 12 of the Uniform Athlete Agents Act illustrates the efforts made by lawmakers to reduce certain aspects of corruption in the industry. In addition, those who control and manage college sports are focused on reforms that are intended not only to ameliorate inequities between student athletes and their institutions but also to remove incentives for agents to engage in dishonest, incompetent, and other forms of inappropriate conduct.

Although progress has been made, much work remains to be done in attempting to stymie corrupt practices by athlete agents. Thus, efforts must first and foremost be aimed at reducing corruption. In addition, reforms should increase access to information about agents by those most likely, directly or indirectly, to be impacted by agent corruption—athletes, colleges and universities, players' unions, and professional sports leagues. A constructive role can be played by each of the principal players most likely to feel the impact of agent irregularities. Finally, reform-minded efforts should be directed toward providing mechanisms to afford relief to victims of agent corruption and to discourage agent conduct that results in unscrupulous behavior.

Athlete Agent Regulations

The uniform act is a positive development in the evolution of the athlete agent industry in that it achieves uniformity. Yet the focus of the Uniform Athlete Agents Act and other existing state athlete agent laws must be broadened if the athlete agent industry is to be policed properly. Athlete agent acts, including the Uniform Athlete Agents Act, are limited in scope; emphasis is placed on regulating agent conduct that may result in the NCAA taking adverse action against colleges and universities. Protecting the interests of these institutions and tangentially the interests of student athletes is laudable. However, this singularity of focus reveals a major shortcoming of such legislation.

As is true of other professionals such as lawyers and architects, if agents are not qualified, they should not be allowed to fully participate in the industry. Moreover, if agents engage in conduct or produce results that depart from a reasonable level of competence, their right to practice should be suspended or terminated. In short, careful consideration should be given to broadening the scope of regulation of the Uniform Athlete Agents Act (and other state athlete agent laws) so as to incorporate provisions aimed at weeding out incompetent agents. Perhaps the act could establish minimum standards of agent competency. Consequently, a prospective agent who fails to meet the standard cannot become licensed as an agent; an agent whose conduct falls below acceptable standards of competence loses the right to participate in the industry.

Continuing Reform of College Athletics

We must face the reality that some people will cheat wherever an economic incentive exists for them to do so. In this regard, the future of the sports agent industry, and particularly its regulation, is closely tied to reforms that occur in college sports, a system that still leaves room within which unscrupulous individuals operate.

The relationships in college sports that create incentives for agents to cheat require restructuring. One way to reduce cheating by agents is to lessen the attractiveness of the improper benefits agents offer to student athletes. Several proposals have been suggested that might indirectly serve as vehicles for accomplishing this objective. These proposals, which seek to balance the inequities that exist in the student athlete/ university relationship by providing compensation to athletes, were recently summarized as follows: "There have been a number of models that have been suggested as means of compensating student-athletes in Division I-A men's football and basketball, in response to concerns regarding inequitable treatment of student-athletes at that level. These various models are largely of four types: (1) revenue-sharing; (2) instituting a professional division within the intercollegiate system; (3) a scholarship plus stipend approach; and (4) the reform approach taken by the NCAA."[1] After providing this summary of reform initiatives, professors Rodney Smith and Robert Walker suggest a fifth model that combines additional grants-in-aid to student athletes with incentives and disincentives, depending on an intercollegiate athletic program's success or lack thereof in graduating its student athletes, and economic incentives for student athletes to graduate within six years.[2]

Let us examine how one of the foregoing proposals might indirectly reduce incentives for agents to engage in improper conduct. Some analysts argue that the time is right for colleges and universities to pay student athletes engaged in big-time intercollegiate athletics a stipend in addition to the scholarships that they currently are permitted to receive. The logical entities to provide these increased funds are, first, the member institutions and, if that is not financially feasible, then the NCAA via a centrally created pool of funds.

The justifications for increased compensation are fairly simplistic. First, from an economic standpoint, should not labor receive a fair share of the contribution it makes to the athletic enterprise? As was set forth by two commentators:

> Institutions have essentially acknowledged the potential profitability of Division I-A men's basketball and football. Salaries for coaches are the largest single expense at the Division I-A level, whereas grants-in-aid (scholarships for student-athletes) are the major expense at all other levels. Head coaches in Division I-A men's basketball and football are often paid more than $1,000,000 per year in personal income from all sources. . . .
>
> Given that student-athletes at this level do not share in the revenues generated by "big-time" men's basketball and football in the same unique manner as the NCAA, conferences, institutions, coaches and administrators, it is not surprising that claims of exploitation and inequitable treatment have arisen.[3]

Second, many of these student athletes actually need additional compensation either for themselves or, in some instances, for their families. At a minimum, the additional amount the student athlete receives should be equal to an amount that brings the spending money available to the student athlete up to that available to the university's average student. If profits are available, is there a better place for them to go? If the effect of a modest stipend is a reduction in unscrupulous payments by others, then all the better for collegiate sports.

The amateurism reforms that the NCAA is exploring are not overly dramatic, but they do strive to address the realities of the day. The dominant belief among NCAA reformers at this point seems to be that receipt of compensation prior to enrollment at an NCAA institution is not the evil to be conquered. The current NCAA focus is on advantages that may be gained by an individual athlete from a competitive standpoint. The concern is in making sure that an individual athlete does not gain a competitive advantage through the quality of athletic competition prior to enrollment. The competitive advantage, the reformers have assessed, should be addressed by reducing the years of NCAA eligibility proportionally with the years spent participating as a professional prior to enrollment.[4]

Cultural and legal impediments stand in the way of adopting any form of compensating student athletes. Included among the practical legal variables that might thwart such a proposal are Title IX, antitrust (if the NCAA imposed a salary cap on or "fixed" the amount of the stipend), tax, and workers' compensation issues.[5] Assuming that these legal obstacles can be traversed, the emphasis on the amateurism principle in the NCAA regulatory system and in the mind-set of the public represents a key impediment. Yet the possibility of paying a stipend to student athletes in certain sports should not offend American sensibilities. As discussed in Chapter 9, the Greek model of athletics allowed athletes to receive compensation.

The granting of stipends will have not only principled opposition but also opposition from those who will merely point to the bottom line.[6] Not all institutions are financially prosperous, of course; some lose money. This fact must be borne in mind in any analysis of increased compensation to the student athlete. Some institutions individually may not be able to foot the bill to provide the student athlete with more funds. A reallocation of the entire NCAA budget might remedy that problem.

Questions also arise concerning a stipend's impact on gender equity in college sports and on nonrevenue-generating sports.[7] Any resources used to provide greater compensation to presumably revenue-producing athletes would reduce the availability of funding for the nonrevenue sports. Legal challenges would likely arise if payments were to run afoul of Title IX. The goal of Title IX is so important that any impact it would have on compensation to revenue-generating athletes is just part of the price that must be paid to bring about equity for women in collegiate sports. With all of this in mind, one coach noted: "I agree it [payment of stipends] would be wonderful if it could be done, but when you're looking at the number of athletic departments that are running in the red already and the fact that if you are going to do it for revenue-producing sports—football and basketball—you are going to have to do it for a similar number of female athletes . . . I just don't think it's feasible."[8] Such restrictions dampen the enthusiasm for paying stipends to student athletes. Nevertheless, paying stipends at a modest level should be more fully explored.[9]

Related to the idea of allowing student athletes to receive stipends is permitting them to receive endorsement income. This proposal seems more problematic, not because athletes would receive income but because the sports agent may begin to play an integral role in the athletes' career at a stage that would, again, encourage cheating. It is difficult to imagine a system that would allow an athlete to work with an agent in a financial transaction as a freshman or sophomore without the agent's beginning to utilize the tactics that have been prevalent near the end of the student athlete's career.

But if the receipt of cash for endorsements is not a problem in itself, should student athletes be able to negotiate endorsement contracts on their own? Can an athlete endorse a local automobile dealership if the owner is a booster or alumnus? What happens if the amount received is disproportionate to what is generally perceived as reasonable for such an endorsement? A solution that has some merit is allowing the endorsement of specific products, such as athletic shoes. These companies would not have an independent incentive, as a booster does, to pay more than the athlete's actual market value. Such endorsements would allow the athlete to receive additional revenues from a natural market source. They would also deal with the fairness issue of coaches receiving shoe endorsement income.

Another income-related suggestion is allowing student athletes to take out loans tied to their athletic potential. Such loans go beyond the loans currently allowed for disability insurance and the like. For these loans, the professional leagues, the individual member institutions, and the NCAA are the logical sources. Although none of the possible funding parties is in the banking business, the investment may prove to be advantageous in the long run. In addition to removing the incentive to take money from an agent, a loan provides an incentive for the athlete to stay in school. Critics of this route maintain that the loans could not be made large enough to compete with what some are willing to pay. This postulation may, in the end, be true.

Much like a bank, and as is the case with existing disability insurance loans, the loans can be based on information received from NCAA or professional scouting sources. Educated guesses are being made every day about a given player's professional prospects. Further, if the professional leagues cooperate, the loan agreement can require automatic repayment to be made to the NCAA from the athlete's salary earned from playing on a professional team. Loans from professional leagues are not as attractive as those from the NCAA because the teams really do not have the same incentive to make the loans that the NCAA does. The ultimate stop for the athlete is the professional leagues, which may not really care whether the athlete stays in school. Either loan program is viable, but the NCAA program, particularly given the NCAA's current prosperity and its desired continued prosperity, seems to be most appropriate. Alternatively, either the NCAA or the pro leagues may be able to develop a relationship with banking institutions that will make loans based on professional athletic potential.

Another proposal that would involve a fundamental change in the structure of college sports is the establishment of professional teams affiliated with colleges and universities. A separate minor league system with home teams centered on campuses seems unattractive. Although it leaves a cleaner taste in the mouths of those who oppose the payment of stipends to amateurs, it removes an incentive from many of our youth to attend college. Predictably, those who would be most negatively impacted would be lower-income individuals. Although it is true that some athletes attend college only to participate in sports anyway, the NCAA is striving against that motivation with its ever-evolving initial eligibility measures.

Reforming college sports should not be feared. It may be the transition itself that is the most difficult step to take. For a long time the tennis world regarded professional athletes as manual laborers. It took "Cash and Carry" Pyle to help change that perception. When he finally convinced the female sensation of the day, Suzanne Lenglen, to accept his offer to turn professional, the press acknowledged that she "was not denigrating herself but uplifting the world of sport."[10]

Professional Sports Leagues

In general, the professional sports leagues are probably the least active entities in the regulating of sports agents. They should utilize their financial resources to educate their athletes regarding agents as well as finances generally. By becoming involved in education, they can play a more affirmative role in this nagging problem. The NFL, for example, has taken a number of steps that align with this need. In both its Rookie Symposium and Business Management and Entrepreneurship programs, the league provides athletes with sound financial information that can be used in their dealings with agents and other financial advisers.

Players' Unions

As discussed in Chapter 10, the unions have the power to deny unscrupulous agents the right to continue practicing their trade. Consistently, the courts have been supportive of the unions when disenfranchised agents have challenged the rights of unions to take such actions.

In addition to the ability to certify and decertify agents, players' unions are the parties with the greatest power to ensure that those who are certified are genuinely qualified. In that regard, whatever test or other instruments that are used to gauge the readiness of a potential agent must have the appropriate level of rigor. In addition to whatever "entry" exam there is, there needs to be adequate continuing education and continuous review of an agent's qualifications.

The tide may be turning away, however, from the complacent union that responds to instances of agent corruption and incompetence only after athletes have been victimized. Players' unions are becoming more proactive in regulating agents. Alarmed by scandals involving corrupt agents and the likelihood that more scandals of the magnitude of that involving Tank Black may arise in the future, the NFLPA is considering whether to adopt a posture more aggressive than it or any players' union has previously taken. In addition to the promulgation of regulations to govern financial advisers, the players' union is considering initiatives that will focus on the "quality of representation" and the "quality of the oversight [the NFLPA] can provide."[11] Because of the explosion in the number of agents that have gained NFLPA certification, the union has taken steps that seem to seek to decrease their numbers. NFLPA officials believe a reduction in the number of agents is necessary to weed out incompetent agents and to lessen the burden imposed on its regulatory mechanisms.[12] Specific strategies that the union is using include increasing the annual dues it charges agents, enhancing the level of difficulty of the examination required for NFLPA certification, and decertifying "an agent who does not negotiate at least one contract over a three year period."[13]

Educational Institutions

As discussed in Chapter 11, colleges and universities have much to lose if they become enmeshed in a sports agent scandal. Apart from the harm to the institutions' reputation is the financial cost in legal fees and sanctions an institution must endure. These direct reasons are why educational institutions must do a better job of policing and educating internally.

Individual institutions need to aggressively take it upon themselves to provide adequate education in this realm to student athletes who will be entertaining this professional option. In years past there was a prominent role at some institutions for an agent-screening panel. If the panels are structured and utilized properly, they can be quite valuable. It appears clear, however, that education outside of the formal panels would help further inform the student athlete. Each institution will have to evaluate its own needs. This institutional obligation must be taken seriously.

Conclusion

The key regulatory parties in this industry—the leagues, NCAA, educational institutions, and legislators—need to work more closely together. The communication between the diverse entities involved is the overall key. From the empirical experience over the past several years, it is evident that no entity acting alone can resolve the problems of the sports agent industry. Communication between sectors is the initial step. Once that communication is in place, constructive change is almost certain.

Even with these changes in place, the problems typified by Walters and Bloom, Tank Black, and scandalous hedge fund promoters will continue to happen to some degree. Where such incidents do occur, or where other laws are broken, the applicable laws must be vigorously enforced. The U.S. Attorney in the Walters-Bloom trial expressed concern over the influence organized crime could have over collegiate and professional sports if rule violations such as payments to athletes continue. He cited the fact that Michael Franzese, a member of the Columbo crime family, was a financier of the Walters-Bloom firm World Sports & Entertainment. Regarding this financing, Franzese told *Sports Illustrated* reporter Bruce Selcraig, "Look, we were business associates. I'm not going to lie and say we weren't. But to say I had anything to do with his sports business, that I controlled it or called the shots, is ridiculous."[14] The district attorney, Anton Valukas, feared that an organized-crime connection of this nature could place pressure on players to shave points or otherwise throw sporting events to serve the purposes of their underworld benefactors.[15] In a similar fashion, the convictions of the likes of Tank Black and Myron Piggie set off warning signals regarding the types of influences that need to be guarded against.

The reality is that sport has become more than an extracurricular activity: sport is now a global business. With the elevation of sports to this higher level, a reevaluation of all the surrounding circumstances must be made, not only in terms of sports agents but also in terms of college sports in general and the level of education that the athletes are receiving.

The passage of the UAAA and SPARTA were certainly milestones. These efforts are critical components of the regulatory matrix that includes players' associations and NCAA rules and regulations. As our discussion demonstrates, however, much more remains to be done.

Notes

Introduction

1. *Palmer Adds New Charges Against Walters, Bloom,* Sports Industry News 239 (July 29, 1988).
2. *See, e.g.,* Steve Fiffer, *Two Sports Agents Convicted of Fraud and Racketeering,* New York Times A-1, col. 1, A-31, col. 3 (April 14, 1989).
3. Rick Morrissey, *Agent's Penalty Would Suit Auburn,* Chicago Tribune 11C (March 5, 2000).
4. *Congress Should Take Action to Regulate Agents Who Represent Athletes and Other Gullible Stars,* San Antonio Express-News 2G (March 12, 2000).
5. ESPN.com, *Bush "Not Worried" About Illegal Benefit Allegations"* (September 16, 2006), http://sports.espn.go.com/ncf/news/story?id=2588347 (last visited October 18, 2007).
6. William Oscar Johnson & Ron Reid, *Some Offers They Couldn't Refuse,* Sports Illustrated 35 (May 21, 1979).
7. Ronald D. Mott & Stephen R. Hagwell, *Student-Athletes: NCAA Rules No Deterrent for Agents,* NCAA News 1 (October 2, 1995).
8. Harvey Araton, *In an Often Shady and Dirty Business, It Is Business as Usual,* New York Times § 8, p. 2, col. 1 (April 2, 2000).
9. Ted Gup, *Playing to Win in Vegas,* Time 56 (April 3, 1989).
10. King Kaufman, *Even if Reggie Bush Cashed in at USC, It Doesn't Mean He's a Bad Guy. Some Rules Deserve to Be Broken,* Salon.com (September 21, 2006).
11. Josh Gotthelf, *Linebacker: Agent Paid Me Cash,* SportsBusiness Journal 1 (July 26, 1999).
12. Phil Taylor & Don Yaeger, *Tangled Web; Marcus Camby Was Both Victim and Villain in His Illicit Dealings with Agents While at UMASS,* Sports Illustrated 66 (September 15, 1997).
13. John Gorman, *"Agent Threatened Me": Bears' Douglass,* Chicago Tribune § 4, p. 1, col. 3 (March 16, 1989). *See* discussion in next chapter.
14. Oliver Williamson, *Markets and Hierarchies* 7 (The Free Press, 1975).
15. John Bannon, *Ex-Agent: "No Clean Programs,"* USA Today C-1, col. 4 (December 17, 1987).
16. Mike Freeman, *Pro Football: Protecting Players from Their Agents,* New York Times § 8, p. 1, col. 1 (July 26, 1998).
17. Bill King, *Playing on the Edge,* SportsBusiness Journal 28 (May 15–21, 2000).

18. *See* Chapter 9.

19. Liz Mullen, *Black Hit with Criminal, Civil Charges*, SportsBusiness Journal 7 (March 6–12, 2000).

20. *Id.*

21. Scott Edelman, *College Can Take Action Against Agents*, New York Times § 8, p. 11, col. 1 (October 15, 1995).

22. NCAA, *Uniform Athlete Agents Act (UAAA) History and Status*, http://www.ncaa.org/wps/portal/!ut/p/kcxml/04_Sj9SPykssy0xPLMnMz0vM0Y_QjzKLN4j3NQDJgFjGpvqRqCKO6AI-YXARX4_83FR9b_0A_YLc0NCIckd FAEuT364!/delta/base64xml/L3dJdyEvUUd3QndNQSEvNElVRS82XzBfTFU!? CONTENT_URL=http://www1.ncaa.org/membership/enforcement/agents/uaaa/history.html (last visited June 2, 2007).

23. David Pickle, *Experience-Based Amateurism Model Presented to Division II Membership*, NCAA News C1 (January 17, 2000).

24. *See* discussion in Chapter 2.

25. Arn Tellem, "Basketball Academy Not Best for Prodigies," Los Angeles Times (May 8, 2007), http://www.latimes.com/sports/highschool/la-sp-tellem8may08, 0,4423380.story?coll=la-headlines-sports-highschool

Chapter 1. Historical and Legal Foundations

1. Gerald Eskenazi, *Red Grange, Football Hero of 1920's Dead at 87*, New York Times B-5, col. 1 (January 29, 1991); Robert C. Berry, William B. Gould, & Paul D. Staudohar, *Labor Relations in Professional Sports* 10 (Auburn House, 1986) (*Labor Relations*); Marc Pachter, *Champions of American Sport* 265–66 (Abrams, 1981).

2. Berry et al, *Labor Relations* at 10 (cited in note 1).

3. *Id.* There were also reports that tennis great Bill Tilden signed with Pyle, which Tilden denied (*Davis Cup Men Deny Signing with Pyle*, New York Times 8 [August 28, 1926]), indicating that even in the beginning there were some negative connotations to being associated with an agent.

4. Arlene Schulman, *Life of the Touring Pro*, New York Times C-2, col. 3 (September 11, 1989).

5. Craig Neff, *Den of Vipers*, Sports Illustrated 76 (October 19, 1987).

6. *See Double Play*, Time 61 (March 25, 1966); Jack Mann, *The $1,000,000 Holdout*, Sports Illustrated 26 (April 4, 1966). *See also All-Star Agent Is a High Scorer*, Business Week 153 (September 20, 1969); *Playing the Money Game*, Time 94 (March 21, 1969).

7. *Double Play*, Time at 61 (cited in note 6).

8. Mann, Sports Illustrated at 26, 28 (cited in note 6).

9. *Double Play*, Time at 61 (cited in note 6).

10. George W. Schubert, Rodney K. Smith, & Jess C. Trentadue, *Sports Law* 123–27 (West, 1986).

11. *See, e.g., Mackey v NFL*, 407 F Supp 1000 (D Minn 1975), aff'd in part & rev'd in part, 543 F2d 606 (8th Cir 1976).

12. *See, e.g., Robertson v NBA*, 389 F Supp 867 (SDNY 1975), aff'd, 556 F2d 682 (2d Cir 1977); *Denver Rockets v All-Pro Management Inc.*, 325 F Supp 1049 (CD Cal 1971).

13. *McCourt v California Sports, Inc.*, 460 F Supp 904 (ED Mich 1978), vacated 600 F2d 1193 (6th Cir 1979).

14. *Mackey*, 543 F2d at 606 (cited in note 11).

15. *Id.* at 609.

16. *Id.* at 622.

17. Roger Noll, *Economics of Sports Leagues*, in Gary A. Uberstine, ed., *Law of Professional and Amateur Sports* § 17.03[4] (Clark Boardman Company Ltd., 1988).

18. *Id.*

19. Larry Weisman, *Expect NFL Salary Cap to Keep Going Through the Roof*, USA Today (July 7, 2006), http://www.usatoday.com/sports/football/nfl/2006-07-07-salary-report_x.htm (last visited July 1, 2007).

20. MLBPA Info, *Frequently Asked Questions*, http://mlbplayers.mlb.com/pa/info/faq.jsp#average (last visited July 1, 2007).

21. Timothy Davis, *Regulating the Athlete-Agent Industry: Intended and Unintended Consequences*, 42 Williamette L Rev 781, 795 (2006).

22. *Id.* at 797.

23. Davis, *Regulating the Athlete-Agent Industry* at 795 (cited in note 21).

24. Daniel Kaplan, *Endorser Bill for Nike Nears $2B*, SportsBusiness Journal 1 (October 9, 2006).

25. Roger Kahn, Introduction to Woolf, *Behind Closed Doors* vii–xiii (New American Library, 1976).

26. *Id.*

27. Mike Trope with S. Delsohn, *Necessary Roughness* (Contemporary Books, 1987).

28. William O. Johnson & Ron Reid, *Some Offers They Couldn't Refuse*, Sports Illustrated 28 (May 21, 1979).

29. Garrett Therolf, *Sports Agent Leigh Steinberg Arrested*, Los Angeles Times (April 14, 2007), http://www.latimes.com/news/local/orange/la-me-steinberg 14apr14,1,7156374.story?coll=la-editions-orange (last visited June 9, 2007).

30. Mark H. McCormack, *What They Don't Teach You at Harvard Business School* 1 (Bantam, 1984); Donald L. Dell, *Minding Other People's Business: Winning Big for Your Clients and Yourself* 1 (Villard, 1989).

31. Jon Saraceno, *King Forges NBA Link*, USA Today 3C, col. 3 (January 16, 1990).

32. Liz Mullen, *Will Agents Get Along at CAA?*, SportsBusiness Journal 5 (July 31, 2006).

33. Bryan Burwell, *Think Williams Got Bad Deal? Don't Try to Tell Him That*, SportsBusiness Journal 54 (October 11–17, 1999).

34. Jarrett Bell, *Rookie Works Hard for His Money Williams' Deal Is Stuffed with Controversial Incentives*, USA Today 3C (November 24, 1999).

35. For a discussion of these and other examples of common agency relationships, *see* Leonard Lakin & Martin Schiff, *The Law of Agency* 2 (Kendall/Hunt, 2d ed 1996) (*Law of Agency*).

36. Restatement (Second) of Agency, § 1(1) (1958).

37. *Id.* at § 1(2).

38. *Id.* at § 1(3).

39. Lakin & Schiff, *Law of Agency* at 1 (cited in note 35).

40. National Conference of Commissioners on Uniform State Laws, *Uniform Athlete Agents Act* 2 (2000).

41. Harold G. Reuschlein & William A. Gregory, *The Law of Agency and Partnership* 11 (West Publishing, 2d ed 1990).

42. Lakin & Schiff, *Law of Agency* at 97 (cited in note 35).

43. Reuschlein & Gregory, *The Law of Agency and Partnership* at 35 (cited in note 41).
44. *Id.*
45. Lakin & Schiff, *Law of Agency* at 97–98 (cited in note 35).
46. *Id.* at 124.
47. *Id.* at 98.
48. *Id.*
49. Interview of Michael B. Siegel, May 17, 2001, Philadelphia, PA.
50. *Id.*
51. *Id.*
52. Lakin & Schiff, *Law of Agency* at 100 (cited in note 35).
53. *Id.* at 27.

Chapter 2. The Business

1. Leigh Steinberg, *Time to Revise Game Rules*, Sporting News 10 (November 16, 1987).
2. *New Role, New Model*, SportsBusiness Journal 1 (May 15–21, 2000).
3. Interview of Reginald Wilkes, September 11, 1989, Philadelphia, PA.
4. Mike Freeman, *Pro Football: Notebook*, New York Times § 8, p. 6 (July 30, 2000).
5. Teresa M. Walker, *Titans Land Pickens: "Misunderstood" Ex-Bengal Receiver Signs Five-Year Deal*, Chattanooga Times/Chattanooga Free Press D1 (July 27, 2000); *NFL Update*, Dallas Morning News 9B (August 1, 2000).
6. Jeffrey Z. Rubin & Frank E. A. Sander, *When Should We Use Agents? Direct vs. Representative Negotiation*, Negotiation Journal 401 (October 1988).
7. Greg Hansen, *NFL See Northcutt as Cornerback*, Arizona Daily Star 10C (March 26, 2000); Nick Cafardo, *Don't Count Out Holmes Run Ravens Free Agent Still May Be Targeted*, Boston Globe D2 (March 31, 2000).
8. Robert H. Ruxin, *An Athlete's Guide to Agents* 17 (Stephen Green, 1993) (*Athlete's Guide*). *See also* Dan Weil, *NBA Do-It-Yourselfers Rare*, SportsBusiness Journal 44 (January 31–February 6, 2000).
9. Bob Hohler, *Red Sox Hit Jackpot, Land Schilling*, Boston Globe A1 (November 29, 2003).
10. Rick Hummel, *Morris Says Cards Were Fair in Negotiations on Contract*, St. Louis Post-Dispatch 18 (January 5, 2002).
11. *Id.*
12. *Id.*
13. *Id.*
14. Roscoe Nance, *Conley Sr. Dives into NBA as Agent*, USA Today 3C (May 8, 2007).
15. Sid Hartman, *Tice: McDaniel Won Most Battles*, Minneapolis Star-Tribune 3C (February 11, 2000).
16. Alan Breznick, *Court Coup for Local Lawyer*, Washington Post F18 (May 17, 1999).
17. *Allen's Method Bad Deal for Agents*, Capital Times 2B (February 11, 1999).
18. Patrick Hruby, *Free Agent? New NBA Rules Alter Player Reprs' Roles*, Washington Times B1 (June 29, 1999).
19. *Allen's Method Bad Deal for Agents*, Capital Times at 2B (cited in note 17).
20. Thomas Heath, *NBA Stars Find Babby Cheaper by the Hour; D.C. Lawyer Bucks Tide of Agent Representation*, Washington Post D4 (May 10, 2000).

21. http://www.wc.com/practice.cfm?practice_ID=130&link=2&pf=1 (last visited June 7, 2007).

22. *Id.*; Liz Mullen, *Babby Signs Battier,* SportsBusiness Journal 5 (May 14–20, 2001).

23. *Id.*

24. *Id.*

25. Richard M. Nichols, *Agent, Lawyer, Agent/Lawyer . . . Who Can Best Represent Student Athletes?* 14 Ent & Sports L J 1 (1996).

26. *Id.*

27. Stacey M. Nahrwold, *Are Professional Athletes Better Served by a Lawyer-Representative Than an Agent? Ask Grant Hill,* 9 Seton Hall J Sport L 431, 441–42 (1999).

28. *Id.* at 445.

29. *Inquiry into Professional Sports,* Final Report, HR Rep No 1786, 94th Cong, 2d Sess 70 (1977).

30. John Culver, Speech to Sports Lawyers Association, Washington, DC (May 12, 1989).

31. Len Elmore, *Turn Out the Lights, Agents' Party Is Over,* SportsBusiness Journal 54 (July 9–15, 2001).

32. *Follow the Bouncing Basketball News, Question of the Day—Do NBA Draft Picks Need Agents?* Sports Business News (July 19, 2001), http://www.sportsbusinessnews.com/basketball/index.asp?sStoryId=1451

33. *Id.*

34. Alan Abrahamson, *Sports and the Agent: Endangered Species?* Los Angeles Times D1 (March 3, 1999).

35. Hruby, Washington Times at B1 (cited in note 18).

36. Interview of William Strickland, May 17, 2001, Philadelphia, PA.

37. Hansen, Arizona Daily Star at 10C (cited in note 7).

38. Mike Strom, *Bonus Baby Incentives Fill Williams Deal,* New Orleans Times-Picayune A1 (May 15, 1999).

39. *Id.*

40. *Id.*

41. *Id.*

42. Alex Marvez, *Williams May Get Better Deal,* South Florida Sun-Sentinel 9C (July 28, 2002).

43. *Id.*

44. Liz Mullen, *Pimpin Ain't Easy, So Why Not Sports?,* SportsBusiness Journal 1 (November 25, 2005).

45. Bryan Burwell, *Think Williams Got a Bad Deal? Don't Try to Tell Him That,* SportsBusiness Journal 54 (October 11–17, 1999).

46. Steve Davis, *This Pronunciation Thing Isn't Exactly Sparking a Controversy,* Dallas Morning News 2B (September 7, 2000).

47. Josh Gotthelf, *Criticized Agent Flunks Test,* SportsBusiness Journal (June 28, 1999), http://www.sportsbusinessjournal.com/index.cfm?fuseaction=search.show_article&articleId=16722&keyword=Leland%20Hardy (last visited June 27, 2007).

48. Josh Getthelf, *Union Suspends 30 Agents Stumped by Test,* SportsBusiness Journal (July 12, 1999), http://www.sportsbusinessjournal.com/index.cfm?fuseaction=search.show_article&articleId=16709&keyword=Leland%20Hardy (last visited June 28, 2007).

49. Mullen, SportsBusiness Journal at 1 (cited in note 44).

50. *See* Donald E. Biederman et al, *Law and Business of the Entertainment Industries* 471 (Auburn House, 1987).

51. *Id.*

52. Kashif, Speech to Black Entertainment and Sports Lawyers Association, Antigua, British West Indies (November 3, 1989).

53. There have been a number of scholarly articles examining various aspects of this field. All give an overview of the role of the athlete agent. Examples of recent scholarship include Thomas J. Arkell, *Agent Interference with College Athletics: What Agents Can and Cannot Do and What Institutions Should Do in Response,* 4 Sports Law J 147 (1997); Jamie E. Brown, *The Battle the Fans Never See: Conflict of Interest for Sports Lawyers,* 7 Georgetown J Legal Ethics 813 (1994); Walter T. Champion, Jr., *Attorneys Qua Sports Agents: An Ethical Conundrum,* 7 Marquette Sports L J 349 (1997); Phillip J. Closius, *Hell Hath No Fury Like a Fan Scorned: State Regulation of Sports Agents,* 30 U Toledo L Rev 511 (1999); Bryan Couch, *How Agent Competition and Corruption Affects Sports and the Athlete-Agent Relationship and What Can Be Done to Control It,* 10 Seton Hall J Sport L 111 (2000); Timothy Davis, *Regulating the Athlete-Agent Industry: Intended and Unintended Consequences,* 42 Willamette L Rev 781 (2006); *Ethics and Sports: Agent Regulation,* 14 Fordham Intell Prop Media & Ent L J 747 (2004); Robert P. Garbarino, *So You Want to Be a Sports Lawyer, or Is It a Player Agent, Player Representative Sports Agents, Contract Advisor, Family Advisor, or Contract Representative?* 11 Villanova Sports & Ent L Forum 11 (1994); Jason Gershwin, *Will Professional Athletes Continue to Choose Their Representation Freely? An Examination of the Enforceability of Non-Compete Agreements Against Sports Agents,* 5 U Pa J Lab & Emp L 585 (2003); Richard T. Karcher, *Solving Problems in the Player Representation Business: Unions Should Be the "Exclusive" Representatives of the Players,* 42 Willamette L Rev 737 (2006); Edward V. King, *Practical Advice for Agents: How to Avoid Being Sued,* 4 Marquette Sports L J 89 (1993); Charles B. Lipscomb & Peter Titlebaum, *Selecting a Sports Agent: The Inside for Athletes & Parents,* 3 Vanderbilt J Ent L & Pract 95 (2001); James Malone & Daren Lipinsky, *The Game Behind the Games: Unscrupulous Agents in College Athletics & California's Miller-Ayala Act,* 17 Loyola Ent L J 413 (1997); Nahrwold, 9 Seton Hall J Sport L at 431 (cited in note 27); Nichols, 14 Ent & Sports L at 1 (cited in note 25); Alec Powers, *The Need to Regulate Sports Agents,* 4 Seton Hall J Sport L 253 (1994); Rob Remis & Diane Sudia, *Statutory Regulation of Agent Gifts to Athletes,* 10 Seton Hall J Sport L 265 (2000); Rob Remis & Diane Sudia, *Athlete Agent Contracts: Legislative Regulation,* 10 Seton Hall J Sport L 317 (2000); Rob Remis & Diane Sudia, *Escaping Athlete Agent Statutory Regulation: Loopholes and Constitutional Defectiveness Based on Tri-Parte Classification of Athletes,* 9 Seton Hall J Sport L 1 (1999); Scott R. Rosner, *Conflicts of Interest and the Shifting Paradigm of Athlete Representation,* UCLA Ent L Rev 193 (2004); Jamie P. A. Shulman, *The NHL Joins In: An Update on Sports Agent Regulation in Professional Team Sports,* 4 Sports Law J 181 (1997); Jan Stiglitz, *A Modest Proposal: Agent Deregulation,* 7 Marquette Sports L J 361 (1997); *Symposium: The Uniform Athlete Agents Act,* 13 Seton Hall J Sport L (2003).

Other articles include Jeffrey P. Crandall, *The Agent-Athlete Relationship in Professional and Amateur Sports: The Inherent Potential for Abuse and the Need for Regulation,* 30 Buffalo L Rev 815 (1981); James J. Giulietti, *Agents of Professional Athletes,* 15 New England L Rev 545 (1980); Adam B. Nimoy & Jackson D. Hamilton, *Attorneys and the California Athlete Agencies Act: The Toll of the Bill,* 7 Hastings Comm & Ent L J 551 (1985); Miriam Benitez, *Of Sports, Agents, and Regulations— The Need for a Different Approach,* 3 Ent & Sports L J 199 (1986); Craig Massey, *The*

Crystal Cruise Cut Short: A Survey of the Increasing Regulatory Influences over the Athlete-Agent in the National Football League, 1 Ent & Sports L J 53 (1984); Len Elmore, *The Agent's Role in Professional Sports: An Athlete's Perspective*, 31 Boston Bar J 613 (1987); Gary Uberstine & Richard J. Grad, *Enforceability of Sports Contracts: A Practitioner's Playbook*, 7 Loyola Ent L J 1 (1987); Dana Alden Fox, *Regulating the Professional Sports Agent: Is California in the Right Ball Park?* 15 Pac L J 1231 (1984); Gary Kohn, *Sports Agents Representing Professional Athletes: Being Certified Means Never Having to Say You're Qualified*, 6 Ent & Sports L J 1 (Winter 1988); Lori J. Lefferts, *The NFL Players Association's Agent Certification Plan: Is It Exempt from Antitrust Review?* 26 Arizona L Rev 699 (1984); Lloyd Z. Remick & David S. Eisen, *The Personal Manager in the Entertainment and Sports Industries*, 3 Ent & Sports L J 57 (1986); Gary Roberts, *Protecting the College Athlete from Unscrupulous Agents*, 5 Sports Lawyer J 8 (Fall 1987); Lionel Sobel, *The Regulation of Sports Agents: An Analytical Primer*, 39 Baylor L Rev 701 (1987); Michael J. Sullivan, *Remedying Athlete-Agent Abuse: A Securities Law Approach*, 2 Ent & Sports L J 53 (1984); Bill Winter, *Is the Sports Lawyer Getting Dunked? (Non-Lawyer Agents in Professional Sports)*, 66 ABA J 701 (June 1980); *Regulation of Sports Agents: Since at First It Hasn't Succeeded, Try Federal Legislation*, Sports Inc. 42 (May 30, 1988). See also John Weistart & C. Lowell, *The Law of Sports* § 3.17 (Michie, 1979).

54. Champion, 7 Marquette Sports L J at 349 (cited in note 53).

55. See, e.g., William M. Bulkeley, *Sports Agents Help Athletes Win—and Keep—Those Super Salaries*, Wall Street Journal § 2, p. 31, col. 4 (March 25, 1985); HR Rep No 1786 at 71 (cited in note 29).

56. David Ware, Speech to the National Football League Players Association agent certification meeting, Washington, DC (April 19, 1989).

57. Abrahamson, Los Angeles Times at D1 (cited in note 34).

58. Hruby, Washington Times at B1 (cited in note 18)

59. Kent Somers, NBA *Example May Diminish Agents' Power*, Arizona Republic C1 (March 24, 1999).

60. Daniel Kaplan, *Lofty Mission or Signing Tool? IMG's Academy Develops Athletes, Facilities and Controversy*, SportsBusiness Journal 3, 42 (March 19–21, 2001).

61. David Falk, Speech at the Seton Hall Sports Law Symposium, Newark, NJ (April 28, 1989).

62. Wayne Henniger, *Octagon Puts Together Many-Sided Vick Strategy*, SportsBusiness Journal 13 (September 17–23, 2001).

63. Interview of Reginald Wilkes (cited in note 3).

64. Telephone interview of Edward V. King, Jr., September 3, 1989, San Francisco, CA.

65. Interview of Merle Scott, November 1, 2000, Philadelphia, PA.

66. *Follow the Bouncing Basketball News, Question of the Day—Do NBA Draft Picks Need Agents*, Sports Business News (July 19, 2001), http://www.sportsbusinessnews.com/basketball/index.asp?sStoryId=1451

67. Abrahamson, Los Angeles Times at D1 (cited in note 34).

68. Davis, Dallas Morning News at 8 (cited in note 46).

Chapter 3. Consolidation

1. See, e.g., Liz Mullen, *Steinberg Case: Secret Agent's Tale*, SportsBusiness Journal 1 (June 18–24, 2001) (outlining the dispute between David Dunn and his former firm, Steinberg, Moorad & Dunn).

2. As of 1999–2000 season, the NBA, NFL, NHL, and MLB comprised 29, 31, 28, and 30 teams, respectively. As of the 1989–90 season, these leagues contained 27, 28, 21, and 26 teams, respectively. The growth in the leagues over the past decade was 7.4 percent, 10.7 percent, 33.3 percent, and 15.4 percent, respectively. This data was compiled based on information obtained from the official website for each league.

3. Bob Woolf, *Agents on Campus*, in Richard Lapchick & John Slaughter, eds., *The Rules of the Game: Ethics in College Sport* 108 (Macmillan for the American Council of Education, 1989).

4. Telephone interviews of respective players' association representatives, February 22, 2001.

5. Timothy Davis, Alfred D. Mathewson, & Kenneth L. Shropshire, eds., *Sports and the Law* 145 (Carolina Academic Press, 1999).

6. *Q & A: David Falk*, SportsBusiness Journal 30 (May 17–23, 1999).

7. http://www.imgworld.com/home/default.sps (last visited November 4, 2006).

8. http://www.octagon.com/worldwide-overview/athletes-and-personalities (last visited June 9, 2007).

9. Liz Mullen, *Assante Close to Deal with Hoops Agent Fegan*, SportsBusiness Journal 1, 47 (July 3–9, 2000).

10. *Assante Strengthens Athlete Representation with Purchase of Leading Basketball Agent*, news release, Assante website, http://www.assante.com/main/aboutAssante/press.cfm?nr_id+nr45.cfm (visited February 3, 2001).

11. Peter Spiegel, *Flesh Peddlers Go Global*, Forbes 189 (March 9, 1998).

12. Richard Alm, *Some Small Sports Marketers Join Big Teams, Others Cherish Control*, Dallas Morning News (December 28, 1999) (1999 WLNR 6295071).

13. *Id.*

14. *Id.*

15. Jim Sullivan, *When It Comes to Pop Concerts, He Is the Player*, Boston Globe N1 (May 16, 1999).

16. *eSuperstars.com Offers a Super Bowl Dream Come True*, Business Wire/edq#/AU: PG#? (December 15, 1999).

17. Michael F. Legg, *SFX Entertainment Company Update*, Prudential Securities Equity Research 4 (December 6, 1999).

18. *eSuperstars.com Offers a Super Bowl Dream Come True*, Business Wire (cited in note 16).

19. Richard Sandomir, *Sale of Agency Opens New Doors for Falk and Clients*, New York Times C-6 (May 6, 1998).

20. *SFX Shares Drop After Buying Streak Attracts Antitrust Scrutiny*, Dow Jones Business News (September 22, 1998).

21. Sandomir, New York Times at C-6 (cited in note 19).

22. Spiegel, Forbes at 189 (cited in note 11).

23. Patrick Haverson, *Shake-up Creates Powerful Players Agents*, Financial Times 14 (September 25, 1998).

24. Sandomir, New York Times at C-6 (cited in note 19).

25. *Id.*

26. *SFX Renames Agents' Business*, Associated Press (December 13, 1999).

27. *SFX Steals the NBA Draft*, Sports Business News, http://www.sportsbusinessnews.com/basketball/index.asp?sStoryId=989 (visited August 30, 2001).

28. Liz Mullen, *Falk-Tellem Combo Trumpets NBA Draft Day Numbers for SFX Sports*, SportsBusiness Journal 21 (July 24–30, 2000).

29. *Id.*

30. *SFX Entertainment Acquires SME,* Business Wire (November 24, 1999).

31. Liz Mullen, *SFX Buys Golf Agency Signature,* SportsBusiness Journal 41 (July 2–8, 2001).

32. Mark Fainaru-Wada & Ron Kroichick, *Agents of Influence,* San Francisco Chronicle C1 (March 11, 2001).

33. Bryan Burwell & Liz Mullen, *SFX: Falk Nearly Walked,* SportsBusiness Journal 4, 43 (April 23–29, 2001).

34. Ethan Smith, *Concert Compass, Could Be Tough Sell,* Wall Street Journal B2 (December 15, 2005).

35. *Whatever Happened To?,* SportsBusiness Journal (October 16, 2006).

36. E. Scott Reckard, *Steinberg to Sell Firm for $120 Million,* Los Angeles Times C-1 (October 28, 1999).

37. Kevin Dougherty, *DPM Now Part of Assante,* Montreal Gazette D-2 (January 13, 2000).

38. Interview of Rand Sacks, January 20, 1999, Philadelphia, PA.

39. Reckard, Los Angeles Times at C-1 (cited in note 36).

40. *Id.*

41. *Id.*

42. *Assante Strengthens Athlete Representation with Purchase of Leading Basketball Agent,* Assante website (cited in note 10).

43. *Id.*

44. *Id.*

45. *What Ever Happened To?,* SportsBusiness Journal at 9, 29 (cited in note 35).

46. Scott R. Rosner, *Conflicts of Interest and the Shifting Paradigm of Athlete Representation,* 11 UCLA Ent L Rev 192, 205 (2004).

47. Liz Mullen, *Hollywood's Climan Joins Legacy Sports,* SportsBusiness Journal 7, 29 (March 7, 2005).

48. Liz Mullen, *Guggenheim Buys Adviser Klarberg's Firm,* SportsBusiness Journal 9, 19 (November 13, 2006).

49. Spiegel, Forbes at 189 (cited in note 11).

50. *Id.*

51. Alm, Dallas Morning News (cited in note 12).

52. Fainaru-Wada & Kroichick, San Francisco Chronicle at C1 (cited in note 32); Liz Mullen, *Final Score from NFL Draft Day's First Round: IMG 6, Assante 5,* SportsBusiness Journal 22 (April 31–May 6, 2001), http://www.imgworld.com/ sports/client_management/athletes.sps

53. *Fortsmann Little to Acquire IMG,* IMG press release (September 30, 2004), http://www.imgworld.com/press_room/fullstory.sps?iType=13708&iNewsid= 109551&iCategoryID=12543

54. Liz Mullen, *Fortsmann Shaking Up IMG Structure,* SportsBusiness Journal 1 (February 7–13, 2005).

55. *Revamped IMG Targets Key Growth Areas,* SportsBusiness Journal 18 (October 16, 2006).

56. Liz Mullen, *IMG Out of Team Sports,* SportsBusiness Journal 1 (July 10, 2006).

57. *Id.*

58. Michael J. Pachuta, *Interpublic Sees Acquisitions, Global Rebound Aiding Sales,* Investor's Business Daily A-22 (June 1, 1999).

59. *Id.*

60. *Id.*

61. Andrew Ross Sorkin, *Some Reshuffling in Sports Marketing*, New York Times D-7 (February 12, 1998).

62. *Interpublic's Offer for Brands Hatch Declared Unconditional*, PR Newswire (December 1, 1999).

63. Stuart Elliot, *Lowe Group Creates the Octagon Brand*, New York Times C-11 (September 27, 1999).

64. *Octagon Announces Unification of Group Branding*, Business Wire (September 27, 1999).

65. *Id.*

66. *Octagon Announces Major Move in Golf Representation Through Partnership with Pros Inc.*, Business Wire\edq#\AU:PG #? (March 3, 1999).

67. *Octagon Announces Unification of Group Branding*, Business Wire (cited in note 64).

68. Liz Mullen, *Octagon's NFL Buy Fills Out the Ticket*, SportsBusiness Journal 9 (December 18–24, 2000).

69. *Octagon Solidifies Baseball Unit with Woolf Associates Baseball Acquisition*, http://www.octagon.com/001214_woolf.html (visited February 3, 2001).

70. Liz Mullen, *Octagon Pushes Its Boundaries with Carlisle Sports Acquisition*, SportsBusiness Journal 10 (August 27–September 2, 2001).

71. John Helyar, *Meet the Newest Super Bowl Player: CAA*, ESPN.com (February 1, 2007), http://sports.espn.go.com/nfl/playoffs06/news/story?id=2751046 (last visited June 9, 2007).

72. http://www.wmgllc.com/management/index.html

73. http://www.wmgllc.com/news/tellem-01_27_06.html

74. *Wasserman Group Acquires SportsNet*, http://www.wmgllc.com/news/sportsnet .html and http://www.wmgllc.com/news/rk_acquisition-11_01_06.html (last visited June 9, 2007).

75. http://blueequity.com/index.shtml

76. Liz Mullen, *Louisville Firm Buys into Sports*, SportsBusiness Journal 1 (August 21, 2006); and Liz Mullen, *Blue Grows into NFL*, SportsBusiness Journal 1 (May 28, 2007).

77. Liz Mullen, *And 1 Signs Isaiah Rider; Wilhelmina Corners Golfer Kuchar*, SportsBusiness Journal 15 (November 27–December 3, 2000).

78. Liz Mullen, *George Looks to Wilhelmina for Face Time*, SportsBusiness Journal 5 (January 1–27, 2002).

79. Liz Mullen, *With Marbury Signing, Wilhelmina Becoming Fashionable in Sports World*, SportsBusiness Journal 21 (September 25–October 1, 2000).

80. *Id.*

81. Liz Mullen, *Hollywood Connection Changes the Game for Agents*, SportsBusiness Journal 1, 46 (August 16–22, 1999).

82. *Id.*

83. Liz Mullen, *NHL Union Also Worried About Old Setup at SFX, Source Says*, SportsBusiness Journal 15 (January 8–14, 2001).

84. *Josh Gotthelf, SFX Deal Would Link Tellem, Falk*, SportsBusiness Journal 1, 46 (August 23–29, 1999).

Chapter 4. The Basics

1. *Q & A: David Falk*, SportsBusiness Journal 30, 31 (May 17–23, 1999).

2. Liz Mullen, *Fehr: Agents' Complaints About Peers Increase*, SportsBusiness Journal 12 (May 20, 2005).

3. Robert H. Ruxin, *An Athlete's Guide to Agents* 34 (Stephen Greene, 1989) (*Athlete's Guide*).
4. Interview of Dr. Michael Jackson, September 11, 1989, in Philadelphia, PA.
5. Bucky Woy, *Sign 'Em Up Bucky: The Adventures of a Sports Agent* 46 (Hawthorn, 1975).
6. Bob Woolf, *Behind Closed Doors* 300 (New American Library, 1976).
7. Bob Cohen, *Few Jerry Maguires: Aspiring Sports Agents Find the Clients Scarce, the Glamour Nonexistent and the Going Tough*, Washington Times C1 (May 4, 2004) (quoting then neophyte agent Adisa Bakari).
8. *Id.*
9. Edward V. King, Jr., *Agents: Do They Help or Hurt the Athlete? Dependency Leads to Abuse*, New York Times S-9, col. 2 (March 5, 1989).
10. Agents generally charge athletes on a percentage basis. The rate varies, but for contract negotiations it is generally less than 5 percent. *See also* George W. Schubert, Rodney K. Smith, & Jess C. Trentadue, *Sports Law* 30 (West, 1986), which notes that flat-rate fees or some combination may be used.
11. National Collegiate Athletic Association, *A Career in Professional Sports: Guidelines That Make Dollars and Sense* 6 (NCAA, 1984) (*Guidelines*).
12. John Powers, *Coaches, Athletes Are Artful Hustlers, Too*, Sporting News 12 (November 16, 1987).
13. Cohen, Washington Times at C1 (quoting experienced agent Tony Agnone) (cited in note 7).
14. Lawrence Taylor & David Falkner, *L.T. Living on the Edge* 74 (Warner, 1987).
15. Richard B. Schmitt, *Suit Spotlights Changed World of Sports Agents*, Wall Street Journal B1, B6 (December 15, 1999).
16. Bruce Selcraig, *The Deal Went Sour*, Sports Illustrated 32 (September 15, 1988).
17. John Bannon, *Ex-Agent: "No Clean Programs,"* USA Today C-1, col. 4 (December 17, 1987).
18. *Guidelines* at 4 (cited in note 11).
19. Jack McCallum & Richard O'Brien, *Singled Out*, Sports Illustrated 18 (July 25, 1994).
20. Earl Gustkey, *Riding Out the Storm*, Los Angeles Times C1 (August 14, 1996).
21. Craig Neff, *Agents of Turmoil*, Sports Illustrated 36 (August 3, 1987).
22. Michael O'Keefe, *Show Them the Trouble: Players Stuck in the Middle as NCAA Attacks Agents*, New York Daily News 69 (March 5, 2000).
23. *Ex Agent for Enis Banned for 2 Years*, New York Times D-7 (October 23, 1998).
24. Craig Neff, *In Hot and Heavy Pursuit*, Sports Illustrated 84, 85 (October 19, 1987).
25. *Agent's Arrest Ordered by Judge*, Atlanta Journal-Constitution 9 (September 1, 1999).
26. *Agent: Players' Contracts Had Bonuses of $75 to $100*, USA Today 9-C, col. 2 (December 16, 1987).
27. *Id.*
28. *Bloom v Harmon*, No. 11059-014 (1987) (Culver, Arb.) at 2.
29. *Id.* at 5.
30. *See* John Gorman, *Sports Agent Case Puts Iowa on Trial, Too*, Chicago Tribune § 4, p. 9, col. 1 (March 8, 1989).
31. Brian Bosworth with Rick Reilly, *The Boz: Confessions of a Modern Anti-Hero* 229 (Charter, 1989).

32. *See* Danny Robbins and Manny Topol, *Influence on the Bench,* Newsday 5 (April 3, 1988).

33. *Id.*

34. L. Jon Wertheim, *Web of Deceit,* Sports Illustrated 80 (May 29, 2000).

35. Michael O'Keefe, *Show Them the Trouble: Players Stuck in Middle as NCAA Attacks Agents,* New York Daily News 69 (March 5, 2000).

36. *Id.*

37. Maryanne Hudson & Elliott Almond, *They Play by Their Own Rules: Colleges: Sports Agents Are Everywhere, and the NCAA Estimates 70% of Current Athletes Have Had Contact with Them,* Los Angeles Times C1 (October 13, 1995).

38. NCAA Division I Committee on Infractions, *California State Unviersity, Fresno Public Infractions Report* (September 10, 2003), http://www1.ncaa.org/membership/governance/division_I/infractions/index/html (follow "Link to Major Infractions," then enter September 10, 2003, in database, then follow link to public report).

39. Liz Mullen, *NFLPA Will Make Agents List Their "Runners,"* SportsBusiness Journal 14 (October 31–November 6, 2005).

40. Michael O'Keefe, *This Piggie Went to Jail: Street Agent Awaits Sentencing for Sins Many Have Committed,* New York Daily News 94 (January 21, 2001); *Piggie Sentenced,* http://sportsillustrated.cnn.com/basketball/college/news/2001/05/30/piggie_sentencing_ap/

41. Interview of Sonny Vaccaro, April 13, 2007, Philadelphia, PA.

42. John Gorman, *"Agent Threatened Me": Bears' Douglass,* Chicago Tribune § 4, p. 1, col. 3 (March 16, 1989).

43. *Id.*

44. *Id.*

45. *See* Ruxin, *Athlete's Guide* at 35–40 (cited in note 3), which outlines the procedure used by UCLA athletes.

46. Phil Taylor & Don Yaeger, *Tangled Web: Marcus Camby Was Both Victim and Villain in His Illicit Dealings with Agents While at UMass,* Sports Illustrated 66 (September 15, 1997).

47. *Id.*

48. *Id.*

49. Rick Hornung, *Hoop Schemes: Toronto Raptors Basketball Player Marcus Camby,* Saturday Night 69 (February 1998).

50. *Id.*

51. *Id.*

52. *Id.*

53. *Id.*

54. *Id.*

55. Dan Shaughnessy, *Regrettably, Camby Expresses No More Regrets,* Boston Globe G1 (November 15, 1997).

56. *Lounsbury Penalized,* Boston Globe F2 (December 3, 1997).

57. Steve Fiffer, *Two Sports Agents Convicted of Fraud and Racketeering,* New York Times A-1, col. 1, A-31, col. 2 (April 14, 1989).

58. Ruxin, *Athlete's Guide* at 29 (cited in note 3).

59. Kenneth L. Shropshire, *In Black and White: Race and Sports in America,* ch 6 (New York University Press, 1996); James G. Sammataro, *Business and Brotherhood, Can They Coincide? A Search into Why Black Athletes Do Not Hire Black Agents,* 42 Howard L J 535 (Spring 1999).

60. *See* the story recounted in Barry Cooper, *Black Sports Agents Beat Odds with Top Clients*, New Pittsburgh Courier A10 (July 13, 1994).

61. Quoted in Phillip M. Hoose, *Necessities: Racial Barriers in American Sports* 29 (Random House, 1989).

62. *Smith v IMG Worldwide, Inc.*, 360 F Supp 2d 681 (ED Pa 2005).

63. *Smith v IMG Worldwide, Inc.*, 437 F Supp 2d 297, 307 (ED Pa 2006).

64. *Id.* at 297, 308.

65. *Id.*

66. Interview of William Strickland, May 17, 2001, Philadelphia, PA.

67. Dan Weil, *For Longtime Partners, Teamwork Pays on the Court, at the Office*, SportsBusiness Journal 24, 25 (February 24–25, 2000).

68. *Id.* at 25.

69. David Aldridge, *Agents of Change See Slow Progess in Sports*, ESPN.com (Feburary 28, 2002), http://sports.espn.go.com/espn/print?id=1342031&type=columnist (last visited June 9, 2007).

70. *Id.*

71. Mark Hyman, *Playing as Rough as Linebacker*, BusinessWeek 92 (September 27, 2004).

72. *Top 10 Agents by League, Based on Salary Represented*, SportsBusiness Journal (August 14, 2006), http://www.sportsbusinessjournal.com/index.cfm?fuseaction=article.printArticles&articleId

73. Weil, SportsBusiness Journal at 25 (cited in note 67).

74. Farrell Evans, *Brother Beware: Eagerly Playing the Race Card, a Few Unscrupulous Black Financial Advisers Are Hurting Athlete-Clients and Legit Minority Businesses*, Sports Illustrated 20 (April 3, 2006).

75. Liz Mullen, *Women Agents? So Far, Only a Handful*, SportsBusiness Journal (October 12, 1998), http://www.sportsbusinessjournal.com/article.cms?articleId=19126&s=1 (visited May 2, 2002).

76. Telephone interview of Athelia Doggette, NFLPA, May 15, 2007,\edq#\AU: CITY?.

77. *Id.*

78. Mullen, SportsBusiness Journal (cited in note 75).

79. Telephone interview of Wendi Huntley, March 28, 2002, Colombus, Ohio.

80. *Id.*

81. Mullen, SportsBusiness Journal at 12 (cited in note 2).

82. *Id.* (quoting the comments of Linda Joplin, who at the time of the report was the chair of the California National Organization for Women's Gender Equity Committee).

83. Telephone interview of Wendi Huntley (cited in note 79).

84. Michael O'Keefe, *Show Them the Trouble: Players Stuck in Middle As NCAA Attacks Agents*, New York Daily News 69 (March 5, 2000).

85. Mike Freeman, *Pro Football: Protecting Players from Their Agents*, New York Times § 8, p. 1 (July 26, 1998).

86. Joan M. O'Connell & Brenton Welling, *How Leigh Steinberg Rises Above His "Sleazoid Profession,"* BusinessWeek 62 (January 14, 1985).

87. Lee Smith, *Scott Boras Saves Baseball*, Men's Journal 86 (April 2001).

88. *Top 10 Agents by League, Based on Salary Represented*, SportsBusiness Journal 18 (August 14, 2006).

89. *Id.* at 89.

90. *Id.*

91. Rick Hurd, *Agents Fight PR Problem T.O.-Rosenhaus Fiasco Gives Industry Black Eye*, Contra Costa Times (Walnut Creek, CA) F4 (December 27, 2005).

92. *Id.*

93. *The 20 Most Influential Sports Agents*, SportsBusiness Journal 16 (August 14, 2006).

94. Len Elmore, *Turn Out the Lights, Agents' Party Is Over*, SportsBusiness Journal 54 (July 9–16, 2001).

95. David Ware, Speech to the National Football League Players Association agent certification meeting, Washington DC (April 19, 1989).

96. John Culver, Speech to the Sports Lawyers Association, Washington, DC (May 12, 1989).

97. Bob Woolf, *Agents on Campus*, in R. Lapchick & J. Slaughter, eds., *The Rules of the Game: Ethics in College Sport* 108 (Macmillan for the American Council of Education, 1989).

98. Ware, Speech (cited in note 95).

99. Interview of Stanley O. King, March 15, 2001, Philadelphia, PA.

100. Transcript of Interview of Kevin Robinson, May 17, 2001, Philadelphia, PA at 2.

101. *Id.* at 4.

102. *Id.* at 6.

103. *Id.* at 4.

104. http://ascentsports.icastsports.com/site_page.asp?page_name=Ascent%20Executives%20Detail&Coachid=10 (last visited June 9, 2007).

105. Freeman, New York Times at § 8, p. 1 (cited in note 85).

Chapter 5. Unscrupulous and Criminal

1. *See* Chapter 4.

2. *See* Chapter 11.

3. Fla Stat § 468.451 (West's Fla Statutes Annotated 2001).

4. *Broker Who Swindled Stars Gets 4 to 12*, Newsday A20 (November 29, 2005).

5. *See* William Nack, *Thrown for Heavy Losses*, Sports Illustrated 40, 41 (March 24, 1986).

6. *Id.*

7. Diana B. Henriques, *Investing It; Making It Harder for Investors to Sue*, New York Times 1 (September 10, 1995).

8. Will Shanley, *Athletes Get Wild Pitches: Financial Scam Artists Often Prey on Wealthy Pros*, Denver Post C1 (February 21, 2006).

9. Craig Neff, *Den of Vipers*, Sports Illustrated 76 (October 19, 1987).

10. Bobby Clay, *Black Agents Compete for Blue Chip Athletes*, Black Enterprise 54 (July 1992).

11. Melissa Isaacson, *New Villain: Financial Adviser*, Chicago Tribune 11 (March 5, 2000).

12. *Id.* at 36.

13. *Id.*

14. Edward T. Pound & Douglas Pasternak, *Money Player: How Some of the NFL's Biggest Stars Got Taken for Millions*, US News & World Report 30 (February 11, 2002).

15. *Id.* at 33.

16. ¶1, Complaint, *Securities and Exchange Commission v Donald D. Lukens*.

17. ¶2. Complaint.

18. *Id.* at 8, ¶20.

19. Pound & Pasternak, US News & World Report at 31 (cited in note 14).

20. *Id.* at 30.

21. Paul Doyle, *Blindside Hit; Trusted Agents, Advisers Find a Way to Scam a Little Off the Top*, Hartford Courant E9 (April 18, 2004).

22. *Id.*

23. *Id.*

24. Neff, Sports Illustrated at 76 (cited in note 9).

25. Doyle, Hartford Courant at E9 (cited in note 21).

26. *Enis' Agent Say He Goes by the Book—The Bible*, Centre Daily Times 1B (August 10, 1998).

27. ¶1, Complaint, *Securities and Exchange Commission v Dunyasha M. Yetts, et al.*

28. *Id.* ¶¶10 and 11.

29. *Id.*

30. *Id.* ¶¶18.

31. Pound & Pasternak, US News & World Report at 35 (cited in note 14).

32. *Id.* at 36.

33. *Securities and Exchange Commission, v. Dunyasha M. Yetts, et al.*, No. C2-01-1263 (SD Ohio) (Litigation Release No. 18167/June 3, 2003), http://www.sec.gov/litigation/litreleases/lr18167.htm (last visited June 9, 2007).

34. *Id.*

35. Bob Cohn, *Caught in the Con Game*, Washington Times C1 (October 10, 2001).

36. Pound & Pasternak, US News & World Report at 30 (cited in note 14).

37. *Id.* at 32.

38. *Id.* at 34.

39. *Id.* at 32.

40. For the most complete discussion on this case prior to adjudication, see L. Jon Wertheim, *Web of Deceit*, Sports Illustrated 80 (May 29, 2000).

41. *Id.*

42. *Id.*

43. *Id.*

44. *Tank Black Ordered to Prison on Money-Laundering Case*, Chattanooga Times D6 (June 15, 2001).

45. *See Former NFL Agent "Tank" Black Pleads Guilty to Money Laundering*, http://www.cbs.sportsline.com/u/wire/stories.0,1169,3373398_59,00.html (visited January 17, 2001).

46. Judy Mathewson, *NFL Former Agent "Tank" Black Conspired to Defraud, Jury Says*, Bloomberg News (February 12, 2002).

47. Ron Work, *Ex-Sports Agent Black Gets Five Years*, Columbia State Record B1 (May 8, 2002).

48. Mike McKee, *Ramsey Resigns from Bar, Investigation Over*, 129 The Recorder 9 (July 8, 2005).

49. Geoffrey C. Arnold, *Players Can Be Easy Money*, The Oregonian E6 (February 14, 2005).

50. Steve Fiffer, *Money Misspent, Witness Says*, New York Times B-11, col. 5 (March 24, 1989).

51. *Id.*

52. David Newton, *High-Profile Stars Defrauded, Indictment Says*, The State (Lexis January 11, 2001).

53. *United States v Marion Darnell Jones, James E. Brown, Willie Williams, Jr., and Andre Lewis,* Indictment, Criminal No 3701-114 (US Dist Ct, D SC January 10, 2001).

54. Newton, The State (cited in note 52).

55. *United States v Marion Darnell Jones, James E. Brown, Willie Williams, Jr., and Andre Lewis* (cited in note 53).

56. David Newton, *Summit Chief Pleads Guilty,* Columbia State B1 (October 22, 2002).

57. *United States v Marion Darnell Jones, James E. Brown, Willie Williams, Jr., and Andre Lewis* (cited in note 53).

58. *Id.* Newton, The State (cited in note 52).

59. *Four Plead Innocent in Alleged Scheme to Defraud Athletes,* The Herald, Rock Hill 2B (January 26, 2001).

60. *S.C. Man Admits Defrauding Client in Pro Athlete Deal,* Charlotte Observer 2B (February 24, 2001).

61. *Around the State,* Charlotte Observer, 2Y (June 19, 2002).

62. Newton, Columbia State at B1 (cited in note 56).

63. Don Dronin, *Carruth's Lawyer Goes on Offensive,* USA Today 11C (November 29, 2000).

64. *Rios Out for 2–3 Months Because of Ankle Injury,* Los Angeles Times part § 4, p. 7 (June 19, 2001).

65. *Adviser to the Stars Gets 12 Years,* Sporting News 35 (January 23, 1989).

66. *Id.*

67. *People v Sorkin,* 407 NYS2d 772 (App Div 1978); and Pete Axthelm, *The Guy with the Edge,* Newsweek 57 (October 3, 1977).

68. Axthelm, *The Guy with the Edge* (cited in note 67).

69. *Id.*

70. Jamie P. A. Shulman, *The NHL Joins In: An Update on Sports Agent Regulation in Professional Team Sports,* 4 Sports Law J 181, 187 (1997).

71. *Baseball Notebook,* Dayton Daily News 3D (February 2, 2001).

72. Newton, The State (cited in note 52).

73. *Wilson Wins,* Associated Press (February 1, 2001).

74. *Id.*

75. Mike Dodd, *Madlock's Ex-agent Claims Legal Victory,* USA Today 6C (August 7, 1991).

76. *Greenberg's Side of the Madlock Suit,* Sporting News 13 (September 2, 1991).

77. Dodd, USA Today at 6C (cited in note 75).

78. Geoff Dougherty, *Chicago Bulls' Scottie Pippen Wins Judgment over Investment Advice,* Chicago Tribune (November 24, 2004) (2004 WLNR 17857601).

79. *Hernandez v Childers,* 806 F Supp 1368 (ED Ill 1992). Other cases involving alleged mismanagement resulting in tax problems for athletes include *Wilson v Commissioner of Internal Revenue,* 1995 WL 649897; and *Willoughby v Commissioner of Internal Revenue,* 1994 WL 444427.

80. *Hilliard v Black,* 125 F Supp 2d 1071, 1074 (ND Fla 2000).

81. *Id.* at 1073.

82. *Williams v CWI, Inc.,* 777 F Supp 1006 (DC 1991).

83. *Id.* at 1007.

84. *Id.*

85. Michael Goodwin & Sam Goldaper, *Enmeshed in a Tangled Web,* New York Times § 5, p. 1, col. 2 (March 15, 1987); Greg Papanek, *A Lot of Hurt,* Sports Illustrated 89 (October 19, 1987).

86. Tom Collins, Address to the Sports Lawyers Association, Los Angeles, CA (May 5, 1990).

87. *See Willoughby*, 1994 (cited in note 79), for a discussion of the player's case against his agent.

88. *Blatt v Farley*, 276 Cal Rptr 612 (1990).

89. 973 SW2d 348 (Tex App 1999), submitted October 16, 1997; opinion delivered June 25, 1998.

90. *Terrell v Childers*, 920 F Supp 854 (ND Ill 1996).

91. *Blatt*, at 612 (cited in note 88).

92. *Clark v Weisberg*, 1999 US Dist LEXIS 11341 (ND Ill 1999).

93. *Id.* at 4.

94. *Clark v Robert W. Baird Co., Inc.*, 2001 US Dist LEXIS 6275 (ND Ill 2001).

95. Jill Lieber, *And One Who Prospered*, Sports Illustrated 96 (October 19, 1987); Earl C. Gottschalk, Sr., *Orel Hershiser Sees a Lot of Pitches Related to Money*, Wall Street Journal p. 1, col. 4 (March 15, 1989).

96. *Brown v Woolf*, 554 F Supp 1206 (SD Ind 1983).

97. *Id.* at 1207.

98. *Id.*

99. *NFLPA Regulations Governing Contract Advisors*, § 4: Agreements Between Contract Advisors and Players; Maximum Fees, p. 9.

100. *Id.* at § 4(B)(3), p. 10.

101. Martin J. Greenberg & James T. Gray, *Sports Law Practice* 975 (Lexis, 2d ed 1998).

102. *NFLPA Regulations Governing Contract Advisors*, § 4(B)(4), p. 10.

103. *Id.*

104. Timothy Davis, *Regulating the Athelte-Agent Industry: Intended and Unintended Consequences*, 42 Williamette L Rev 781, 826 (2006).

105. *MLBPA Regulations Governing Player Agents*, § 4(F).

Chapter 6. Conflicts of Interest

1. See Chapter 1.

2. Leonard Lakin & Martin Schiff, *The Law of Agency* 97 (Kendall/Hunt, 2d ed 1996) (*Law of Agency*).

3. *Id.* at 27.

4. *Reggie White's $1.5 Million Suit*, Sports Industry News 229 (July 28, 1989). The suit served as leverage in White's bid for a contract renegotiation.

5. Ron Borges & Larry Tye, *Patriots VP Faces Charges*, Boston Globe 33 (April 4, 1992).

6. *Detroit Lions, Inc. v Argovitz*, 580 F Supp 542 (ED Mich 1984).

7. *Id.* at 546.

8. *Id.* at 547.

9. *Detroit Lions*, at 547–48 (cited in note 6); *see generally* Lakin & Schiff, *Law of Agency* at 98 (cited in note 2).

10. Glen Macnow, *Chief of NHL Union Is on Thin Ice*, Philadelphia Inquirer, D-1, col. 1 (July 16, 1989).

11. Craig Neff, *Den of Vipers*, Sports Illustrated 84 (October 19, 1987).

12. This hypothetical scenario is based on a situation involving athletes who played for the Kansas City Royals Major League Baseball team in 1981. It is

discussed in Jamie E. Brown, *The Battle the Fans Never See: Conflicts of Interest for Sports Lawyers*, Note, 7 Georgetown J Legal Ethics, 813 (1994).
  13. *Id.* at 817.
  14. *Id.*
  15. Rob Remis, *Analysis of Civil and Criminal Penalties in Athlete Agent Statutes and Support for the Imposition of Civil and Criminal Liability Upon Athletes*, 8 Seton Hall J Sport L 1, 31 n 121 (1998).
  16. Brown, Georgetown J Legal Ethics at 813 (cited in note 12).
  17. Restatement (Second) of Agency § 387 (1958).
  18. *NBPA Regulations Governing Player Agents* 5–6 (as amended June 1991).
  19. *NHLPA Regulations Governing Agent Certification*, June 25, 2002.
  20. Andy Bernstein, *IMG Cuts Ties to NHL After Conflict Alleged*, SportsBusiness Journal 1, 41 (April 16–22, 2001).
  21. *Id.*
  22. Andy Bernstein, *Structure Still Shifting at SFX*, SportsBusiness Journal 10 (June 4–10), 2001.
  23. Liz Mullen, *Union Attorneys Giving SFX's New Baseball Company a Good Going-over*, SportsBusiness Journal 19 (April 9–15, 2001).
  24. Liz Mullen, *Fired Agents Blame Losses on SFX Merger*, SportsBusiness Journal 1, 31 (February 12–18 2001).
  25. Mark Hyman & Skip Rozin, *Sparks Fly at SFX*, BusinessWeek 68, A4 (June 25, 2001).
  26. *See* Jack McCallum, *I Own You*, Sports Illustrated 50 (February 14, 2000).
  27. *NBPA Regulations Governing Player Agents* 5–6 (as amended June 1991).

Chapter 7. Ethics

  1. Walter T. Champion, *Attorneys qua Sports Agents: An Ethical Conundrum*, 7 Marquette Sports L J 349, 359 (1997).
  2. Robert E. Fraley & F. Russell Harwell, *Ethics and the Sports Lawyer: A Comprehensive Approach*, 13 J Legal Prof, 9, 53 (1988).
  3. *Id.*
  4. Comment, *The Agent-Athlete Relationship in Professional and Amateur Sports: The Inherent Potential for Abuse and the Need for Regulation*, 30 Buffalo L Rev 815, 823 n 37 (1981).
  5. John A. Walton, *Conflicts for Sports and Entertainment Attorneys: The Good News, the Bad News and the Ugly Consequences*, 5 Villanova Sports & Ent L J 259, 261 (1998).
  6. *Id.* at 264.
  7. *Id.* at 261.
  8. *Id.* at 263.
  9. Fraley & Harwell, 13 J Legal Prof at 74–75 (cited in note 2).
  10. Walton, 5 Villanova Sports & Ent L J at 273 (cited in note 5).
  11. Annotated Model Rules Rule 1.7 (commentary at 11) (1983).
  12. Fraley & Harwell, 13 J Legal Prof at 73–74 (cited in note 2).
  13. *NBPA Regulations Governing Player Agents* 5–6 (as amended June 1991).
  14. Fraley & Harwell, 13 J Legal Prof at 74–76 (cited in note 2).
  15. Jamie E. Brown, *The Battle the Fans Never See: Conflicts of Interest for Sports Lawyers*, 7 Georgetown J Legal Ethics, 813, 818 (1994).

16. Walton, 5 Villanova Sports & Ent L J at 263 (cited in note 5).

17. *Detroit Lions, Inc. v Argovitz*, 580 F Supp 542 (ED Mich 1984).

18. *Id.* at 548.

19. *Id.*

20. John C. Weistart & Cym H. Lowell, *The Law of Sports* 53 (1985 Supplement).

21. *Id.* at § 3.19, at Supp. 53 (1985).

22. Fraley & Harwell, 13 J Legal Prof at 19 n 23 (cited in note 2).

23. *Id.* at 19 n 24.

24. ISBA Advisory Opinion on Professional Conduct, Opinion No. 700 (November 4, 1980).

25. *Cuyahoga County Bar Association v Glenn*, 649 NE2d 1213 (Ohio 1995).

26. *In the Matter of Fredrick J. Henley, Jr.*, 478 SE2d 134 (Ga 1996).

27. Paul T. Dee, *Ethical Aspects of Representing Professional Athletes*, 3 Marquette Sports L J 111, 113 (1992).

28. *In the Matter of a Member of the State Bar of Arizona, James J. Dwight*, 573 P2d 481 (Ariz 1977).

29. *Id.* at 484.

30. *Id.*

31. *Kelly v State Bar of California*, 808 P2d 808 (Cal 1991).

32. *Id.* at 517.

33. *Id.*

34. *In re Pappas*, 768 P2d 1161, 1166 (Ariz 1988).

35. Michael A. Weiss, *The Regulation of Sports Agents: Fact or Fiction?* 1 Sports Law J 329, 349 (1994); Curtis D. Rypma, Note, *Sports Agents Representing Athletes: The Need for Comprehensive State Legislation*, 24 Valparaiso Univ L Rev 481, 407 (1990).

36. Fraley & Harwell, 13 J Legal Prof at 41–42 (cited in note 2).

37. *In the Matter of the Application of Steven B. Jackman for Admission to the Bar*, 761 A2d 1103, 1106 (NJ 2000)

38. *Id.*

39. *Birbrower, Montalbano, Condon & Frank P.C. v The Superior Court of Santa Clara County*, 949 P2d 1 (Cal 1998).

40. *Id.* at 6.

41. ISBA Advisory Opinion on Professional Conduct, Opinion No. 700 (November 4, 1980).

42. Model Rules of Professional Conduct, Rule 7.3(a).

Chapter 8. Agent Wars

1. Leonard Lakin & Martin Schiff, *The Law of Agency* at 101 (Kendall/Hunt, 2d ed 1996) (*Law of Agency*).

2. *"Tank" Beats the Rap Star*, Ottawa Sun 72 (November 3, 2004).

3. *Id.*

4. Mike Freeman, *Pro Football, Protecting Players from Their Agents*, New York Times § 8, p. 1 (July 26, 1998).

5. *Gandler v Nazarov*, 1995 WL 363814 (SDNY).

6. *Id.*

7. 898 SW2d 98 (Mo Ct App 1995).

8. Lakin & Schiff, *Law of Agency* at 109 (cited in note 1).

9. *Id.* at 124.

10. *Id.*

11. *Zinn v Parrish*, 644 F2d 360 (7th Cir 1981).

12. *Id.* at 361.

13. *Id.* at 362.

14. *Id.* at 364.

15. *Id.* at 366.

16. *Athletes and Artists, Inc. v Millen*, 1999 US Dist LEXIS 11991 (SDNY).

17. *Id.* at 16.

18. *Id.* at 8.

19. National Football League Players Standard Representation Agreement § 12.

20. *Id.*

21. *Pro Tect Management Corp. v Worley*, 1991 US Dist LEXIS 13058 (SDNY).

22. Liz Mullen, *Rosenhaus Targeted by Lawsuit*, SportsBusiness Journal 6 (September 19, 2005).

23. *Rosenhaus v Star Sports, Inc.*, 929 So2d 40 (Fla Ct App 2006).

24. *Speakers of Sports, Inc. v ProServ, Inc.*, 178 F3d 862 (7th Cir 1999).

25. *Id.* at 864.

26. *Id.*

27. *Id.* at 865.

28. *Wright v Bonds*, 117 F3d 1427, 1997 US App LEXIS 24340 (9th Cir 1997) (unpublished opinion).

29. Bryan Couch, *How Agent Competition and Corruption Affects Sports and the Athlete-Agent Relationship and What Can Be Done to Control It*, 10 Seton Hall J Sport L 111, 119 (2000). Other examples of allegations by an agent that another agent improperly interfered with his or her client include *Roundball Enterprises, Inc. v Richardson*, 616 F Supp 1537 (SDNY 1985) (sports representation firm alleged that agent Patrick Healy improperly persuaded basketball player Michael Ray Richardson to terminate his contract with Roundball and sign a representation agreement with Healy's sports management firm).

30. *Beverly Hills Sports Council v Wright*, 2002 Cal App Unpub LEXIS 9628.

31. *Manton v California Sports, Inc.*, 493 F Supp 496 (ND Ga 1980).

32. Liz Mullen, *Financial Advisor Sues Audit Firm Hired by NBPA*, SportsBusiness Journal 6 (February 26, 2007).

33. Liz Mullen, *Countersuit: Agent Stalled My Career*, SportsBusiness Journal 10 (October 6, 2003).

34. *Faigin v Kelly*, 184 F 3d 67, 74 (1st Cir 1999).

35. *Id.* at 73.

36. *Id.* at 74.

37. *Weinberg v Silber*, 140 F Supp 2d 712 (ND Tex 2001).

38. *Jacobs v ProSports Management of the South, Inc.*, 243 BR 836, 845 (MD Fla 2000).

39. Liz Mullen, *Steinberg Case: Secret Agent's Tale*, SportsBusiness Journal 1 (June 18–24, 2001).

40. Liz Mullen, *Agent Lawsuit File Kept Open*, SportsBusiness Journal 6 (July 16–22, 2001).

41. *Id.*

42. *See* Liz Mullen, *Union Claims Role in Agency Lawsuit*, SportsBusiness Journal 1 (July 9–15, 2001).

43. *Id.* at 52.

44. Liz Mullen, *Restraining Order Issued Against Dunn*, SportsBusiness Journal 42 (August 20–26, 2001).

45. Liz Mullen, *21 Players Back Dunn in Fight with Steinberg*, SportsBusiness Journal 3 (August 27–September 2, 2001).

46. *Steinberg Moorad & Dunn Inc. v Dunn*, 136 Fed App 6 (9th Cir 2005).

47. *Id.* at 5.

48. Liz Mullen, *NFL Union Wins a Round in Fight to Discipline Agent Dunn*, SportsBusiness Journal 14 (March 13, 2006).

49. *Id.*

50. Liz Mullen, *NFLPA Set to Resume Disciplinary Action Against Agent Dunn*, SportsBusiness Journal 14 (May 15, 2006).

51. Liz Mullen, *Dunn's Bankrupcty Maneuver Played into Supension Union Says*, SportsBusiness Journal 20 (December 4, 2005).

Chapter 9. The Last Amateurs on Earth

1. David C. Young, *The Olympic Myth of Greek Amateur Athletics* 7 (Ares, 1985). For a critical view of the amateurism ideal in intercollegiate athletics, *see* Walter Byers, *Unsportsmanlike Conduct: Exploiting College Athletes* (University of Michigan Press, 1995). Byers served as executive director of the NCAA from 1951 to 1987. Another critical assessment of the incorporation of the amateur ideal into American intercollegiate athletics as manifested in the NCAA regulatory system can be found in Allen L. Sack & Ellen J. Staurowsky, *College Athletes for Hire: The Evolution and Legacy of the NCAA's Amateur Myth* (Praeger, 1998).

2. John C. Weistart & Cym H. Lowell, *The Law of Sports* p. 7, § 1.04 (Michie, 1979) (*Law of Sports*).

3. National Collegiate Athletic Association, 2006–7 Manual art. 2.9 [hereinafter NCAA Manual].

4. NCAA Manual art. 2.9.

5. Weistart & Lowell, *Law of Sports* at 7, § 1.04 (cited in note 2).

6. NCAA Manual art. 12.1.2(a) & (b).

7. Howard J. Savage, *American College Athletics* (Carnegie Foundation for the Advancement of Teaching, 1929).

8. *Id.* at 34.

9. Young, *Olympic Myth* at 7 (cited in note 1).

10. *Id.* at 1. Young notes later that in a single running event the winner received enough money to buy six or seven slaves, one hundred sheep, or three houses. *Id.* at 127.

11. *Id.* at 7.

12. Eugene A. Glader, *Amateurism and Athletics* (Leisure Press, 1978).

13. Young, *Olympic Myth* at 7 (cited in note 1).

14. *Id.* at 8.

15. *Id.*

16. *Id.* at 9 n 3. Young maintains further that this was not, in fact, the first revival of the Olympics. He writes that as early as 1870 a modern Olympiad took place in Athens and cash prizes were awarded. *Id.* at 31.

17. *Id.* at 9.

18. *Id.* at 10.

19. *Id.* at 9.

20. *Id.* at 12.

21. *Id.* at 12–13.

22. *Id.* at 13.

23. *Id.* at 14.

24. Marc Pachter, *Champions of American Sport* 195 (Abrams, 1981).

25. *Id.*

26. Young, *Olympic Myth* at 87 n 84 (cited in note 1).

27. *Id.* at 86, citing Avery Brundage, "Why the Olympic Games?" in United States Olympic Committee, *Report: Games of the XIVth Olympiad, London, England* 23ff. (1948).

28. Young, *Olympic Myth* at 87 n 84 (cited in note 1).

29. *Id.*

30. *Id.* at 100, citing H. Hewitt Griftin, *Athletics* 13–14 (George Bell, 1891), and H. F. Wilkinson, *Modern Athletics* 16 (Frederick Warne, 1868).

31. Young, *Olympic Myth* at 19 (cited in note 1).

32. Glader, *Amateurism and Athletics* at 15 (cited in note 12); Ronald A. Smith, *Sports and Freedom: The Rise of Big-Time College Athletics* 166 (Oxford University Press, 1988).

33. Smith, *Sports and Freedom* at 166 (cited in note 32).

34. Glader, *Amateurism and Athletics* at 17 (cited in note 12).

35. Smith, *Sports and Freedom* at 165–66 (cited in note 32).

36. Savage, *American College Athletics* at 36 (cited in note 7).

37. Young, *Olympic Myth* at 22 (cited in note 1).

38. Smith, *Sports and Freedom* at 169 (cited in note 32), citing Alexander Agassiz, *Rowing Fifty Years Ago*, Harvard Graduates Magazine 458 (March 1907); Charles W. Eliot, *In Praise of Rowing*, 15 Harvard Graduates Magazine 532 (March 1907); and B. W. Crowninshield, *Boating*, in F. O. Vaille & H. A. Clark, *The Harvard Book* vol. 2, p. 263 (Welch, Bigelow, 1875).

39. Smith, *Sports and Freedom* at 171 (cited in note 32).

40. *Id.* at 188.

41. *Id.*

42. *Id.*

43. *Id.* at 174.

44. Savage, *American College Athletics* at 42 (cited in note 7).

45. "Eligibility Rules," NCAA Constitution (1906), art. VII.

46. Paul Lawrence, *Unsportsmanlike Conduct: The National Collegiate Athletic Association and the Business of College Football* 24 (Praeger, 1987).

47. *Id.* at 43.

48. *Walters and Bloom v Fullwood and Kickliter*, 675 F Supp 155 (SDNY 1987).

49. *Id.* at 163.

50. *National Collegiate Athletic Association v Board of Regents of the University of Oklahoma*, 468 US 85 (1984).

51. *Id.* at 96 (emphasis added).

52. *Gaines v NCAA*, 746 F Supp 738 (MD Tenn 1990).

53. *Id.* at 744 (emphasis added).

54. *Banks v NCAA*, 977 F2d 1081 (7th Cir 1991).

55. *Id.* at 1091 (emphasis added).

56. *Id.*

57. NCAA Manual art. 12.1.2.

58. NCAA Manual art. 12.1.2.1.1.

59. NCAA Manual art. 12.3.1.2.

60. NCAA Manual art. 12.1.2(g).

61. 2000–2001 NCAA Manual art. 15.02.4.

62. 2000–2001 NCAA Manual art. 15.02.4.

63. 2000–2001 NCAA Manual art. 15.02.04.

64. 2000–2001 NCAA Manual art. 15.02.4.

65. 2000–2001 NCAA Manual art. 15.02.4(d).

66. 2006–7 NCAA Manual § 15.2.7, at 197.

67. *Id.*

Chapter 10. Knights of Columbus Rules?

1. Jack Falla, *NCAA: The Voice of College Sports* 13 (NCAA, 1981).

2. Richard D. Schultz, Speech to Sports Lawyers Association, Washington, DC (May 12, 1989).

3. 2006–7 NCAA Division I Manual § 12.3.1 at 73.

4. *Id.*

5. Mike Sullivan & Craig Neff, *Shame on You, SMU,* Sports Illustrated 18 (March 19, 1987).

6. *$1.8 Million in Losses Faced by Kentucky Under Probation,* Sports Industry News 157 (May 26, 1989).

7. Schultz, Speech (cited in note 2).

8. NCAA, *Memorandum to Individuals Acting in the Capacity of Player Agents* (September 2, 1988) (hereafter cited as NCAA memorandum).

9. Mike Trope with Steve Delsohn, *Necessary Roughness* 68 (Contemporary Books, 1987).

10. Bruce Selcraig, *Agents of Violence,* Sports Illustrated 25 (April 6, 1987).

11. Ben Brown, *Jury Selection Begins in Agents' Trial,* USA Today 1C, col. 2 (March 1, 1989).

12. Diana Sudia & Rob Remis, *The History Behind Athlete Agent Regulation and the "Slam Dunking of Statutory Hurdles,"* 8 Villanova Sports & Ent L J 67, 72 (2001).

13. Schultz, Speech (cited in note 2).

14. 29 USC § 141 *et seq.* (1982). For discussion of the applicability of the NLRA to sports, *see* Robert C. Berry, William B. Gould, & Paul D. Staudohar, *Labor Relations in Professional Sports* 31–34 (Auburn House, 1986).

15. *NFLPA Regulations Governing Contract Advisors* (hereafter cited as NFLPA Regulations); *MLBPA Regulations Governing Player Agents* (hereafter MLBPA Regulations); and *National Basketball Players Association Regulations Governing Player Agents* (hereafter NBPA Regulations).

16. *Collins v National Basketball Players Association,* 850 F Supp 1468 (D Colo 1991).

17. *Collins v National Basketball Players Association,* 976 F2d 740 (10th Cir 1992) (unpublished opinion).

18. *Collins,* 850 F Supp 1468 (cited in note 16).

19. Regulations Governing Contract Advisors, *2005 Amendments to the NFLPA Regulations* (May 16, 2005).

20. MLBPA Regulations at 3.

21. In 1988 the NBPA decertified one agent for improprieties and declared all basketball-related contracts negotiated by that agent void. *See Agent Has His Certification Suspended by NBA Union,* Philadelphia Inquirer E-5, col. 4 (May 31, 1988). Similarly, the *Philadelphia Inquirer* reported that the NFLPA had decertified a sports agent for alleged problems in "the handling of clients' funds." *See* Glen Macnow, *Becoming an Agent,* Philadelphia Inquirer A-12, col. 2 (August 23, 1987). Robert Ruxin also writes that the NFLPA refused to renew an agent's

certification because he forged a power of attorney. *See* Robert H. Ruxin, *An Athlete's Guide to Agents* 86 (Stephen Greene, 1989). The NFLPA maintains that confidential hearings have been held regarding other agents as well.

22. Lionel Sobel, *The Regulation of Sports Agents: An Analytical Primer*, 39 Baylor L Rev 727 (1987). The agreement is enforced with teams in collective bargaining agreements.

23. MLBPA Regulations at 2, citing 29 USC § 141 *et seq.* (1982).

24. *Id.* at 2, citing MLB Collective Bargaining Agreement, art. II.

25. *Id.* at 2, citing MLB Collective Bargaining Agreement, art. IV. One agent publicly decertified under the program was Jerry Kapstein, not for any improprieties but because he took a management position within the San Diego Padres organization. *Kapstein Decertified*, New York Times A-28, col. 2 (November 3, 1989). Gene Orza of the MLBPA noted that in the first nine months only one team had negotiated with an agent that was not certified, and in that case the team official admitted that negotiating with the uncertified agent had been unintentional. *See* Gene Orza, Speech to Sports Lawyers Association, Washington, DC (May 12, 1989).

26. 1992 US App LEXIS 24069 (10th Cir 1992) (unpublished opinion).

27. *Id.* at 7.

28. 87 F Supp 2d 1 (DDC 2000).

29. 92 F Supp 2d 918 (D Minn 2000).

30. *NFL Notes*, Washington Post \edq#\AU:PG#?(December 11, 1996).

31. Nicholas J. Cotsonika, *Agent Blames U-M's Carr for NFL Union* Sanctions, Detroit Free Press 1C (February 23, 1999).

32. *Id.* at 1C.

33. Liz Mullen, *Tank Fires Back: Black Claims Players He Defrauded Owe Him Money,* SportsBusiness Journal 13 (February 11, 2002).

34. Liz Mullen, *NFLPA Committee Votes to Suspend Agents Jerome Stanley, Neil Cornrich,* SportsBusiness Journal 13 (January 10, 2005).

35. *Id.*

36. Nate Allen, *Agent Resigns Under Pressure from NBA Players Association,* Mark's Sports Law News (March 14, 2001), www.sportslawnews.com/archive/Articles%202000/defaziodecert.htm

37. *Dunn and NFLPA Agree Suspension Will Last 18 Months,* SportsBusiness Journal 4 (November 27, 2006).

38. *Id.*

39. Liz Mullen, *NFLPA Issues One Year Suspensions for Branion, Sandhu,* SportsBusiness Journal 13 (April 9, 2007).

40. *Id.*

41. Liz Mullen, *Source: NFLPA Files Complaint Against Arrington's Agent,* SportsBusiness Journal 14 (January 23, 2006).

42. NFLPA Regulations Memo, *2005 Amendments to the NFLPA Regulations* (May 16, 2005).

43. Liz Mullen, *One-in-Three Rule's Arrival May Decertify About 150 NFL Agents,* SportsBusiness Journal 14 (September 26–October 2, 2005).

44. Liz Mullen, *NFLPA Thinks Rules Have Trimmed Agent Roster by at Least 240,* SportsBusiness Journal 14 (October 31–November 6, 2005).

45. NFLPA Regulations Memo, *SRA Disclosure for Recruiting Assistance Payments* (November 22, 2004).

46. Liz Mullen, *NFLPA Will Make Agents List Their "Runners,"* SportsBusiness Journal 5 (April 5–11, 2004).

47. Oversight Hearing on "The Arbitration Process of the National Football League Players Association," *Testimony of Richard T. Karcher* (December 7, 2006).

48. NFLPA, *2007 Amendments to the NFLPA Regulations Governing Contract Advisors*, April 4, 2007.

49. *Id.*

50. *Id.*

51. Sobel, *Regulation of Sports Agents* at 732 (cited in note 22).

52. Doug Allen, Memorandum to NFLPA contract advisers, November 1988.

53. Sobel, *Regulation of Sports Agents* at 735 (cited in note 22).

54. Orza, Speech (cited in note 25).

55. NFLPA Regulations and Code of Conduct Governing Registered Player Financial Advisors 3 (2002).

56. Introduction, NFLPA Regulations and Code of Conduct Governing Registered Player Financial Advisors, at 2 (2002).

57. *Id.*

58. *Id.* at 5.

59. *Id.* at 8.

60. *Id.* at 9, § II(C)—Professional Qualifications.

61. *Id.* at 10, § II(E)—Legal Standing.

62. *Id.* at 10, § III(A)—Criminal Record.

63. *Id.* at 11, § III(D)—Civil Judgments.

64. *Id.* at 12, § III(I).

65. *Id.* at 13, § III(G).

66. *Id.* at 13, § IV.

67. *Id.* at 14, § IV(B)(II).

68. *Id.* at 15, § IV(B)(II).

69. *Id.* at § II(D)—Insurance.

70. *Stephen D. Atwater v National Football League Players Association*, 2007 WL 1020848 (ND Ga).

71. *See* Gene Rosenblatt, *Agent Interests: Can ARPA Do the Job?* Sports Inc. 98 (November 16, 1987).

Chapter 11. The Laws

1. Katherine Waugh, *Shake 'Em Hard in the Sports Side*, National Law Journal 8 (April 3, 1989).

2. Uniform Athlete Agents Act (2000).

3. 18 USC 1961 *et seq.* (1988).

4. John Gorman, *Lawyers Testify They Gave Lawyers Wrong Information*, Chicago Tribune § 4, p. 2, col. 5 (March 30, 1989).

5. Waugh, National Law Journal at 8 (cited in note 1).

6. *Criminal Penalties Imposed in Agent Contract Case*, Sports Industry News 125 (April 28, 1989).

7. *Clark v Robert W. Baird, Co.*, 142 F Supp 2d 1065 (ND Ill 2001).

8. 18 F3d 899 (11th Cir 1994).

9. *Id.* at 914.

10. Robert H. Ruxin, *An Athlete's Guide to Agents* 90 (Stephen Greene, 1989).

11. Glenn Burleigh, *Sports Law and Representation: More Agents Than Players in Lucrative Field?* 133 Chicago Daily Law Bulletin (October 7, 1987). *See, e.g.*, Robert C. Berry, William B. Gould, & Paul D. Stadohar, *Labor Relations in Professional Sports*

255–56 (Auburn House, 1986), which notes that, regarding franchise relocations, "Congress will not at length do nothing and leave the disposition of the antitrust problems to the courts under existing law."

12. 15 USCA §§ 7801–7807 (2004).

13. Bill Sing, *Despite Reforms, Abuses Still Suspected on Wall St.*, Los Angeles Times p. 1, col. 3 (December 24, 1988).

14. *Former Agent Convicted*, New York Times B-87, col. 6 (March 2, 1978); *Abernethy v State*, 545 So 2d 185 (Ala Crim App 1988).

15. *See* discussion in Chapter 5.

16. Pre-UAAA statutes were *Ala Code* §§ 8-26-1 to -41 (2000); *Ariz Rev Stat* §§ 15-1761 to -1765 (2000); *Ark Code Ann* §§ 17-16-101 to -207 (Lexis 1999); *Cal Bus & Prof Code* §§ 6106.7, 18895 to 18897.97 (West 2000); *Colo Rev Stat Ann* §§ 23-16-101 to -108 (2000); *Conn Gen Stat.* §§ 20-553 to -569 (1999); *Fla Stat Ann* §§ 468.451 to .457 (West 2001); *Ga Code Ann* §§ 43-4A-3 to -20 (Supp 2001); *Ind Code Ann* §§ 35-46-4-1 to -4 (1998); *Iowa Code Ann* § 9A.1 to .12 (1995); *Kan Stat Ann* §§ 44-1501 to -1515 (2000); *Ky Rev Stat Ann* §§ 164.680–.689 (Michie 1999); *La Rev Stat Ann* §§ 4.420–433 (West 2001); *Md Code Ann Bus Reg* 4-401 to -426 (1999); *Mich Comp Laws* § 750.411e (Lexis 2001); *Minn Stat* § 325E.33 (1995); *Miss Code Ann* §§ 73-41-1 to -23 (2000); *Mo Rev Stat* §§ 317.018, 436.200–.212 (Supp 2001); *New Rev Stat* 398.065–.255 (2000); *NC Gen Stat* §§ 78C-71 to -81 (1999); *ND Cent Code* §§ 9-15-01 to -05 (2001); *Ohio Rev Code Ann* §§ 4771.01–.99 (Anderson 2000); *Okla Stat Ann* tit 70, §§ 821.61–.71 (1997); *Ore Rev Stat* tit 52, §§ 702.005–.057 (1999); 5 *Pa Cons Stat* §§ 3301–3312 (2000); *SC Code Ann* §§ 16-1-90, 16-1-100, 59-102-10 to -50 (2000); *Tenn Code Ann* §§ 49-7-2112 to -2121 (2000); *Tex Occ Code Ann* §§ 2051.001–.553 (Vernon 2000).

17. HB 1251, 56th Leg, 1st Reg Sess (Wash 1999).

18. Miss Code Ann § 73-67-1 (2001) (repealing existing agent statute and replacing it with the Uniform Athlete Agents Act).

19. *Alabama to Forfeit $250,000 to N.C.A.A.*, New York Times B-l, col. 5 (December 16, 1987).

20. Richard P. Woods & Michael R. Mills, *Tortious Interference with an Athletic Scholarship: A University's Remedy for the Unscrupulous Sports Agent*, 40 Alabama L Rev (1988).

21. Jack Cavanaugh, *UMass and UConn Lose '96 Honors*, New York Times (May 9, 1997).

22. *Id.*

23. Ala Code, § 8-26-1.1.

24. The following series of pre-UAAA articles provide detailed analysis of athlete agent statutes: Rob Remis, *Analysis of Civil and Criminal Penalties in Athlete Agent Statutes and Support for the Imposition of Civil and Criminal Liability Upon Athletes*, 8 Seton Hall J Sport L 1 (1998); Rob Remis, *The Art of Being a Sports Agent in More than One State: Analysis of Registration and Reporting Requirements and Development of a Model Strategy*, 8 Seton Hall J Sport L 419 (1998); Rob Remis & Diane Sudia, *Escaping Athlete Agent Statutory Regulation: Loopholes and Constitutional Defectiveness Based on Tri-Parte Classification of Athletes*, 9 Seton Hall J Sport L 1 (1999); Diane Sudia & Rob Remis, *Athlete Agent Solicitation of Athlete Clients: Statutory Authorization and Prohibition*, 10 Seton Hall J Sport L 205 (2000); Diane Sudia & Rob Remis, *Statutory Regulation of Agent Gifts to Athletes*, 10 Seton Hall J Sport L 265 (2000); Diane Sudia & Rob Remis, *Athlete Agent Contract: Legislative Regulation*, 10 Seton Hall J Sport L 317 (2000).

25. *See* Edward V. King, Jr., *Dependency Leads to Abuse*, New York Times § 8–9, col. 2 (March 5, 1989).

26. *See, e.g.*, Cal Bus & Prof Code § 18895.2(2)(a); Fla Stat Ann § 468.452(2); La Rev Stat Ann § 430; Miss Code Ann § 73-41-2 1; NC Gen Stat § 78C-2(1)(c); Okla Stat Ann tit 70, § 821.71.

27. *See, e.g.*, Ala Code § 8-26-2(2); Iowa Code Ann § 9A.2(2); Ken Rev Stat Ann § 164.680(3)(b); La Rev Stat Ann § 4:421(2); Ohio Rev Code Ann § 4771.01(B)(2); Tenn Code Ann § 49-7-2111(2).

28. *Texas Fines Former Heisman Winner Firm Under Agent Law*, NCAA News 2 (December 27, 1989).

29. *Id.*

30. Danny Robbins, *Agent Fined, Suspended by State*, Houston Chronicle 4 (January 19, 1996).

31. Franz Lidz & Richard O'Brien, *Seminole Justice*, Sports Illustrated, 9 (August 8, 1994).

32. Jack McCallum & Richard O'Brien, *Singled Out*, Sports Illustrated 15 (July 25, 1994).

33. *Limogate Finally Runs Its Course*, South Florida Sun-Sentinel 8 (June 23, 1999).

34. *Agent's Arrest Ordered by Judge*, Atlanta Journal and Constitution E9 (September 1, 1999).

35. *Man Impersonates Jarvis' Agent*, Raleigh News and Observer C7 (May 26, 2000).

36. Chris Harry, *Attorney Pleads Out in UF Case*, Orlando Sentinel C3 (May 25, 2000.)

37. *See, e.g.*, *Taylor v Wake Forest University*, 191 SE 2d 379 (NC Ct App 1972) cert. den. 192 SE 2d 197; *Begley v Corporation of Mercer University*, 367 F Supp 908 (ED Tenn 1973); Derek Quinn Jones, Note, *Educating Misguided Student Athletes: An Application of Contract Theory*, 85 Columbia L Rev 96 (1985). *See also* Woods & Mills, 40 Alabama L Rev at 141 (cited in note 20).

38. Scott Edelman, *Colleges Can Take Action Against Agents*, New York Times 11 (October 15, 1995).

39. *Id.*

40. *Id.*

41. *Id.* Remis, 8 Seton Hall J Sport L at 419, 449 (cited in note 24). These panels are also permitted to advise student athletes regarding professional careers; provide information to assist athletes in obtaining a loan for purchasing insurance to guard against a disabling injury; and review a proposed contract with a professional team.

42. *Id.*

43. Diane Sudia & Rob Remis, *The History Behind Athlete Agent Regulation and the "Slam Dunking of Statutory Hurdles,"* 8 Villanova Sports & Ent L J 67, 88 (2001).

44. *Id.* at 67, 85.

45. *Id.* at 67, 86. For a thorough discussion of vagueness concerns with athlete agent laws, *see* Remis & Sudia, 9 Seton Hall J Sport L at 1 (cited in note 24).

46. Gary Kohn, *Sports Agents Representing Professional Athletes: Being Certified Means Never Having to Say You're Qualified*, 6 Ent & Sports Lawyer 1 (Winter 1988).

47. *City of Oakland v Oakland Raiders*, 174 Cal App 3d 414 (1985). For a thorough discussion of the related preemption and federalism issue as well as the use of the supremacy clause, *see* Paul Wolfson, *Preemption and Federalism: The*

Missing Link, Hastings Constitutional L Quarterly 69 (Fall 1988). *See also Partee v San Diego Chargers Football Co.,* 34 Cal App 3d 378, 194 *Cal Rptr* 367, 668 P2d 674 (1983), which reaches a similar decision in holding that the NFL requires nationally uniform regulation and that it would be unnecessarily burdened if state antitrust laws applied.

48. *Walters, Alabama Settle Dispute over Signings,* Sports Industry News 156 (May 20, 1988).

49. Craig Neff, *Soft Time,* Sports Illustrated 13 (May 23, 1988).

50. *Agent Conviction Thrown Out by Alabama Appeals Panel,* Sports Industry News 5 (January 6, 1989). *Abernethy v State,* 545 So 2d 185 (Ala Ct App 1988).

Chapter 12. A Uniform Approach

1. Robert N. Davis, *Exploring the Contours of Agent Regulation: The Uniform Athlete Agents Act,* 8 Villanova Sports & Ent L J 1 (2001) (providing a detailed discussion of the legislative history of the act).

2. There are currently more than 140 uniform laws. *See* Directory of Uniform Acts and Codes, U.L.A. (1989 West Supp.).

3. *See, e.g.,* Uniform Arbitration Act, Explanation, 7 U.L.A. IV (1985).

4. Davis, 8 Villanova Sports & Ent L J at 3 (cited in note 1) (quoting NC-CUSL's 1999–2000 Reference Book). The National Conference of Commissioners on Uniform State Law was organized in 1892. The objective of the conference is to promote uniformity in state law on all subjects on which the states agree uniformity is desirable.

5. The majority of states provide the governor or legislature with express legislative authority to appoint an average of four commissioners for three-year terms.

6. Davis, 8 Villanova Sports & Ent L J at 3 (cited in note 1).

7. *Id.* at 5 (quoting letter from Richard C. Hite, Chairman, Study Committee, to Study Committee Members [July 23, 1996] [on file with author]).

8. *Id.* at 4.

9. *Id.* at 5 (quoting letter from Bion Gregory, President, NCCUSL, to Richard C. Hite, Chairman, Study Committee [June 14, 1996] [on file with author]).

10. *Id.* at 5–6 (quoting letter from Richard C. Hite, Chairman, Study Committee, to Study Committee Members [July 23, 1996] [on file with author]).

11. *Id.* at 6.

12. *Id.*

13. *Prefatory Note,* Uniform Athlete Agents Act 6 (2000) [hereafter UAAA].

14. *Id.* at 5–6.

15. *Id.* at 6.

16. § 2 (2), UAAA.

17. *Prefatory Note,* UAAA.

18. *Prefatory Note,* UAAA.

19. § 5, UAAA.

20. *Prefatory Note,* UAAA.

21. Davis, 8 Villanova Sports & Ent L J at 9 (cited in note 1).

22. § 9, UAAA.

23. Davis, 8 Villanova Sports & Ent L J at 13 (cited in note 1).

24. § 5 (b), UAAA.

25. § 4 (c), UAAA.

26. *Prefatory Note*, UAAA.

27. § 10 (6)(c), UAAA.

28. § 10 (6)(d), UAAA.

29. *Prefatory Note*, UAAA.

30. § 11 (a) & (b).

31. *Prefatory Note*, UAAA.

32. § 13, UAAA.

33. § 14, UAAA.

34. § 15, UAAA.

35. *Prefatory Note*, UAAA.

36. § 16, cmt, UAAA.

37. § 17, UAAA.

38. Phillip J. Closius, *Hell Hath No Fury Like a Fan Scorned: State Regulation of Sports Agents*, 30 U Toledo L Rev 511, 520 (1999).

39. Diane Sudia & Rob Remis, *Athlete Agent Legislation in the New Millennium: State Statutes and the Uniform Athlete Agents Act*, 11 Seton Hall J Sport L 263, 279 (2001).

40. *Indictment: Man Sent LSU Players Texts for Agent*, Sporting News.com (April 13, 2007), http://www.sportingnews.com/yourturn/viewtopic.php?t=196820 (last visited June 9, 2007).

41. Adrian Angelette, *La. Law Allows Agent-Athlete Contact Within Rules*, Baton Rouge Advocate A1 (October 26, 2006).

42. Timothy Davis, *Regulating the Athlete-Agent Industry: Intended and Unintended Consequences*, 42 Willamette L Rev 781, 814–15 (2006).

43. *Prefatory Note*, UAAA.

44. Davis, 8 Villanova Sports & Ent L J at 17 (cited in note 1).

45. Diane Sudia & Rob Remis, *The History Behind Athlete Agent Regulation and the "Slam Dunking of Statutory Hurdles,"* 8 Villanova Sports & Ent L J 67, 91 (2001).

46. Davis, 42 Willamette L Rev at 815 (cited in note 42).

Chapter 13. Conclusion

1. Rodney K. Smith & Robert D. Walker, *From Inequity to Opportunity: Keeping the Promises Made to Big-Time Intercollegiate Student Athletes*, 1 Nevada L J 160, 166 (2001).

2. *Id.* at 187–92.

3. *Id.* at 167.

4. Kenneth L. Shropshire, *The Erosion of the NCAA Amateurism Model*, Antitrust 46 (Spring 2000).

5. A fine summary of these possible legal impediments may be found in Smith & Walker, 1 Nevada L J at 166 (cited in note 1).

6. *See* David Pickle, *Experience-Based Amateurism Model Presented to Division II Membership*, NCAA News C1 (January 17, 2000).

7. Title IX of the Civil Rights Act of 1964, as amended by the Education Amendments of 1972.

8. Daniel Feigen, *Green with Envy: Athletes Earn College and NCAA Money, but What's in It for Them?* Houston Chronicle 1 (March 31, 1991).

9. Even these, if at a fixed level, could be subject to antitrust scrutiny. For a discussion of those potential issues, *see Sports and Antitrust: Should College Students Be Paid to Play?* 65 Notre Dame L Rev 206 (1990); and Note, *Sherman Act Invalidation of NCAA Amateurism Rules*, 105 Harvard L Rev 1299 (1992).

10. Ted Tinling, *Tinling: Sixty Years in Tennis* 61 (Sidgwick & Jackson, 1983).

11. Mike Freeman, *Pro Football: Players Union Taking Steps to Exert More Control over Agents*, New York Times § 8, p. 5 (March 10, 2002).

12. *Id.*

13. *See* NFLPA website, http://www.nflpa.org/RulesAndRegs/AgentCertification .aspx

14. Dan Moldea, *Interference: How Organized Crime Influences Professional Football* 409 (William Morrow, 1989).

15. *Valukas Warns Mafia May Invade College Sports, Agents' Ranks*, Sports Industry News 125 (April 28, 1989).

Index

Sports teams are indexed by city.

Abdul-Jabbar, Kareem, 84
Abernethy, Jim, 5, 58, 148, 155
Advantage International, 41, 48
African American agents, 35–36, 63–66,
   78–79
African American athletes, 62–66
agent fees: and agent statutes, 154–55; and
   athletes' earnings, 69–70; and competition, 56–57; and contracts, 26, 33, 38,
   68, 86, 183n.10; excessive, 85–87; and
   players' associations, 86–87
agents. *See* agent wars; attorney agents;
   problem agents; sports agents; sports
   agents' business
agent wars, 107–16; acrimony among
   agents, 17, 113–16; agent competition,
   38, 55; agents against agents, 110–13,
   192n.29; agents against athletes,
   107–10; agents against teams, 112–13;
   interference with contractual relationships, 138
Aikman, Troy, 45
Ainge, Danny, 24
Air Jordan athletic shoes, 33
Alabama, athlete agent statutes, 148
Alfortish, Sean, 151
Allen, Ray, 24–25, 27
Allen, Terry, 78
Amateur Athletic Club of England, 121
Amateur Athletic Union (AAU), 7, 60
amateurism, 117–27; American collegiate,
   6, 119–20, 122–25, 193n.1; ancient
   Greek, 6, 117–21, 125, 193n.10,

193n.16; and compensation, 166–70,
   201n.9; defined, 117–18, 120–21; English, 120–23; loss of amateur status,
   118; NCAA ideal of, 6, 117–18, 124–25,
   148–49, 193n.1; NCAA review of, 7;
   NCAA rules of, 6–7, 117–18, 121,
   123–27; and noncompensation, 6,
   118–25; Olympic, 119–21, 125, 193n.16;
   vs. professional sports, 118, 122–23,
   169–70
Amateur Sports Act, 144
American Basketball Association, 13
American Basketball League (ABL),
   17, 67
American Football League, 13
Americans with Disabilities Act (ADA), 26
Ammirati Puris Lintas, 48
Anderson, Ray, 78–79
Aniston, Jennifer, 49
antitrust, 43, 51–52, 137, 168, 198n.11,
   200n.47
APA, 48
API Group (London), 48
Argovitz, Jerry, 89–90, 99–100
Arizona, courts on attorney ethics, 102–3
Arizona Diamondbacks, 115
Arkansas, athlete agent statutes, 148
Arli$$, 1, 22
Armato, Leonard, 26
Arrington, LaVar, 138
Artists Management Group, 51
Ascent Sports Management, 71
Ashe, Arthur, 16

Assante: consolidation's effects on, 5,
36–37, 40–42, 45–47; and Steinberg, 40,
45–46, 115
Association of Representatives of Professional Athletes (ARPA), 143
athlete agent statutes: and the commerce
clause, 153–54; and conflicts of interest
and excessive fees, 154–55; and free
speech, 154; impact of, 150–51; jurisdictional issues with, 152–53; narrow focus
of, 72; of states, 7, 148; vagueness of, 153
Athletes and Artists (A&A), 43, 110
Athletes First, 114–15, 138
Atkins, Steve, 2–3
Atlanta Falcons, 16, 34, 108
attorney agents: contracts negotiated by,
25–28; entrance into the business, 70;
ethics and conflicts of interest, 97–106;
multiple representation by, 99–100,
103–4; solicitation by, 105–6; standards
governing, 101; unauthorized practice
and attorney status, 100–106
Atwater, Steve, 76, 142–43
autograph relationships with products, 33

Babby, Lon, 25–26, 32, 35
bank fraud, 80–81, 146
Banks, Charles, 75
Banks v. NCAA, 125
Barnes, Roosevelt, 46, 64
Barnett, Mike, 94
Bartkowski, Steve, 16
Bartlestein, Mark, 74
baseball, professional vs. amateur, 122. *See
also* MLB
basketball academies for high school
players, 7
Bates, Bill, 76
Battie, Tony, 25
Battier, Shane, 25
Baxter, Fred, 81
Bell, Ricky, 15
Belle, Albert, 43–44
Beltran, Carlos, 68
Berman, Chris, 43
Berthelsen, Richard, 78–79, 115
Beverly Hills Sports Council (BHSC), 112
Billups, Chauncey, 67
*Birbrower, Montalbano, Condon & Frank,
P.C. v. The Supreme Court of Santa Clara
County*, 104–5

Black, Ivery, 57
Black, William ("Tank"): accused of payments to athletes, 59, 78; Vince Carter
sued by, 107; decertification of, 137–38;
illegal activities and prosecution of, 6,
17–18, 72, 78–79, 148, 155, 172; lawsuits
against, 83, 107; mismanagement by,
78–79; on the NFLPA, 137; Rutledge
on, 4; and David Ware, 69
Blackman, Martin, 15
*Black v. National Football League Players Asso-
ciation*, 137
Bledsoe, Drew, 45, 114–15
Bloom, Lloyd: improper actions and prose-
cution of, 6, 17–18; payments to ath-
letes, 58; and Norby Walters, 63, 155
(see also *U.S. v. Walters-Bloom*)
Blue Equity, 42, 50
Bob Woolf Associates, 49
Boesky, Ivan, 147
Boldin, Anquan, 111
Bond, Nelson, 143
Bond, Robert, 114
Bonds, Barry, 112
Boorstin, Daniel L., 123
Boras, Scott, 67–68
Boros, Julius, 56
Boston Red Sox, 80–81
Bosworth, Brian, 58
Bowens, Tim, 81
Bradley, Bill, 147
branding, 42, 44
Brands Hatch Leisure, 48
Branion, Joby, 138
Brett, George, 24
Brieant, Charles L., 125
British Amateur Rowing Association, 121
Bronner, Jim, 95
Brooks, Michael, 58
Brooks, Robert, 79
Brown, Andrew, 85–86
Brown, James E., 80–82
Brown, Kevin, 68
Brown, Kwame, 44
Brown, Mary K., 11
Brundage, Avery, 120–21
Brunner, Scott, 91
Bruschi, Tedy, 24
Bryant, Kobe, 43–44
Bush, Reggie, 2–3, 58
Byers, Walter, 193n.1

CAA (Creative Artists Agency), 17, 32–33, 47; client list of, 49; consolidation's effects on, 5, 37, 42, 45, 49, 51
Caffey, Jason, 79–80
Cage, Nicolas, 49
Calhoun, Lee, 120
California: athlete agent statutes, 148, 151–52; attorney statutes, 105; California Supreme Court, 102, 104–5
Cambridge University, 122–23
Camby, Janice, 61
Camby, Marcus, 4, 6, 61–62, 149
Campbell, Earl, 15
Canadian Football League (CFL), 91
Canadian Major Junior Hockey Club, 94
Carlisle Sports Management, 49
Carnegie Foundation, 119
Caron, Robert, 6–7, 58, 137, 151–52
Carroll, Wesley, 151
Carter, Cris, 146
Carter, Kevin, 114
Carter, Vince, 6, 34, 78, 107
Carucci, Vic, 113
Catchings, Tamika, 25–26
CBS, 110
Cebrun, Nate, 2, 151
Champion, Walter, 97
Chang, Michael, 48
Chicago Bears, 11, 101
Chicago Tribune, 60
Childress, Josh, 25
Cincinnati Bengals, 6, 23, 109
Cincinnati Red Stockings, 122
City of Oakland v. Oakland Raiders, 154
Clark, Ray, 41
Clark, Vincent, 85, 146
Clark v. Robert W. Baird, Inc., 85, 146
Clear Channel Communications, 44–45, 94–95
Clemens, Roger, 44
Cleveland Browns, 138
Clifton, Greg, 47
Climan, Sandy, 46
Close, Casey, 17, 47
Collins, Kerry, 114–15
Collins, Tom, 84
Collins v. National Basketball Players Association, 137
Colorado, athlete agent statutes, 148
commerce clause, 153–54
commercials, 15, 34. *See also* endorsements

communication, 171–72
Condon, Tom, 17, 47, 49, 64, 108
conflicts of interest, 88–96; agent self-interest and financial interests, 88–93; and athlete agent statutes, 154–55; and attorney agents, 97–106; and consolidation, 51; defined, 88; multiple representation and other conflicts, 90–93, 99–100; and the NBPA, 95, 99; players' association regulations of, 93–96; Restatement (Second) of the Law of Agency on, 93
Conley, Mike, Jr., 25
Conley, Mike, Sr., 25
Connecticut, athlete agent statutes, 148
consolidation of sports agency firms, 37–52; and antitrust, 51–52; Assante, 5, 36–37, 40–42, 45–47; Blue Equity, 42, 50; CAA, 5, 37, 42, 45, 49, 51; and conflicts of interest, 51; factors affecting, 38–42; full-service firms affected by, 36–37; IMG, 5, 37, 42, 47; Octagon, 5, 37, 41–42, 47–49; persistence of, 5; SFX, 5–6, 36–37, 41–45; Synergy, 50–51; WMG, 5, 42, 50
contracts, players': with agents, defined, 19; and agent fees, 26, 33, 38, 68, 86, 183n.10; agent-negotiated, 23–24, 27–28; agents' duties beyond, 28–29, 31–32 (*see also* full-service firms); athlete termination of, 110–11; attorney-negotiated, 25–28; family or friends' negotiation of, 24–25, 27; full-service firms' negotiation of, 33; incentives in, 29–30; and legal relationship, 18–21; reserve and option clauses in, 12–13; self-negotiated, 24, 27–28; UAAA on, 160–61
Cornrich, Neil, 138–39
Courrege, Joe, 76
Craighill, Frank, 41
Creative Artists Agency. *See* CAA
Crockett, Ray, 65, 142–43
Croshere, Austin, 46
CSI (London), 48
Csonka, Larry, 13
Culver, John, 27
Cummings, Von, 85
Curry, Eddy, 44
Curt Flood Act, 144
Cuyahoga County Bar Association v. Glenn, 101

Dallas Stars, 94–95
Darden, Calvin, 65, 73
Davis, Dale, 46
Davis, Jerry A., 84
Davis, Ron, 59
Davis, Stephen, 80–81, 114
Davis, Terrell, 29
DeFazio, Sal, 138
De La Hoya, Oscar, 84
Dell, Donald, 16–17, 50
Dent, Richard, 101
Department of Justice, 43
Detroit Lions, 69
Detroit Lions, Inc. v. Argovitz, 89–90, 99–100
Detroit Pistons, 26
Dickerson, Eric, 76
DiFonzo, Luigi, 78
Dishman, Cris, 77–78
Dogra, Ben, 17, 22, 45, 49
Dorsett, Tony, 15
Douglas, Maurice, 60
drug trafficking, 78–79
Drysdale, Don, 11–12
Dudley, Chris, 46
Duffy, Bill, 65
Duncan, Tim, 25
Dunn, David, 114–16, 138–39
Dwight, In re (Arizona Supreme Court), 102

Eagleson, Alan, 90
earn-outs, 40, 42–43
Edwards, Vince, 11
Eisley, Howard, 46
Elmore, Len, 27–28, 68–69
Elway, John, 13
endorsements: athlete's relationship with the product, 33; Blackman's role in, 15; fees for, 14; and full-service firms, 33, 35; and sports-entertainment synergy, 33, 43
Engelhard, Hadley, 113
English model of amateurism, 120–23
Enis, Curtis, 58
entertainment industry: agents' roles in, 30–31; sports' synergy with, 33, 43, 50–51
Erving, Julius, 15
ESQ, 104–5
eSuperstars.com, 41
extreme sports, 49

Faigin, A. J., 113
Falk, David, 17, 33, 38–39, 41–44, 55, 95–96
Falk Associates Management Enterprises (FAME), 41, 43
Farley, John, 84
Farr, D'Marco, 76
Federal Arbitration Act, 137
Federal Bureau of Investigation (FBI), 78
federal regulation of sports agents, 30–31. *See also* UAAA
Federal Trade Commission (FTC), 147, 164
Fegan, Dan, 40, 45
Fegan & Associates, 40, 46
Fehr, Don, 55
Fenech, Craig, 155
Ferraro, James, 151
fiduciary relationships, 19–20, 93, 107, 142
financial advisers, 140–42
Fisher, Jeff, 23
Flammini Group (Italy), 49
Fleischer, Larry, 90
Fleisher, Eric, 58
Florida: athlete agent statutes, 72, 151; investigations and prosecutions of agents, 78, 148, 151
Florida State University, 2, 151
Forte, Patrick, 88
Fortsmann, Ted, 37, 47
Fortsmann Little, 47
Foster, George, 82
Fox, Kenneth, 146
Fox network, 110
Francis, Steve, 25
Franklin, James, 79, 83
Franzese, Michael, 145, 172
Fredrick J. Henley, Jr., In the Matter of (Georgia Supreme Court), 101
free speech, 154
Fresno State University, 59
Fried, Jeff, 25
Frykholm, Linda, 77
Fuchs, Michael, 78
full-service firms: African American and female agents affected by, 35–36; alternatives to, 34; competition with, 34–35; and conflicts of interest, 34; consolidation's effects on, 36–37 (*see also* consolidation of sports agency firms); and endorsements, 33, 35; services offered, 32–33,

38–39; and sports-entertainment synergy, 33, 43, 50–51. *See also specific firms*

Gaines, Travelle, 163
Gaines v. NCAA, 125
Gandler, Mark, 108
Garciaparra, Nomar, 43–44
Garner, Charlie, 81
Garnett, Kevin, 67
Garrity, Pat, 25, 32
Garvey, Edward, 25
General Motors, 138
General Talent International, 62–63
Genske, Greg, 46
George, Eddie, 50
Georgia Supreme Court, 101
Giambi, Jason, 44
Gilbert, Sean, 76
Gilhooley, Robert, 95
Gillette, John W., Jr., 76, 146
Giordano, Leslie, 66
Glavine, Tom, 49
Global Sports & Entertainment, 75–76
golf, 16, 44, 48
Golub, Howard J., 82
Gonzalez, Juan, 95
good faith, 20–21, 88–90, 93, 97–99, 110
Gould, Jimmy, 137
Grange, Harold ("Red"), 11
Grant, Tom, 60
Greek model of amateurism, 6, 117–21, 125, 193n.10, 193n.16
Greenberg, Steve, 82
Greg Norman Production, 44
Gretzky, Wayne, 94
Griffin, Eddie, 44
Grossman, Jay, 45

Hardy, Leland, 18, 28–30
Harmon, Ron, 58
Harrington, Al, 67
Harris, Harold, 120–21
Harvard University, 122–23
Hayes, J. William, 11
Haywood, Brendan, 67
Healy, Patrick, 192n.29
Hendricks, Alan, 43, 45
Hendricks, Randall, 43, 45, 95
Hendricks Management Company, 43–44
Henley, Fredrick J., Jr., In the Matter of (Georgia Supreme Court), 101

Hernandez, Keith, 83
Hershiser, Orel, 85
Hicks, Tom, 94–95
Hill, Grant, 25–26
Hill, Greg, 3
Hilliard, Ike, 78–79, 83
Hogan, James, 122
holdouts, 11
Holdsclaw, Chamique, 25–26
Holmes, Jon, 43
Houston Gamblers, 89–90, 113
Houston Oilers, 12
Howard Law Journal, 63
Hudson, Eldridge, 3
Hunt, Waymon, 83
Huntley, Wendi, 66–67

Illinois Code of Professional Responsibility, 101
Illinois State Bar Association, 101, 105
Indianapolis Racers, 85–86
Integrated Sports International (ISI), 44
Internal Revenue Service (IRS), 78, 83
International Creative Management (ICM), 51
International Management Associates (IMA), 65
International Management Group (IMG): consolidation's effects on, 5, 37, 42, 47; founding of, 16; as full-service firm, 32–34, 39; income management by, 85; ownership of, 17, 47; and players' associations, 94; size of, 47
Internet, 40–41, 46
Interpublic Group, 41–42, 47–48
Iowa, athlete agent statutes, 148
Ivy League schools, 122–23

Jackson, Janet, 62–63
Jackson, Jesse, 78–79
Jackson, Dr. Michael, 56
Jackson, Samuel L., 73
Jacobs, Lawrence, 114
Jenkins, Corey, 80–81
Jerry Maguire, 1, 22, 68
Jocketty, Walt, 24
Johnson, Earvin ("Magic"), 112–13
Johnson, Peter, 47
Johnson, Rob, 114–15
Jones, Marion D., 80–82
Jones, Sean, 77–78

Jones v. Childers, 146
Joplin, Linda, 185n.82
Jordan, Michael, 33, 43–44, 95

Kansas City Royals, 91, 189–90n.12
Kapstein, Jerry, 196n.25
Karlis, Rich, 82
Kashif, 31
Katz, Adam, 50
Kearse, Jevon, 4
Keating, Ed, 56
Kelly, Jim, 90, 113
Kelly v. State Bar of California, 102
Kemp, Jack, 147
Kendricks v. Grant Thornton International, 84
Kersey, Jerome, 46
Kiick, Jim, 13
King, Don, 17
King, Edward V., Jr., 34, 56, 150
King, Kirk, 149
King, Shaun, 81
King, Stanley O., 70
Kirwan, Pat, 139
Kite, Tom, 48
Klarberg, Barry, 46
Klarberg, Raiola and Associates, 46
Klosterman, Don, 12
Koch Tavares (Brazil), 48
Koufax, Sandy, 11–12
Kournikova, Anna, 48
Kreiter, Keith, 28
Kuchar, Matt, 50

LaBelle, Patti, 62–63
Laboy, C. J., 163
LaFave, Arthur J., 47
laws. *See* athlete agent statutes; regulation of sports agents
Lawson, Safarrah, 113
lawyers as agents. *See* attorney agents
Leaf, Ryan, 114–15
Legacy Sports, 46
Lenglen, Suzanne, 11, 170
Leonard, Justin, 48
Levine, Michael, 49
Levy, Joel, 80
Lewis, Andre, 81
Lindros, Eric, 24–25
Linta, Joe, 67
Live Nation, 44–45

Livingston, Cliff, 59
Lombardi, Vince, 12
Long, Howie, 58
Loring Ward, 46
Los Angeles Lakers, 112–13
Louisiana, investigations of agents, 78, 162–63
Louisiana State University (LSU), 162–63
Lounsbury, John, 4, 6, 61–62
Love, Davis, III, 48
Lowe, Frank, 48–49
Lowe Group, 48
loyalty, duty of, 20–21, 88, 90, 93, 97–98
Luchnick, Lance Jay, 59
Lueddeke, David, 146
Lukens, Donald, 75–76, 146, 154
Lum, Robert, 82–83
Lustig, Greg, 113
Lynch, John, 114–15

Mackey v. National Football League, 13
Maddox, Gary, 85
Madlock, Bill, 82
mail fraud, 6, 80–81, 144–46
Major League Baseball. *See* MLB
Major League Baseball Collective Bargaining Agreement, 136–37, 196n.25
Major League Baseball Players Association. *See* MLBPA
Manning, Peyton, 33, 65
Manton, John, 112–13
Marbury, Stephon, 3, 50
Marion, Shawn, 46
Marquee Group, 41, 43
Martin, Kenyon, 46
Maximum Sports Management, 46
Maxwell, Cedric, 82
Mays, Willie, 11
McCann-Erickson World Group, 48
McCormack, Mark, 16–17, 37, 47. *See also* International Management Group
McCray, Nikki, 25–26
McGrew, Reggie, 4
McKenzie, Raleigh, 77
McKey, Derrick, 58
McRae, Hal, 91
M. D. Gillis & Associates, 46
media, 2, 14, 31, 34, 40
Michaels, Al, 43
Michaels, Michael, 2
Michigan, athlete agent statutes, 148

Milken, Michael, 147
Millen, Matt, 110
Miller, Andre, 25
Miller, Andy, 67
Miller, Percy ("Master P"), 30, 92–93
Miller Lite, 15
Mills, A. J., Jr., 70
Mills, Jack, 71
Milwaukee Bucks, 25
Minnesota Twins, 25
Misle, Howard, 108
Mississippi, athlete agent statutes, 148
Mitchell, Brian, 77
MLB (Major League Baseball): African
    Americans in, 65; and female agents,
    66; number of agents and players in, 18
    (table), 38; number of teams and
    leagues in, 180n.2; salaries of players, 68
MLBPA (Major League Baseball Players
    Association): and agent fees, 87; agent
    regulations and certification by, 135–36,
    196n.25; educational goals of, 140;
    founding of, 135; *MLBPA Regulations
    Governing Player Agents*, 87
Model Penal Code, 157
Model Rules of Professional Conduct
    (American Bar Association), 26–27,
    98–99
money laundering, 5, 78–81, 146
Monk, Art, 77
Montreal Alouettes, 15
Moon, Warren, 91
Moorad, Jeff, 115, 137
Moorad & Dunn, 41, 45–46, 114–15
Moore, Ricky, 149
Mora, Melvin, 25
Morris, Matt, 24
motor sports, 48
Motzkin, Richard, 50
Mourning, Alonzo, 44
Muhleman Marketing, 47
Mutombo, Dikembe, 44

Nalley, Jeffrey S., 58, 137
Namath, Joe, 13
NASCAR, 47
National Basketball Association. *See* NBA
National Basketball Players Association. *See*
    NBPA
National Collegiate Athletic Association.
    See NCAA

National Conference of Commissioners on
    Uniform State Laws (NCCUSL), 7,
    157–62, 200nn.4–5
National Football League. *See* NFL
National Football League Management
    Council, 137
National Football League Players Associa-
    tion. *See* NFLPA
National Hockey League. *See* NHL
National Hockey League Players Associa-
    tion. *See* NHLPA
National Labor Relations Act (NLRA),
    135–36
Nazarov, Andrei, 108
NBA (National Basketball Association):
    African Americans in, 65; vs. American
    Football League, 13; and contract self-
    negotiation, 27–28; and female agents,
    66; number of agents and players in, 18
    (table), 38; number of teams and
    leagues in, 180n.2; salaries of players,
    14, 38
NBC, 110
NBPA (National Basketball Players Associa-
    tion): and agent fees, 87; agent regula-
    tions and certification by, 135–36, 140,
    195n.21; auditors hired by, 113; and
    conflicts of interest, 95, 99; founding of,
    135; Don King certified as agent by, 17;
    NBPA Regulations Governing Player Agents,
    93–94
NCAA (National Collegiate Athletic Associ-
    ation): amateur ideal of, 6; authority of,
    133–34; employment rules of, 126–27;
    founding of, 131; and loans to athletes,
    57; member institutions of, 151–52;
    NCAA Manual, 132; non-agent rule by,
    2, 125; number of members, 131; play-
    ers on rules of, 3; reforms by, 166–70;
    rules and regulations of, 74, 108,
    131–35, 145; sanctions by, 59, 72,
    132–33, 149–51; and the UAAA, 7, 158,
    165–66; voluntary agent registration by,
    134–35. *See also* amateurism
NCAA v. Board of Regents, 125
Nelson, Chris, 25
New England Patriots, 24
New Jersey Supreme Court, 104
New Orleans Saints, 18–19, 29–30
Newport, Jeffrey, 150
Newsday, 59

Newton, Fairron, 81, 146
New York Athletic Club, 122
New York Giants, 91
New York state laws, 148
New York Times, 63, 107–8
NFL (National Football League): African Americans in, 65; Business Management program, 170; and consolidation, 51; Entrepreneurship program, 170; and female agents, 66; and financial advisers, 140–43; number of agents and players in, 18 (table), 38; number of teams and leagues in, 180n.2; Rookie Symposium, 170; salaries of players, 13–14, 29, 38; and UAAA, 158; vs. USFL, 13
NFL Collective Bargaining Agreement, 137
NFLPA (National Football League Players Association): on agent fees, 86–87; agent regulations and certification by, 19, 30, 59, 108, 135–36, 139–40, 171, 195–96n.21; arbitration system, 108; disciplining of agents by, 77, 115–16, 137–39; on financial advisers, 75, 140–43; founding of, 135; *NFLPA Regulations and Code of Conduct Governing Registered Player Financial Advisers*, 86, 140–41; and rookies, 140; Standard Representation Agreement, 19, 110–11
NHL (National Hockey League): African Americans in, 65; and consolidation, 51; and female agents, 66; number of agents and players in, 18 (table), 38; number of teams and leagues in, 180n.2; salaries of players, 14, 38; and UAAA, 158
NHLPA (National Hockey League Players Association), 66, 90, 94–95, 135–36
NHLPA Regulations Governing Agent Certification, 94
Nicklaus, Jack, 16
Nike, 14, 33, 51, 60
NKS Management, 46
Nokia, 47
No Limit Sports, 30
Noll, Roger, 13
notification requirements, 159, 162–63
Nuchow, Howard, 49

Oakland Raiders, 154
Octagon: client list of, 49; consolidation's effects on, 5, 37, 41–42, 47–49; as

full-service firm, 32–33, 39; Vick's representation by, 33–34
Oden, Greg, 25
Ohio: athlete agent statutes, 148, 152–53; Ohio Supreme Court, 101
Olympics, 119–21, 125, 193n.16
O'Malley, Walter, 12
Omnicom Group, 41
O'Neal, Shaquille, 26, 73
O'Neil, Terry, 18
Options Plus Financial Services, 81
organized crime, 145, 172. *See also* RICO
Ornstein, Mike, 2
Orr, Louis, 82
Orr, Terry, 77
Orza, Gene, 87, 140, 196n.25
Ovitz, Michael, 51
Owens, Terrell, 1, 68
Oxford University, 122–23

Palmer, Arnold, 16, 33
Palmer, Carson, 13, 139
Palmer, Paul, 1–2, 80
Parker, Eugene, 22, 45–46, 64
Parker, Scott, 46
Parrish, Lance, 82
Parrish, Lemar, 109–10
Pascoe, Alan, 48
Peters, Brian, 46
PGA Tour of America, 44
Philadelphia Eagles, 68, 88
Philadelphia Inquirer, 195n.21
Philpott, Bills & Stoll, 46
Phoenix Coyotes, 94
Pickens, Bruce, 108–9
Pickens, Carl, 23–24
Pierce, Palmer E., 124
Piggie, Myron, 17–18, 59–60, 144–45, 172
Pippen, Scottie, 82–83
Player, Gary, 16
players' associations: and agent fees, 86; agent regulations certification by, 135–40, 171, 195–96n.21, 196n.25; and education, 170; reform of, 170–71; revenues affected by, 14; sanctions by, 136–37. *See also specific associations*
Plummer, Jake, 45
Plunkett, Jim, 15
PMI (Professional Management, Inc.), 4, 78–79, 83, 107
Porter, Chris, 2, 58

Porter, Kevin, 148
Poston, Carl, 65, 138–39
Poston, Kevin, 65
problem agents, 72–87; excessive fees by,
    85–87; income mismanagement by,
    72–80; lawsuits against, 80, 82–85; legal
    mechanisms for, 80–85; legislative solu-
    tions for, 72; overview of, 1–2, 72–73;
    prosecution of, 80–82
Professional Management, Inc. *See* PMI
ProServ, 4, 16–17, 39, 41, 43, 62, 111–12
Pros Inc., 48
ProSports Management, 114
Puma, 107
Pyle, Charles C. ("Cash and Carry"), 11,
    170, 174n.3
Pyne, George, 47

Radke, Brad, 25
Ramsey, Githaiga, 79–80
Ray, Chris, 25
recruitment, 55–71; agent-client interac-
    tion in, 57, 60–61, 66–67; of agents,
    41–42; agents' view of, 57, 67–71; com-
    petition, 55–58, 70–71 (*see also* agent
    wars); ethics in, 57; gender barrier in,
    66–67; payments to, and solicitation of,
    athletes, 1–5, 57–62, 76, 78, 118; racial
    undertones of, 62–66; techniques for,
    57–59. *See also* conflicts of interest;
    problem agents
Reebok, 14
reform of collegiate athletics, 166–70. *See
    also* UAAA
regulation of sports agents, 131–43; by
    ARPA, 143; athlete agent statutes, 7,
    148–52; by educational institutions,
    151–52; federal regulations, 30–31,
    144–47 (*see also* UAAA); NCAA efforts,
    131–35; NFLPA financial adviser regula-
    tions, 140–43; by players' associations,
    135–40; and reform of collegiate sports,
    166–70; registration, 109, 134–35,
    140–42, 149–52, 155, 159–60, 162–63;
    self-regulation, 143; state regulations,
    148; before UAAA legislation, 148–50,
    152–55
Reich, Tom, 50
Reich & Katz, 50
Restatement (Second) of the Law of
    Agency, 19, 93

Rice, Simeon, 76
Richardson, Michael Ray, 192n.29
RICO (Racketeer Influenced and Corrupt
    Organizations Act), 85, 144–46
Ridnour, Luke, 25
Ringo, Jim, 12
Robertson, Pat, 76
Robert W. Baird Co., 85, 146
Robinson, David, 48
Robinson, Frank, 57
Robinson, Kevin, 70–71
Rocker, John, 44
Rodgers, Johnny, 15, 150
Rodriguez, Alex, 67–68
Rodriguez, Ivan, 111–12
Rogers, George, 58
Rohrer, Jeff, 76
Rone, David, 49
rookies, 28, 35, 69–70, 140
Roosevelt, Theodore, 131
Rose, Malik, 25
Rosenhaus, Drew, 1, 22, 68, 111
Roundball Enterprises, Inc. v. Richardson,
    192n.29
rowing, 122
Rozelle Rule, 13
Rozier, Mike, 57
Rubin, Jeffrey Z., 23–24
runners (street agents), 7, 59–60, 139, 159
Russell, Byron, 75–76
Ruth, Babe, 11
Rutledge, Johnny, 3–4, 55
Ruxin, Robert, 63, 195–96n.21

salaries of players, 13–14, 29, 38
sanctions: against attorney agents, 98, 101;
    cost of, 171; "death penalty" and proba-
    tion, 133; decertification, 136; via fed-
    eral legislation, 146–47; against Fresno
    State University, 59; by the NCAA, 59,
    72, 132–33, 149–51; by players' associa-
    tions, 136–37; by the UAAA, 160, 163;
    against Norby Walters, 145
Sander, Frank E. A., 23–24
Sanders, Barry, 69
Sanders, Deion, 46
Sanderson, Derek, 15
Sandhu, Zeke, 138
San Francisco 49ers, 137
San Francisco Giants, 24
Santiago, Benito, 49

Sarnoff, Ken, 111
Savage, Howard J., 119, 121
Schaffer, Peter, 50
Schembechler, Bo, 6
Schiller, Harvey, 46
Schilling, Curt, 24
Schubert, George W., 12
Schultz, Richard, 133–35
Scott, Merle, 34
Sean Michael Edwards Design (SME), 44
Securities and Exchange Commission (SEC), 75–79, 141, 146
Segal, Joel, 50, 137
Selcraig, Bruce, 172
SFX, 17; and Clear Channel, 44–45, 94–95; client list of, 44; consolidation's effects on, 5–6, 36–37, 41–45; reorganization of, 94–95
Sharpe, Shannon, 76
Sharpe, Sterling, 78
Shea & Gould, 145
Sheffield, Gary, 24
Shefsky, Lloyd, 147
Sherman Act, 13
Shorey, Paul, 119–20
Siegel, Michael B., 20
Signature Sports Group, 44
Silber, Howard, 114
Simmons, Brian, 77
Sims, Billy, 89–90. See also *Detroit Lions, Inc. v. Argovitz*
Singletary, Mike, 24
Slaughter, Fred, 63–64
Smith, Alex, 13
Smith, C. Lamont, 50, 64, 69
Smith, Emmitt, 46
Smith, Joe, 46
Smith, Robert, 77
Smith, Rodney K., 12, 166
Smith, Ronald A., 121–23
Sorkin, Richard, 82, 148, 155–56
Southern Methodist University (SMU), 133
SPARTA (Sports Agent Responsibility and Trust Act), 30–31, 57, 59, 147, 163–64, 172
Speakers of Sport, 111–12
Spears, Wesley, 4, 6, 61–62
Sports Agent Responsibility and Trust Act. *See* SPARTA
sports agents: African American, 35–36, 63–66, 78–79; attorneys as (*see* attorney

agents); defined, 19; female, 17, 35–36, 66–67; illegal activities and prosecution of, 4–8; legal basis of relationship with principals, 18–21; mergers among, 17 (*see also* consolidation of sports agency firms); number of agents and players, 18 (table), 38; opportunism of, 5; payments to athletes by, 1–5, 57–62, 74, 118; registration of, 109, 134–35, 140–42, 149–52, 155, 159–60, 162–63; revenues for, 37–39; stereotypes of, 22, 67–68. *See also* agent fees; agent wars; problem agents
sports agents' business, 22–36; agents' view of, 67–71; duties of agents, 28–29, 31–32 (*see also* full-service firms); and entertainment industry, 33, 43; and financial advisers, 74–77; gender barrier in, 66–67; history of, 11–18; need for an agent, 23–32; racial undertones of, 62–66, 78–79. *See also* agent fees; full-service firms; recruitment
SportsBusiness Journal, 65–67
SportsCenter, 22
Sports Illustrated, 11, 58, 66, 85
Sports Industry News, 133
Sports Lawyers Association (SLA), 147
Sports Management Group, 17
Sports Marketing and Television International, 41
SportsNet, 50
Sports Plus, 17
Sportstars, 17
Sprewell, Latrell, 22, 65, 73
Staley, Duce, 78
Stanley, Jerome, 138
Station, Larry, 58
statutes. *See* athlete agent statutes; regulation of sports agents
Steinberg, Leigh: on the agent business, 22, 67; and Assante, 40, 45–46, 115; on consolidation, 45–46; and Dunn, 114–16, 138; as early agent, 16; in legal disputes, 137; multiple representation by, 91; reputation of, 16, 41–42, 56; on the sports-entertainment synergy, 43; Ricky Williams's contract negotiated by, 29–30
Steinberg, Moorad & Dunn, 41, 45, 114–15
Steiner, Jim, 17, 45, 49
Stephens, Tony, 43

Stern, David, 7
Stern, Harry, 73
St. John, Dan, 114
St. Louis Cardinals, 24
street agents. *See* runners
Strickland, Bill, 28, 31, 50, 59, 65, 164
Sugar, Bob, 68
Sullivan & Sperbeck, 49
Summit Management Group, 80–82, 145–46
Super Bowl, 14, 16
Superstars, 17
Surhoff, B. J., 49
Synergy, 50–51

Taplin, Charles, 162–63
Taylor, Fred, 4, 78–79, 83
Taylor, Lawrence, 57
Taylor, Reggie, 81
Team America, 108
Technical Equities, 73
television, 13–16, 30, 45–46, 51, 72, 110
Telfair, Sebastian, 67
Tellem, Arn, 7, 17, 22, 45
Tellem & Associates, 41, 43–44, 50
Temple University, 56, 152
Tennessee Titans, 23
tennis, 11, 16–17, 50, 170, 174n.3
Terrell, Charles ("Walt"), 84
Texaco, 47
Texas, athlete agent statutes, 148, 150
Texas Christian University, 58
Texas Rangers, 67–68, 94–95
Thomas, Derrick, 138
Thomas, Kurt, 75–76
Thomas, Zach, 65
Thorpe, Jim, 120
Tilden, Bill, 174n.3
Time, 3, 12
Title IX, 168
Tony Rosenberg Promotions, 44
Toomer, Amani, 114–15
Total Economic Athletic Management of America, Inc. v. Pickens, 108
Total Economic Management of America, 150
Trentadue, Jess C., 12
Trope, Mike, 2–3; *Necessary Roughness*, 15–16, 134
Trost, Lonn, 145
Twitty, Alfred ("Tweet"), 4, 79

UAAA (Uniform Athlete Agents Act): on the agent's relationship with the principal, 19, 21; goals and rationale of, 7; key provisions of, 159–62; legislation before, 148–50, 152–55; and the NCAA, 7, 158, 165–66; NCCUSL and development of, 7, 157–62, 200nn.4–5; number of uniform laws, 200n.2; promulgation of, 30–31, 162; reception of, 163–64; scope of, 165–66; and SPARTA, 147, 163–64; and state agent-specific statutes, 72; states' adoption of, 7
UEFA Cup, 48
Uniform Commercial Code, 157
Uniform Probate Code, 157
unions, 14, 38, 75, 90, 94, 99, 135–37, 158, 170–71. *See also* players' associations
United States Attorney's Office, 78
United States Football League (USFL), 13, 89
United States Supreme Court, 125, 146
University of Alabama, 149, 155
University of Connecticut, 62, 149
University of Florida, 3–4, 80, 151
University of Kentucky, 133
University of Massachusetts, 149
University of Miami, 151
University of Southern California (USC), 2, 6–7, 137, 145, 151–52
USFL, 13
U.S. News and World Report, 75, 77–78
U.S. v. Walters-Bloom, 60, 80, 144–46, 172
US West, 47

Vaccaro, Sonny, 7, 60
Valukas, Anton, 172
Vereen, Ben, 62–63
Vick, Michael, 33–34

Waddy, Wayne, 58
Walker, Larry, 44
Walker, Robert, 166
Wall Street Journal, 58
Walsh, Bill, 22
Walsh, Christy, 11
Walters, Norby: Black stars represented by, 62–63; improper actions and prosecution of, 6, 17–18, 155; on NCAA rules, 134; payments to athletes, 1, 58; on recruitment, 57
Walters, Shawn, 58

Walters and Bloom v. Fullwood and Kickliter,
    124–25, 156
Walton, John, 99
Ware, Andre, 150
Ware, David, 31, 65, 69–70
Warfield, Paul, 13
Warrick, Peter, 6
Warwick, Dionne, 6
Washington Redskins, 77, 114, 138–39
Washington state, athlete agent statutes, 148
Washington Wizards, 95
Wasserman Media Group (WMG), 5,
    32–33, 37, 42, 50
Watson, Jamie, 81
Weeks, Rickie, 25
Weinberg, Steve, 114
Weisberg, Michael A., 85
Wells, David, 49
Wendell, Turk, 49
White, Frank, 91
White, Reggie, 88
White v. National Football League, 137
Wichard, Gary, 111, 137
Wilhelmina Artist Management, 50–51
Wilhelmina Models, 58
Wilkes, Reginald, 23, 34
Wilkins, Dominique, 25
William Morris Agency, 30, 51
Williams, Reginald, 83–84
Williams, Ricky, 18–20, 28–30
Williams & Connolly, 25
Williamson, Oliver, 5
Williams v. CWI, Inc., 83–84
Willoughby, Bill, 84

Wilson, Earl, 15, 56
Wilson, Mookie, 80, 82
Wimbledon Tennis Championships, 11, 16
Winfield, Antoine, 74, 77
wire fraud, 6, 60, 76, 79–80
WMG. *See* Wasserman Media Group
Women's National Basketball Association
    (WNBA), and female agents, 67
women's professional sports, 17, 67
Woods, Tiger, 33, 47
Woodson, Charles, 80
Woolf, Bob, 15, 37–38, 56, 85–86
workers' compensation, 26, 168
World Championship of Wrestling, 44
World Football League, 13
World Hockey Association (WHA), 85
World Sports & Entertainment, 172
Worldwide Financial Group, 77
Worldwide Football, 50
World Wide Sports Group, 77
Worley, Patrick, 111
Woy, Bucky, 56
Wright, Kirk, 65–66, 73, 143
Wright, Roderic, 112

Yale University, 122–23
Yastrzemski, Carl, 15
Yetts, Dunyasha, 74, 76–77, 137–38, 146
Young, Chris, 25
Young, David C., 6, 117–21, 125, 193n.10,
    193n.16

Zatkoff, Lawrence, 79
Zinn, Leo, 109–10

Acknowledgments

A number of people were helpful directly and indirectly in researching this and earlier editions of the book. An incomplete list includes Allen Saunderson, Wendi Huntley, Ray Anderson, Stanley King, Craig Fenech, Charles Grantham, Michael Jackson, Edward V. King, Jr., Pam Lester, Ash Narayan, Roger Noll, Jeff Orleans, Phil dePiciotto, Reginald Wilkes, Wayne Wilson, Michael Siegel, Greg Smith, Bill Strickland, John Carlos, André Colona, Reginald Turner, Scott Rosner, Sonny Vaccaro, and Kevin Young. Invaluable research assistance was provided by Jason Buchanan, Kim Chainey, Brian Conley, Tiffany Fujioka, David Ginzer, Nicole King, Nancy Ladson, Jeffrey Lepchenske, Roslyn Levine, Paul McNamara, Henry Moniz, Kelly Motycka, Michael Rivera, Michael Ryan, Melissa Shingles, Kevin Robinson, and Sankar Suryanarayan. Important research assistance and writing was provided in Chapter 3, "Consolidation," by Marc Chodock, a one-time student of Professor Shropshire's.

This book is a collaboration of two men who followed similar yet different paths from inner-city Southern League schools in Los Angeles (Professor Shropshire at Dorsey and Professor Davis at Washington) to Stanford University to law school, private practice, and then the academy. We observed each other's work from afar as we both pursued sports in scholarship. The names looked curiously familiar, but it was years before we contacted each other. This work constitutes our second collaboration in the area of sports law and business, the first being *A Modern Sports Law Anthology*.

Professor Shropshire would like to thank Kellen Winslow for an expensive, firsthand exposure to the business. Expensive but fun and informative.

We would both particularly like to thank our families for being supportive on yet another project. For Tim, that's wife Ida and daughter Adia. For Kenneth, it's Diane and their children, Theresa and Sam.